The Nation-State and Transnational Corporations in Conflict

edited by
Jon P. Gunnemann

Published in cooperation with the
Council on Religion and International Affairs

The Praeger Special Studies program—
utilizing the most modern and efficient book
production techniques and a selective
worldwide distribution network—makes
available to the academic, government, and
business communities significant, timely
research in U.S. and international economic, social, and political development.

The Nation-State and Transnational Corporations in Conflict
With Special Reference to Latin America

Praeger Publishers   New York   Washington   London

PRAEGER SPECIAL STUDIES IN INTERNATIONAL ECONOMICS AND DEVELOPMENT

Library of Congress Cataloging in Publication Data
Main entry under title:

The Nation-state and transnational corporations in
        conflict, with special reference to Latin America.

        (Praeger special studies in international economics
and development)
        Includes index.
        1. International business enterprises--Addresses,
essays, lectures. 2. Corporation, Foreign--Latin
America--Adresses, essays, lectures. 3. Underdeveloped
areas--Corporations, Foreign--Addresses, essays, lectures.
I. Gunnemann, Jon P
HD69.I7N37   338.8'8   75-3623
ISBN 0-275-05200-1

PRAEGER PUBLISHERS
111 Fourth Avenue, New York, N.Y. 10003, U.S.A.

Published in the United States of America in 1975
by Praeger Publishers, Inc.

Printed in the United States of America

The Council on Religion and International Affairs (CRIA) was founded in 1914 by Andrew Carnegie in an effort to bring religious principles to bear on the problems of world peace. Through a basic program of conferences and publications CRIA has through the years played a small but vital role in attempting to bring moral precepts to international affairs as envisaged by its founder.

Several years ago, together with many other philanthropic and nonprofit institutions, CRIA began to study its portfolio, which contains securities of international corporations, from a moral perspective. Discussions attending its social investment concerns resulted in the conviction that CRIA should and could further the important and difficult discussion on the ethics of investment by organizing a seminar. Out of this first seminar came the book People/Profits: The Ethics of Investment. The current volume is the result of a second such seminar. These two seminars in turn have helped CRIA to embark on a full-scale Corporate Consultation Program, which concerns itself with the social responsibility of multinational corporations.

FOREWORD

A. William Loos

James Finn .

The subjects of corporate responsibility and the broader, more general one of the transnational corporation have, during the past decade, moved to stage center. A number of voluntary agencies have studied these subjects closely, and some of the agencies have confronted the corporations with sharply differing views of what social responsibility demands. Corporations themselves, partly due to this persistent prodding by voluntary organizations, have devoted considerable attention to what their obligations are, not only to their stockholders, to whom they need to return a profit, but to the general public.

All discussion of the transnational corporation must, of course, be placed in a global context. But even when considering domestic corporations, it is impossible, on this star we call the earth, to escape the interdependence that ties together all peoples, all institutions, all corporations.

The direct relevance of the work of the Council on Religion and International Affairs (CRIA) at this point becomes most apparent. Since its founding in 1914 by Andrew Carnegie CRIA has been dedicated to working for international peace with justice. In light of the enormous global power of the corporation, and most especially of the transnational corporation, CRIA has undertaken to study if and how the corporation and the transnational corporation can be instruments in achieving a larger measure of justice.

One method CRIA has used in this endeavor is the small consultation which brings together 15 corporate executives on the policy-making level from the U.S.A. and other countries and 15 persons from organized labor, from government, from international organizations, from academia, from the religious community.

This volume is the third to issue from these CRIA consultations. The first is People/Profits: The Ethics of Investment (published by CRIA, 1972); the second, The Multinational Corporation and Social Policy (published by Praeger, 1974). This book is the first in a new ongoing program of consultations and research dealing with issues relative to "The Nation-State and Transnational Corporations in Conflict." The consultation of which this book is one product focused its discussion on Latin America.

CRIA is benefited from the collaboration of the Aspen Institute for Humanistic Studies, although the program and choice of participants for the consultation, as well as the preparation of this volume, have been the responsibility of CRIA alone.

CRIA expresses its profound appreciation to certain individuals who helped to make the consultation a valuable experience for all who took part and who have contributed most significantly to this volume.

Our thanks go first to Jon P. Gunnemann of the Department of Religious Studies, Pennsylvania State University, who contributed enormously to the consultation with his brilliant summary and analysis at its close, but even more for the perspicacious editing he did of the transcript of the consultation—an extremely difficult and at times onerous task.

We are especially grateful to the following persons: To William J. Barnds, Chairman of the CRIA Executive Committee, for his perceptive, firm, and constructive moderating of the consultation.

To two distinguished participants for the papers on the general theme with which they opened the consultation: Miguel Wionczek, Director de la Secretaria Tecnica, Place Nacional de Ciencia y Tecnologia, CONACYT, Mexico City, and Carl A. Gerstacker, Chairman of Dow Chemical Company, and to a distinguished international servant, Luis Escobar, Special Representative for Inter-American Organizations, World Bank, for his closing paper.

To three corporate executives who presented case studies as a basis for group discussion: Luis Alcala Sucre, former president, Mene Grande Oil Co., Gulf Oil subsidiary in Venezuela; Robert A. Bennett, Vice President-Americas, IBM World Trade Corporation; and Harlow W. Gage, Vice President, General Motors Corporation, and General Manager, GM Overseas Operations Division.

To Charles W. Powers, Associate Professor, Yale Divinity School, who stimulated the lively exchange of opinions by emphasizing at the start of each discussion session those questions and problems that required special attention.

To six commentators on presentations: Theodore H. Moran, The Brookings Institution; Burke Marshall, Deputy Dean, Yale University Law School; Ronald E. Muller, Assistant Professor of Economics, The American University; James A. Joseph, Vice President for Corporate Action, Cummins Engine Company; and Anthony Wiener, The Hudson Institute.

To Florence Norton, research editor of Worldview, for her meticulous, painstaking, and imaginative copyediting of the manuscript; and to Ulrike Klopfer, assistant to the CRIA president, for carrying through so faithfully the unenviable task of coordinating the many steps in getting material from tape recording to a form approved by the participants.

Finally, to Michael P. Sloan, special assistant to the CRIA president, whose vision, planning, and consultation with many people

in different disciplines led to the three-year project and to the particular consultation on which this book is based.

The literature on the transnational corporation is growing, but
slowly. CRIA is pleased to make a contribution from its special
perspective, the ethics of interinstitutional activity. It is our deep
and continuing hope that this moral emphasis will make a significant
contribution during these dangerously troubled times to the growth of
international peace with justice.

A. William Loos
President, CRIA
1 January 1956–31 December 1974

James Finn
Director of Publications, CRIA
Editor, Worldview

PARTICIPANTS IN THE CONSULTATION

Held at the Aspen Institute, Colorado, 15-19 September 1973

William J. Barnds
Senior Research Fellow
Council on Foreign Relations
58 East 68 Street
New York, N.Y. 10021

Robert A. Bennett
Vice President-Americas
IBM World Trade Corporation
821 United Nations Plaza
New York, N.Y. 10017

E.N. Brandt
Director
Business Communications
Dow Chemical Company
2020 Dow Center
Midland, Michigan 48640

Joseph G. Canavan
General Motors Corporation
767 Fifth Avenue
New York, N.Y. 10022

Alphonse De Rosso
Senior Advisor
Public Affairs Department
Exxon Corporation
1251 Avenue of the Americas
New York, N.Y. 10020

Herbert H. Dow
Secretary
Dow Chemical Company
2030 Dow Center
Midland, Michigan 48640

Luis Escobar
Special Representative for
  Inter-American Organizations
International Bank for Reconstruction
  and Development (World Bank)
1818 H Street, N.W.
Washington, D.C. 20433

Harlow W. Gage
General Manager
GM Overseas Operations Division
767 Fifth Avenue
New York, N.Y. 10022

Carl A. Gerstacker
Chairman, Dow Chemical Company
2030 Dow Center
Midland, Michigan 48640

Jon P. Gunnemann
Assistant Professor of Religion
Pennsylvania State University
University Park, Pennsylvania 16802

Terrance Hanold
Chairman, Executive Committee
The Pillsbury Company
Minneapolis, Minnesota 55402

Elizabeth R. Jager
Economist
AFL-CIO
Washington, D.C. 20006

James A. Joseph
Vice President for Corporate Action
Cummins Engine Company
Columbus, Indiana 47201

Moorhead C. Kennedy
Director
Office of Investment Affairs
Bureau of Economic and
  Business Affairs
Department of State
Washington, D. C. 20520

Burke Marshall
Deputy Dean
Yale University Law School
New Haven, Connecticut 06520

David Moore
Ph. D. candidate
The American University
Washington, D. C. 20016

Theodore H. Moran
Research Associate
Project on MNCs and U. S.
  Foreign Policy
The Brookings Institution
1775 Massachusetts Avenue
Washington, D. C. 20036

Ronald E. Muller
Assistant Professor of
  Economics
The American University
Washington, D. C. 20016

Paul M. Neuhauser
Associate Dean
University of Iowa Law School
Iowa City, Iowa
(Chairman, Executive Council's
  Committee on Social Criteria
  for Investments, Episcopal
  Church)

H. B. Nicholson
Senior Vice President
Coca-Cola Company
310 North Avenue, N. W.
Atlanta, Georgia 30313

Charles W. Powers
Associate Professor of Social Ethics
Yale Divinity School
New Haven, Connecticut 06511

Thomas E. Quigley
Division for Latin America
U. S. Catholic Conference
1430 K Street, N. W.
Washington, D. C. 20005

Victor G. Reuther
UAW (retired)
3701 Porter Street, N. W.
Washington, D. C. 20016

Stanley H. Ruttenberg
Ruttenberg and Associates
1211 Connecticut Avenue, N. W.
Washington, D. C. 20036

Howard Schomer
World Issues, United Church Board
  for World Ministries
475 Riverside Drive
New York, N. Y. 10027

Luis Alcala Sucre
Gulf Oil Company-Latin America
P. O. Box 910
Coral Gables, Florida 33134

Reginald Tuggle
Ph. D. student at Yale University
119 Main Street
West Haven, Connecticut 06156

Anthony Wiener
The Hudson Institute
Quaker Ridge Road
Croton-on-Hudson, N.Y. 10520

Miguel Wionczek
Director de la Secretaria Tecnica
Place Nacional de Ciencia y Tecnologia
CONACYT
Av. Insurgentes Sur #1814
Mexico City, D.F., Mexico

Aspen Institute Staff
P.O. Box 219
Aspen, Colorado 81611
A.A. Jordan
Director

CRIA Staff
170 East 64 Street
New York, N.Y. 10021
A. William Loos
President
James Finn
Director of Publications
Michael P. Sloan
Special Assistant to the President

CORPORATE CONSULTATION PROGRAM ASSOCIATES
OF
COUNCIL ON RELIGION AND INTERNATIONAL AFFAIRS

American Can Company
Behrman, Jack N.
Cassell, Anna J.
Cummins Engine Company
D&R Fund
Dow Chemical Company
David Dubinsky Foundation
Exxon Corporation
Ford Motor Company
Francis, The Rev. Everett W.
General Motors Corporation
General Service Foundation
Hanold, Terrance
Harper, David
International Business Machines Corporation
Lee, James E.
Eli Lilly and Company
Lutheran Church in America
Milliken, Frank R.
Quigley, Thomas E.
Ruttenberg, Stanley H.
Stackhouse, Max L.
Stone Container Corporation
Tuggle, Reginald
United Auto Workers
United Church Board for Homeland Ministries
United Church Board for World Ministries
Westinghouse Electric Corporation
Women's Division of the Board of Global Ministries (Methodist)

CONTENTS

LIST OF TABLES AND FIGURES

FIGURES

INTRODUCTION
Jon P. Gunnemann

It is increasingly evident that multinational corporations (MNCs) are the most important structures in contemporary international economic affairs. These institutions, very new in their structure, financing, and operation, are the chief conduits for the transfer of capital and technology, for the training and exchange of managers, for information flow and marketing knowledge, and for access to markets. They are prodigious in size: By the end of 1972 four of the largest had "sales volume in excess of the one-billion dollar level."[1]

Beyond these threshold factual statements, however, there is little agreement on the impact of the multinational corporation or on what, if anything, should be done to regulate it. Champions of the MNC argue that, through the functions described in the preceding paragraph, it provides vital social services. It can raise the income of less developed countries (LDCs), develop natural resources, educate management and labor, promote production and abundance—in short, the MNC is a master instrument of economic and social development, promoting international harmony and equality. But the critics argue differently. For them the MNC is a structure that prevents the genuine flow of technology (keeping it for home base countries), that contributes to distributional inequality within an LDC, that creates serious balance-of-payments problems for host and home countries, and that has the potential for disrupting the international monetary structure. Thus John Kenneth Galbraith writes that the multinational system "internationalizes the tendency to inequality,"[2] and a United Nations report warns, "There is no doubt that multinational corporations could precipitate a currency crisis if they were to move only a small proportion of their assets from one currency to another."[3]

Two events, one just before and the other just after the CRIA conference, dramatized the dry statistics that lend support to either side of the debate. We arrived in Aspen just after the overthrow and death of Salvador Allende in Chile. That tragic event brought to an end a political and economic struggle that in one country combined the major elements of a larger drama taking place throughout Latin America and a greater portion of the world. Chile was one nexus of interaction between the "more developed nations" and the "less developed nations"; of the great debate between capitalism and socialism; and of the interplay between the giant multinational corporations and the claims and thrusts of nations struggling to assert their own paths of modernization.

For some, the Chilean situation was a vivid demonstration of the willful power of national governments attempting to work against the grain of modern economic patterns and institutions. The Allende government had foolishly cut itself off from international ties and economic progress by nationalizing the international institutions (and that without just recompense). For others the same event was an example of the arrogance and threat of the multinationals—for these, it was charged, had disrupted the Chilean economy and society before Allende and had interfered directly in the Chilean political and economic process during the Allende regime, thus bearing considerable responsibility for its demise. For all of us, the Chilean situation created a sense of urgency and served as a sober reminder that all of our abstract conceptions about politics and economics, about sovereignty and statistical accuracy, ultimately had to be translated into human terms. Whatever opinions we held about the multinational corporations, we could not shunt aside the sometimes hidden fact that they are human institutions, having a profound impact on human lives and subject to human control and decisions.

Looking back to Chile, then, we saw the multinational corporation as one very significant actor in the drama of Latin American development. But we did not anticipate in any way what would happen in the next few months in the Middle East. There, a war among relatively small countries had an impact on all the industrial nations of the world far beyond what such a war would normally have had. The reason was oil, and the fact that a few nations were able for some time to bring the industrial nations to their knees underscored mightily a central theme we addressed at the conference: The chief characteristic of modern economic structures is interdependence, and at the core of our interdependence stand the multinational corporations—but as nations we have not come to terms either with this interdependence or with these massive new economic structures.

There is of course nothing new in the fact that politics and economics are closely intertwined, nor in the frequent economic cause of international strife. Nor is it new that international economic ties and influences are expressed through the vehicle of economic corporations. What was new was that the huge oil companies involved in the Middle East did not all make a simple claim to represent the economic interests of a single country. Indeed, there was a news story that some oil companies, nominally based in the United States, had agreed with some Middle East nations to cut off oil supplies to U.S. military units. Although this report was not later verified, its plausibility was itself revealing. It seemed that the ancient identity of military and economic forces had been shattered and that multinational corporations had become international actors without clear national allegiance.

Is such a situation possible? And is it desirable? These in some fashion were the overriding questions of our conference. On one hand corporate managers represented themselves as citizens of the world, providing the vital channel for capital and technology flow, facilitating production and growth toward abundance; yet on the other they continued to use designations such as "host country" and "home country" and stressed the importance of abiding by local customs and standards rather than imposing international standards on host-country situations. Critics of the multinationals, when they came from less developed countries, tended to view the corporation as a tool of foreign domination, but there were also critics, especially from the labor unions in the United States, who claimed that these same corporations did not heed sufficiently the claims and interests of domestic constituencies. In short, it is difficult to claim "world citizenship" when there is no international community in which to hold membership, and yet it is clear that the multinational corporations are operating in a fashion that prevents their control and use by any one sovereign state.

The modern multinational corporation is, then, an anomalous structure, which does not fit easily into past patterns of nation-state economic and political analysis. When analysis is made, it tends to reflect the perspective that arises from one level of attachment to the corporation. As in the Indian story of the blind men, each of whom describes an elephant on the basis of the anatomical part he happens to touch, we get only a partial picture, and the whole is understood in light of that part.

It was in the hope of fleshing out the entire anatomy of the multinational corporation that CRIA brought together such a diverse group of people. It is unlikely that so many parts of that particular anatomy had been in one room before. People representing the following institutions, professions, or interests were present: U.S. and Latin American managers of MNCs, the World Bank, the Center for Latin American Monetary Studies, U.S. consulting institutes and think tanks, labor unions, the State Department, professors of law, churchmen with involvement in Latin America, economists, and professors of ethics. While this list does not exhaust the interests and groups intertwined with the operation of multinationals, it does cover a great deal of ground, and it gives some indication of the complexities of the institution under study.

Consider the modern corporation itself. Efforts in recent years to define "corporate responsibility" and to place the corporation within a larger picture of the public interest (that is, to discover the relationship with other dimensions of political, social, and economic life) have met with a welter of threshold legal and analytical problems. With respect to the question, Who is responsible? a variety of answers can be given: the owners, the managers, the structure as a whole. The well-known separation of ownership and control compounds the difficulties of locating responsibility, as does the alleged diffuse character of corporate decision-making. With respect to the question, To whom is the corporation responsible? the legal priority of the shareholder (in economic questions) competes with many other "constituencies": consumers, labor, suppliers, the government, the general public. To these two broad areas of problems we must add the inherent difficulties of defining corporate social responsibility (Are all questions of corporate responsibility translatable into economic terms, or do some defy such analysis? Does corporate responsibility extend beyond a concern for the impact of corporate activity itself—self-regulation—to positive "citizenship" duties?); and last but not least, we must consider that the business community itself cannot decide what the corporation is up to: Is it interested in profit, or long-range growth, or institutional flexibility and stability? Or are all these simply different dimensions and translations of one goal?

When we move to the multinational corporation, we have simply to multiply these difficulties several times. This is literally the case when locating constituencies, but it also applies roughly to the areas of ownership complexity, diffusion of planning and decision-making, and translation of terms. It is not difficult to imagine that a group of people representing so many of these multiplicities would have difficulty agreeing on the shape of the whole. To return to the earlier elephant metaphor, the fear would be that we would discover not four legs, a trunk, and a tail, but many legs, trunks, and tails as well as some previously unheard-of appendages. In light of this, questions of ethics and accountability would be especially confused.

THE CRIA CONSULTATION AND THE
STRUCTURE OF THE BOOK

In spite of the threshold difficulties, the consultation at Aspen did not break down. Not everything that was hoped for was accomplished, nor did the discussion follow at all points the structure set down for it, but patterns of concern did emerge.

It was a hope of the planners of the consultation that as a group we could move in the direction of formulating an international code of conduct for multinational corporations. Such a formulation was not forthcoming, but we did move in the direction of discovering the preconditions for such a code, as well as the kinds of considerations it would have to include. And it became clearer as we threaded through the issues that a code alone is probably too narrow to meet the needs;

ultimately institutions have to be established to regulate bargaining and to collect and disseminate information. These points are scat- tered throughout the book but come to some focus in Part IV.

Our path to some agreements and common concerns was winding and hilly—and there were frequent wrong turns that required back-tracking. The consultation had been structured around case studies—an effort to move from the concrete to the more general. Yet the discussion almost always moved immediately to the general and even to the abstract, and particular cases were frequently left in suspension only to be woven back into the discussion as general themes were discussed.

Natural clusterings of interests did emerge. The most obvious of those grouped around the four natural "actors" in the multinational drama: the MNCs themselves, the host countries, the home countries, and the international community. But these clusterings never held up in sustained fashion under critical analysis. The MNCs are a diverse lot, being different in structure and operation from home country to home country (for example, the United States, Japan, Germany) and from industry to industry (extraction, manufacturing, computer and information processing, and so on). We could not decide on how to define host country interests: in terms of the government, the labor unions, or the masses of the people. Home country interests broke down as easily between government and unions, or between foreign policy and domestic needs. It was suggested further, but never agreed upon, that international labor groups had more commonality than did national communities, and that MNCs had actually created internationalism in labor. And we could not discover an international community.

What happened, of course, is what usually happens when conflicting interests meet in one room. Each accuses the others of masking their own interests and being unable to see the whole, and thus all the multiplicities suggested earlier are exacerbated. I do not intend here to suggest that the consultation was marked by excessive hostility—on the contrary, there were discoveries of unexpected agreements among unlikely parties, and the heated debates never created acrimony. But there were heated debates as well as gentle ones, and within these the conflicts of interest were clear.

The problem is that interests and their realization are matters of power, and power is one of the most elusive of social terms. I have been at a number of consultations on related themes and am always struck by the disavowal of power on the part of almost every participant. It is always the other fellow who has the power, and that power is usually capriciously or unwisely wielded. So the corporate manager claims that governments have all the power and that host governments can do almost as they like. The host countries claim that the massive corporations represent direct threats to their sovereignty. And so the Chilean experience becomes an example of the unbridled and irresponsible power of both host governments and of foreign-based corporations.

If power is an elusive idea, are we reduced to pure subjectivity in understanding it? I think not. The consultation very early focused on power and the shifting of power relations as the crux of the issue in understanding multinationals and the problems of accountability. This was evident in the first two presentations, which stand at the beginning of Part I, and the issue was further clarified in the ensuing analysis and discussion. What we could not agree on was who was benefiting from the shifts in power and what terms ought to be used in describing the process. Yet it was precisely these disagreements that began to fall into patterns.

The first pattern was this: In our discussion of the impact of MNCs on nation-states (and vice versa), there were those who tended to emphasize the political and legal dimensions of that impact and there were those who tended to emphasize the economic dimensions. This is not to say that those who tended one way denied the existence of the other dimension. It was rather a case of wanting to translate the one mode of power into the terms of the other mode of power. For example, those who tended to emphasize the political and legal side of power would say of the economic side, "It is true, of course, that the economic impact is there. But if you want to regulate this, or if you are going to establish canons of behavior and channels of responsibility, you are going to have to do it in terms of existing legal structures and constraints and in terms of political and quasi-political groupings, that is, in terms of the constituencies which are relevant to a given situation." In contrast, those who leaned toward the economic mode of impact would say, "It is true that legal structures and constituencies exist, but if you focus on those you will miss what is actually happening. Structural economic changes are taking place that cannot be discovered through legal and political analysis—in fact, emphasis on constituencies and legal structures may even mask the economic realities. What we need to do is to develop the analytical economic tools to understand the economic structure and its changes, and then perhaps attend to the legal and political issues."

This natural division of emphasis came out early in the group's discussion. One group wanted to translate power relations into the vocabulary of law and politics, the other into the vocabulary of economics. But two other modes of translation broke through at various times in the discussion, most often when attempts were made to discuss power in ethical terms. The first found expression in the desire to measure the total cultural impact of MNCs on nation-states. These voices wanted to focus on questions of cultural disruption (or cultural

advance), on the effect of transforming agrarian economies to industrial economies with the concomitant population shifts from village
to urban centers, on the instilling of the work ethic or the consumer
ethic, and so on. The other mode of handling ethical issues was to
discuss the conscious, day-to-day conduct of a corporation in its
various activities: its treatment of employees, its pollution (or
nonpollution) of the environment, the kind of involvement it had in
political processes, its attitude toward graft and bribery—in short,
these voices tended to view the moral dimensions of MNC power in
terms of a fairly traditional view of business responsibility. And it
should be pointed out that some believed that all discussion of power
had normative or ethical dimensions, whereas others seemed to hold
that power was amoral.

It would be a mistake to assume that any participant ever fell
clearly into any one of the four modes of translating questions of
power—most covered all four at one time or another. But the
emphases were usually clear, and many of the apparent disagreements were a consequence of talking out of different translations of
the problem of power. As the discussion progressed, certain "natural"
groupings within each mode of translation became evident as a consequence of the different experiences and histories of the participants,
but at the same time there was progress in understanding among the
various translations.

In the conclusion of the book, which is essentially the summary
given at the end of the consultation, I try to explore both the philosophical assumptions of the four translations and the significance of
the experiential histories that undergird each. For the structure of
the book I have used only the first two modes of understanding power:
the political-legal and the economic. The clusters of discussion were
strongest around these, and they form Parts II and III, respectively.
The other two modes of understanding, the cultural impact and the
day-to-day conduct, are threaded throughout the presentations and
discussions. Part I, which sets the groundwork for what comes after
by focusing on shifting power, in fact stood at the beginning of the
consultation and Part IV stood at the end. But in Parts II and III, I
have rearranged many of the presentations and ensuing discussions
to fit the thematic patterns.

All except one of the major divisions of the book are begun with
formal presentations. Some of these were papers prepared for the
consultation; some were analytical responses made at the consultation itself. In addition I have included a great deal of the transcript
of discussion, because it was in open debate that many of the issues
took sharpest focus. In these debates I have tried to retain as much
of the original language as possible, deleting only material that was
repetitive or totally extraneous to the issue at hand. This means that

the material contained herein covers a spectrum from the formal paper prepared with care to the informal statement made in the heat of argument. It is my hope that the reader will keep in mind this fact and remember that the participants have graciously consented to open their informal words to public scrutiny. While each has looked at, and approved, what is included here of his or her speech, none has had the opportunity I have had—to look over the whole with hindsight and <u>then</u> to write in the quiet of his study.

The reader may wish to read the concluding chapter first as a way of becoming acquainted with the issues. But almost every presentation or section stands on its own, and the reader may go through the book, selecting according to his interests. Two case studies are included as appendixes. As indicated earlier, the discussion showed a marked tendency to move away from the particular, and thus the cases did not fit the flow of the book as now structured. But the cases did provide valuable starting points and were used "in progress" as it were. They are included both for full reading and for reference.

I am deeply indebted to all the consultation participants for what they taught me in our days together and for consenting to my use of their words and ideas. The structure I have developed, to the extent that it is helpful, had its origin in the conference itself, in the attempts by many along the way to give shape to our deliberations. I owe special thanks to Charles W. Powers, my friend and colleague, who in long hours of conversation continually contributed ideas and sharpened distinctions. To the extent that the structure inhibits or falls short of the many contributions herein, I alone bear responsibility.

NOTES

1. Kathleen Teltsch, "U.N. to Study Multinationals," New York Times, August 13, 1973. For more complete and up-to-date statistics on multinationals see the section by Ronald Muller in Part III below.

2. John Kenneth Galbraith, Economics and the Public Purpose, quoted by C. L. Sulzberger, "The Enormous Unknown," New York Times, September 22, 1973.

3. Quoted by Teltsch, op. cit.

The Nation-State and Transnational Corporations in Conflict

THE MULTINATIONAL CORPORATION AND THE NATION-STATE: A PROBLEM OF SHIFTING POWER AND CHANGING INTERESTS

The consultation opened with two papers presenting contrasting views of the multinational corporation and Latin American countries. The issues raised in these papers provided a dramatic focus for much of the discussion in the next days, and they thus serve as an excellent starting point. Together with an analysis by Theodore H. Moran, they constitute Chapter 1.

The first paper, by Carl A. Gerstacker, chairman of the board of Dow Chemical, is a case study of Dow's experience in Chile. Dow was among a number of foreign companies whose operations in Chile were nationalized by the Allende government. The second paper, by Miguel Wionczek of the Center for Latin American Monetary Studies, outlines the central issues and problems faced by the lesser developed countries in dealing with multinational corporations.

Theodore H. Moran of the Brookings Institution places the two views in a framework of two opposing perspectives, economic nationalism and dependencia, out of which conflicting parties interpret the same process. In his mind, these opposing perspectives are at the root of most disagreements about multinationals and are the chief obstacles in attempts to gain international accords and regulations.

Chapter 2 is comprised of discussion of issues that came out of the introductory papers. The conference participants quickly agreed that the power relations between a host country and a multinational firm change with time, as do the interests of each. Given the fact that these power shifts frequently lead to open conflict and losses on both sides, one of the earliest questions asked was whether it was worth it for either side to continue to work together. The reader will discover that this question was soon passed with a clear if not unqualified "yes."

The discussion then turned to patterns of phased withdrawal by MNCs and to the problem of renegotiating contracts and initial agreements as power shifts and interests change. More questions are raised than answered—as might be expected in an opening session.

1

AN OPENING DIALOGUE: TWO PERSPECTIVES ON THE MULTINATIONAL CORPORATION IN LATIN AMERICA

DOW CHEMICAL'S EXPERIENCE IN CHILE
Carl A. Gerstacker

Importance of Historical Antecedents

As you know, most of the nations located south of the United States were discovered and colonized by Spain and Portugal. The Roman Catholic Church had a very active role in this colonization and in the educational field through its missionaries, schools, and universities.

The countries we loosely lump together as "Latin America" differ radically from one another. Although united by certain cultural and spiritual bonds because of the common traditions derived from their Iberian ancestry and Roman Catholic religious formation and background, each republic considers itself a distinctly separate and independent nation having its own particular national characteristics and traditions. All the Latin American nations of the Western Hemisphere speak Spanish except Brazil, where Portuguese is spoken, and Haiti, which is French-speaking. All are proud of their particular traditions and history.

They somehow dislike being grouped together as one "uniform mass" located "South of the Rio Grande" called "Latin America." They each prefer to be considered a part of "Las Americas" and subconsciously resent the name we chose for our nation, "The United States of America." You will frequently see the U.S.A. mentioned in documents, writings, and articles as "The United States of North America." And when they refer to us as individuals, we are norteamericanos.

Mexico's official name is "Estados Unidos de Mexico." Brazil's name is "Estados Unidos do Brasil."

A strong individualism—leading one's life in one's own way without too much regard for others—is one of the principal characteristics of the Latino and probably the basic reason he is so intensely patriotic, fiercely nationalistic, and yet, simultaneously, a perennial "oppositionist" in politics.

In 1900 there appeared what has been called the most influential book ever written by a Latin American author. The author was a Uruguayan, Jose Enrique Rodo, and his book was called <u>Ariel</u>. Rodo's book, virtually unknown in North America, is one of the sources of anti-U.S. feeling in Latin American intellectual and university circles.

In this book Rodo admonishes his countrymen for being imitators of the U.S. model of democracy and its practice, and he tells them that Latin America must develop its own intellectual aristocracy, one that will stand firmly against the basically materialistic impact of U.S. ideals. He says that Latin Americans may be attracted by the material achievements of the United States but that Latinos have a more mature judgment and a sounder grasp of human, spiritual, and cultural values than their North American counterparts and should have more sense than to devote their lives to the pursuit of purely materialistic goals.

Rodo's aims were not political—in fact he contended that North and South America complement each other and could and should work together—but his book gained wide circulation in Latin America.

I cite Rodo as merely one example of a host of historical antecedents to what I am about to say concerning the role of the multinational companies in the less developed countries and specifically in Latin America.

We cannot escape from history; and Latin Americans appear reluctant to accept help from foreigners, outwardly reluctant to be associated with foreign interests. This makes the role of the multinational company more difficult. We must not make the mistake of underestimating the influence of history or the importance of cultural heritage.

I want to discuss this problem with you today. First, I will talk about my impressions from a recent trip to South America and give you some of my general observations about doing business there from the viewpoint of an executive of a multinational company.

Later I will discuss the experience of Dow Chemical in Chile.

Impressions of South America

I spent the month of May on business in South America, mostly in Brazil, where one sees evidence of booming prosperity everywhere.

5

There are more skyscrapers, more factories, more highways, more
hotels, all modern and new. You see an abundance of all kinds of
consumer products and people buying them. Those who are well-to-do
live on a scale comparable to anywhere else in the world, and they
with their children are ready to take off for a weekend at beach resorts
as readily and easily as any of us. In a business sense I was struck
by the great numbers of Japanese businessmen, and I was told that
before long the Japanese will be the foremost rivals of the North
Americans as the predominant foreign investors in Brazil.

Great highway networks are being built to "open up the interior, "
the Matto Grosso, the Amazon, to farming, trade, commerce, and
industrial development. This amazing prosperity and feverish activity
has developed from political stability, which creates a favorable economic climate for both national and international investments.

As those of you familar with Latin America know, it is extremely
rare for a Latin American to feel that he is a Latin American; if he
is a Brazilian, he feels no affinity or kinship with a Guatemalan; if he
is a Uruguayan, he may see the Bolivian as a misguided foreigner; and
if he is an Argentinian, he may feel very lucky, because all the other
Latinos are not quite as "civilized" as the Argentines. This heightened
sense of nationalism is an aspect of Latin America that North Americans tend to overlook.

Companies like Dow Chemical that have international operations
in almost every country in the area must move their employees about
the hemisphere as their skills and abilities are needed, and our experience is that these narrower nationalistic feelings are being softened
as men and families carry on their jobs and move from one nation to
another. There is really no other institution, in fact, that is developing Latin Americans with a sense of being Latin Americans in
anything approaching the numbers being developed by the multinational
companies. If the Latin American countries of this hemisphere are
to develop in harmony and with a strong sense of the need for different
nationalities to work with each other, this type of individual is greatly
needed.

When Simon Bolivar called the first international conference of
the Latin American States in Panama in 1826, representatives of only
four nations attended. Fortunately, in our day the Organization of
American States is pursuing Bolivar's ideals of international cooperation in the Americas with considerably more success.

It may be worth recalling that Bolivar died a disillusioned man,
his dreams of greatness for his continent shattered. You may recall
his remarkable prediction that "many tyrants will rise upon my tomb, "
and his bitter comment that "America is ungovernable; he who serves
a revolution ploughs the sea. " A year before his death he wrote,
"There is no good faith in America, nor among the nations of America.

Treaties are scraps of paper; constitutions are printed matter; elections are battles, freedom becomes anarchy, and life a torment." You will notice that Bolivar uses "America" in referring to all of the nations of the hemisphere, and not only the U.S.A.

Bolivar freed a large portion of South America from Spanish rule, but he failed in his efforts to replace it with a workable political system. The Spanish colonial territories were not yet ready to develop a sophisticated government apparatus. In such circumstances the doors were open for strong nationalistic feelings that led to the division of the liberated Spanish colonies into many independent nations instead of a "United States of Latin America."

What went wrong? Most of the main flow of Latin American history seems to be a story of ineffectual parliamentary democracy that lasts for a while, becomes shaky, and then is suspended upon the arrival of a strong man, usually a military leader, who sometimes is a benevolent despot and sometimes an autocratic tyrant but usually rules or influences his nation for a long time. Eventually he weakens or the younger officers rebel, and off he goes into exile. And the nation goes back to republican institutions, elects a new parliament, and begins the unfortunate cycle again.

The Brazilians, with their delicious sense of humor, have a saying: "Brazil grows only at night, after the politicians have gone to sleep." The saying contains a lot of truth; the politicians have been doing a poor job everywhere. The great men in Latin American history, the Bolivars, the San Martins, the Juarezes, and the Pedro II's, have been patriotic exceptions to this pattern.

The complexity of the Latin American's character makes him more difficult for us to understand. He can be tolerant and tyrannical at the same time. The Latin American is proud and passionate, devoted to the principle of the supremacy of the individual, and he has inherited an unwillingness to compromise or to make concessions, which can be a serious problem. With him, things are placed on the personal basis. Political issues become clear to him only when they are translated into terms of persons rather than parties.

There is still illiteracy in some Latin American countries today, and this should be one of the first targets of those interested in a prosperous Latin American future. The lack of democratic political know-how is bad enough, but the lack of modern technological education is worse.

It is pleasant to dream of the great bounds forward that could take place in Latin America with a fully developed population. I believe Latin America could be the paradise of gold that Cortes and Pizarro thought they had found, if the technical educational level were brought to a higher plane.

7

A general and substantial raising of this educational level is the most needed single thing in Latin America today. The peasant and farming classes should be educated to become the draftsmen and technicians of a new middle class, and the middle classes should be developed to be the professionals, technocrats, and managers of this new upper class. A revolution of learning would change it all and make life better for all the people.

We live in a technocratic world. Those countries that have and use the best technology in the best way are those that are most prosperous. Those who do not acquire all-round technology and use it properly will be surpassed by those who do before too many years go by. Without a more numerous educated population the Latin American republics will have difficulty in putting the technology of others to work and will not develop the means and the skills to create a technology of their own. They will soon lose out, if this is so, in the competition between the nations in a steadily shrinking world.

The example of Brazilian rubber production is a good case in point. In 1900 virtually all the world's rubber came from northeastern Brazil, whose wild rubber trees were the world's only source of natural rubber at that time. With a monopoly on the market, there was nothing to worry about. But an Englishman smuggled some rubber seeds out and planted them in London, and from there some young rubber plants were taken to Ceylon. By 1912 the Far East was supplying most of the world's rubber. Almost overnight the whole fabulously prosperous Amazon rubber business of Brazil fell into ruins. This industry had depended on untrained laborers who braved the dangers and privations of the raw jungle to extract rubber from wild trees. The entire business was virtually unsupervised.

In the Far East, on the other hand, the rubber trees were planted in orderly rows, carefully tended by men trained to do this, in plantations whose operations were presided over by trained technicians. Not only was the yield per tree and per man much higher and the product of more consistent quality, but the workers were well housed, fed, and provided with medical care. It is no wonder that the jungle operation of the Brazilian rubber trade, which in theory should be much less costly—without any overhead to speak of—was forced out of business in a few short years. The difference was training.

This is a fairly primitive example of the value of technology and of trained technicians, but perhaps it makes my point: Brazil could just as well have developed the technology and the prosperity it would have carried with it if Brazil had had the trained people to do so. Here again we have another powerful argument in favor of multinational company operations in developing countries—because the multinational companies are in the business not only of creating technology but of putting it to use wherever in the world it can best serve.

But the multinational companies cannot do much without a reasonable level of local modern education. We can bring in foreign technicians and managers, but for the long run we much prefer the local nationals, who must be developed to take over the operations and should have acquired some basic education to enable them to improve on it and reach the higher technological specialities needed.

It therefore seems to me that the nations in Latin America should take a quantum jump in the technical educational field. The newest, most modern methods of education are coming into use in the more developed nations, so it is a perfect time to build new schools, to install new educational methods and techniques, and leap into the future educationally.

Will Latin America see a new Golden Age? I believe it is fully possible if such an educational system is rapidly developed in a major way.

Chile: A Case Study

Bolivar, a century and a half ago, predicted that Chile would be a great country because being so far away it had not been contaminated by "the ancient vices of Europe and Asia." Chile is in many ways unique among the Latin American republics, and the experience of Dow Chemical in Chile has been unique in many ways as well.

Chile is the longest country in the world, stretching for a fantastic 2,600 miles along the Pacific and Ande. coast in western South America, but it is seldom more than 100 miles wide at any point. Its 10 million people are a mixture of many races. By and large it has been a model of political stability and democracy since the days of Bernardo O'Higgins, the hero of Chilean independence. Economically and industrially the country has been affected by overdependence on a single source of income, a weakness common to many countries of Latin America.

About a century ago it was discovered that the rich natural nitrate deposits in the far north of Chile were a great fertilizer, and after going to war with Peru and Bolivia to secure these deposits, Chile entered what is now referred to as the "Age of Fertilizer." For about 40 years nitrates were the major export of the country and the pillar of its economy. Then during World War I the Germans invented synthetic nitrates, and by the early 1920s the Chilean nitrate business disappeared.

At about this time the great Chilean copper ore deposits were acquired by two large U.S. companies, Kennecott and Anaconda, and the rapid development of the Chilean copper deposits shortly took up the slack left by the collapse of the nitrate markets. By 1964 more than 80 percent of the country's export earnings came from copper, and the taxes paid by the mining companies accounted for more than half of the government's income.

In 1964 Eduardo Frei was elected president of Chile by a record vote margin over a Marxist named Salvador Allende, and the Frei government began planning the industrial and technological renaissance of Chile.

One of its basic interests was petrochemicals. Empresa Nacional del Petroleo (ENAP), the government oil agency, wanted to develop ethylene, a petroleum by-product, as a key raw material for a host of chemicals, plastics, and fibers. Petroquimica Chilena (PQC), another wholly owned government entity, was planning a caustic soda/chlorine plant at Concepcion; chlorine would be in excess supply in the caustic production process, so a profitable outlet for chlorine was needed. This combination of Chilean ethylene and chlorine availability provided a great potential for manufacturing several of the more useful plastic materials.

That was why Dow was invited into the act. In June 1965 we received a letter from Corporacion de Fomento (CORFO), the excellent industrial development agency of the Chilean Government, inquiring whether Dow would be interested in participating in a joint venture with Chile for the production of two plastics—low-density polyethylene and polyvinyl chloride. We were interested, although we did not know very much about Chile; we had no local operations, no offices, only a local independent distributor representing us. Further, we have never been very enthusiastic about joint ventures, and we had no experience in ventures where the other portion of the operation was owned by a government.

Our response was that we were interested in the joint venture if we could have a controlling interest so that we could protect our exceptional technology and ensure the proper efficient management of the business. As the negotiations progressed and proposals and counterproposals were considered, Dow discovered that it was one of a total of 17 chemical companies of many nations being considered as partner for this proposal and that the Chileans were gradually narrowing down the candidates. By October 1966, however, Dow had developed with the Chilean Government agencies the proposal eventually adopted, so we were ready to go ahead when the government finally selected Dow Chemical and approved and accepted this proposal.

During the negotiations we put a great deal of emphasis on the fact that we wanted to install an efficient, technologically advanced joint-venture enterprise that would not only make money for Dow but also for Chile and become the leader in developing for Chile a plastics industry. We did not sugarcoat the fact that we wanted to make a profit. So this profitability concept was expressly written into the master agreement we signed with the Chilean Government. I remember one of the Chilean representatives saying to me, "We realize that Dow Chemical is not the American Red Cross. We recognize that you cannot invest in and operate this venture unless you obtain earnings for your many stockholders."

When President Frei signed the decree approving this investment, we entered into a partnership with the Chilean Government in which Dow owned 70 percent of Petroquimica-Dow S.A. or Petrodow, the joint venture, and the other 30 percent was owned by the Chilean Government entities, ENAP and PQC.

The financing of this $31 million project was rather unique. ENAP and PQC paid for their shares in escudos in cash (the equivalent of $4 million), and Dow invested $8 million in cash and $2 million by transferring know-how and technology. The remaining $17 million of the capital needed was obtained by the joint-venture company through loans made by the Export-Import Bank and the Bank of America, with CORFO as guarantor.

Under the terms of the master agreement, Dow was also to be paid for the technical services and engineering required for building the plants, was to be paid royalties for the process technologies provided to the venture, for continuing know-how during 10 years from start-up, and for other financial considerations. The Chilean Government guaranteed the availability of national raw materials at competitive prices to the joint venture company and gave assurances that Petrodow would receive duty protection, that reasonable price stabilization would be maintained, and that other commercial considerations would be provided.

In 1968 construction began at Concepcion in Chile of what Dow planned would be the finest petrochemical complex in the Andes, a model of its kind, and the seedbed for a thriving plastics industry in the southern part of the South American continent. It was called the Petrodow complex. By the middle of 1970 its construction was virtually complete. Production began in the fall of that year, and from an operational viewpoint the plant was an immediate success. We felt we had given birth to a real winner, and we were beginning to see the opportunity to make solid contributions to Chile—and earnings for Dow's investment. We moved ahead with plans to invest in a polystyrene plant, fully owned by Dow, at Santiago.

However, a new variable entered the picture: the 1970 presidential elections. As Eduardo Frei could not be reelected, the race became a three-way contest. Jorge Alessandri, who had been president from 1958 to 1964, represented the right-of-center National Party; Radomiro Tomic was the candidate of Frei's leftist Christian

Democratic Party; and on the far left was Salvador Allende, the Marxist, who had three times before been a loser in Chilean presidential elections.

Alessandri was considered the odds-on favorite. The pollsters were giving him 55 percent of the votes in the preelection polls, and very few political observers gave Tomic and Allende any chance.

What happened is now considered one of the more stunning electoral upsets in history. Allende won only 36.2 percent of the popular vote but squeaked in first, just ahead of Alessandri. The Chilean Congress ratified his election in October 1970 with the support of Tomic. Chile suddenly found itself being governed by the Unidad Popular, a coalition of Marxists and Socialists. It soon became obvious that drastic changes were to come.

Most dramatically, in the business world the U.S. copper companies, which controlled more than 90 percent of the Chilean copper deposits, were expropriated without compensation. Ford, General Motors, Du Pont, and others lost their holdings.

Unfortunately for Chile, Allende's Marxist economic and political policies did not result in progress for Chile. Industrial output fell off rapidly. Large numbers of technically educated and professional Chileans left their country for other countries.

During the early months of the Allende regime the Petrodow operation continued its normal and expected growth, without any interference. Our relationship with the Chilean Government representatives and authorities from 1965 to 1970 had been cordial and excellent. But as the new Allende representatives were introduced, these relations began to cool down, and before long, with no change in attitude on our part, the cordiality of the Chilean Government representatives waned. It was 23 months from the time Allende took over until the two Dow operations were suddenly requisitioned without prior notice.

Let me describe briefly how this takeover happened: In December 1971 the Allende government gave us the first indication of its new objectives by a letter requesting the opening of "conversations" concerning its wish to restructure the stock ownership of Petrodow to increase its voting power to 51 percent instead of 30 percent. We did not welcome this suggestion but did indicate our willingness to talk. We pointed out first of all that we were happy to continue in partnership but that there was a serious stumbling block to such discussions, which was that the Allende government was responsible for about $2 million in arrears in the payments by the joint-venture company to Dow Chemical for royalties and payments for the construction and engineering of the plants. We felt these payments should be honored before any serious talks began. During the ensuing months several meetings took place that were not very satisfactory.

Then in September 1972 the union workers of Petrodow staged a walkout over an alleged labor grievance involving the right to assign supervisory personnel. After heavy negotiation, a settlement was almost reached, but then the union came back with a new batch of demands. Again and again settlements were prevented during this work stoppage because the labor union would make last-minute changes in its uncompromising position. We have since learned that the union was acting at the suggestion of socialist government representatives, who were apparently using these tactics in an effort to pressure Dow.

As this confusing situation continued the Petrodow plants remained on strike, and when it was entering its third week, the whole nation was hit by the national strike that tied up the entire country, brought about by public protests against shortages, economic conditions, government policies, and related matters. During the two weeks that followed several hundred Chilean companies were "requisitioned" by the government on the pretext that "they were unable to operate normally." Among the hundreds of plants that were unable to ship their product—because the entire transport system of the country was on strike—were the two Petrodow plants in Concepcion and the Dow Quimica Chilena polystyrene plant in Santiago. They were therefore among those taken over by the government on October 18, 1972.

We were both shocked and offended by this sudden and unprovoked takeover. We had always honored our Chilean commitments, and this illegal action was unjustified. When a government openly violates binding agreements and decrees, questions and doubts are raised.

We appealed through the Chilean courts, and in December 1972 the Controller General, who by law must support the legal grounds for such requisitions, ruled that the seizures were "not in conformance with the law" and rejected the requisitions. The government appealed, and the Controller General of Chile earlier this year again declared that both requisitions had no legal basis.

One unusual aspect of our experience was that when the Chilean Government requisitioned the Petrodow complex, the Chilean salaried and technical employees went out on strike—against the takeover by the Chilean Government. And they stayed out, in protest against the seizure of the plants. They told the government they considered Dow technology essential and Dow management and operations techniques vital to the successful operation of the plant. It made little difference. Today, almost a year later, we are aware that there is little hope of recovering our Chilean plants.

As a footnote to this sad story, let me give you a rough breakdown of what has happened to our 131 Chilean employees as of September 1973. Of the total, 65 decided to leave Chile, and 66 stayed in their homeland. Of those who left Chile 32 requested employment and have been relocated in jobs in other countries, mostly in Latin America

13

but 12 in the United States. Twenty have found jobs with other companies with our cooperation, as requested by each of them, and six have found jobs on their own. Three are in other countries seeking new jobs. Of the 66 who stayed in Chile, 40 have moved to jobs with other Chilean companies. Eight were not in the job market (girls who got married, students who returned to school, and the like), and 18, we have heard, are still seeking jobs in Chile. The plants that we began operating less than three years ago now stand idle, and the bright hopes for a Chilean industrial renaissance have suffered.

There are those who might say that Dow was saddened to leave Chile only because it has lost the opportunity to obtain profits there. This is not true. We always feel that we are at our best when we are working with excellent people; and when we are helping people develop into effective employees, they and Dow together are usually making the most money.

The Lessons from the Chilean Experience

Among other things, I believe we learned that Dow's behavior in Chile was in every respect exemplary—a model of how a multinational company should conduct itself in a developing country. We contributed our very best technology, which the country wanted and badly needed. In the process our employee relations were outstanding. And quite late in the day even representatives of the government were expressing satisfaction with our technological achievements. We were repeatedly praised by Chilean businessmen, economists, and in the press as an example of how a foreign company ought to conduct itself.

The conclusion is that the very best plans and intentions can come to an unhappy ending when an extremist political government takes over control of a democratic nation with whose previous democratic government you have carefully developed all proper and legal requirements.

As a case study the Chile experience raises some interesting points.

The Role of the Multinational Company

The first is that the multinational company is an efficient economic instrument, and it should therefore be used for economic purposes. The basic universal problem in the developing nations, in one form or another and to one degree or another, is the need to improve the living conditions of all the people. The multinational company role should be primarily geared to this problem—that is, to the problem of producing more goods, more foodstuffs, more products and services, and thereby raising the overall living standards of the whole population of the host country.

The multinational company is admirably equipped for this role. By and large, what the developing countries have in abundance is people, and in varying amounts, natural resources. What they lack is capital, technology, markets, and management; and these are what the multinational company can bring to these countries. It is in fact the only institution that can bring to them all of these essential things in one package.

So I believe the primary role of the multinational company should be aimed at developing and employing local people and resources to raise the local living standard, this being done in close cooperation with the local government authorities and in accordance with the laws of the country. In return the local government should be willing to provide adequate compensation for the multinational company to encourage its efforts, fully recognizing that we are owned by stockholders who expect reasonable returns on their equity and that we are not charitable organizations. We must obtain earnings for our stockholders.

My second point has to do with complete education. I have already discussed this question, so let me only summarize. The second greatest universal problem of many of the developing countries is a lack of a modern, technological educational system available to all. The Brazilian Government, for example, has recognized this and is currently undertaking a major educational effort, with more than 1.5 million adults participating actively in a basic education program.

The multinational companies are technically oriented and can usefully supplement the educational efforts of the host countries in the technology field. We already train professionals and technicians to run our plants of course, and we also train local people as business, marketing, industrial managers, to become the managers of those operations and plants. But a broader effort than this is called for, because I think also that it is essential to teach farmers to use advanced methods (and the advanced products we have to offer), and we should also be teaching the people, the consuming public, how to use more sophisticated products. We should also be supporting the university-level training in the host countries; a chemical company, for example, should be willing to provide help to local schools of chemistry and chemical engineering.

In brief, I believe the multinational companies must emphasize their educational role in the developing nations and help these nations raise their educational levels as rapidly as possible. I do not see this as altruistic; I see it as enlightened self-interest.

We are contending in many places with the revolution of rising expectations. When you show people a better life and develop in them the notion that they can live that better life, it is not very long before they insist on living that better life now—not tomorrow. We have little problem showing the better life and planting the idea that it's possible, but we do have problems keeping up with the demand for better things. The people in the developing countries often go through crises of this sort. Our problem in years to come may well turn out to be whether we in the more developed nations can keep up with the demands from the underdeveloped nations to achieve a living standard similar to what we have in the developed countries. The multinational companies can do much to reduce the gap. In fact they can probably do more than any other institution I know of, but a better understanding of their role must be achieved in order to give them the freedom to exercise that role.

In conclusion, one further comment: I believe the multinational companies would welcome standard international rules to work by, together with a code of international standards governing their proper treatment by the host nations—some internationally approved method of governing the relationships between the nation states and the multinational companies and settling their disputes in an impartial court. In my opinion the need for such a set of international rules of the game is becoming clear.

As we continue to develop this subject, perhaps we will all come to the same conclusion—that international rules are needed. This is one aspect of the problem I hope we can discuss more fully. We need a great deal of constructive and creative thought on this aspect of the problem.

The countries of Latin America have much to offer the world. They may not be world-record-beaters in science, in business, in democratic institutions, or in following strict international legal codes. But they can teach the rest of the world all there is to know about things like friendship, the art of conversation, racial equality, individualism, and the fact that people are more important than things. We can learn much from each other. If we do, the future of the world will be better and brighter.

MULTINATIONALS AND THE LDCs
Miguel S. Wionczek

We are meeting at a time when the concern about the growing unregulated impact of multinational corporations upon the world economy and particularly upon the political, social, and economic life of the LDCs is felt everywhere. According to the latest estimates, at least some 500 books, essays, and articles have been written in the past few years on that subject by political scientists, sociologists, and economists of many nationalities. While most of this literature has its origin in the United States and Western Europe, multinationals are also the subject of analytical research and very often of extremely violent attacks in Latin America, Asia, and Africa.

While it is obviously impossible to find a consensus among all those who study the interrelationship between multinationals, national economies, and world politics, there is a growing body of agreement among people concerned with the growth and the spread of multinationals in the LDCs. Most of the people in the LDCs, both social scientists and political men, seem to agree that because of their sheer size and their ability largely to ignore the objectives of the weak nation-states, multinational firms are sources of many conflicts. Moreover, the present regulatory mechanisms in force in their countries of origin (the United States, Western Europe, and Japan) are useless for the peaceful resolution of conflicts that involve multinationals and the governments of the weak host countries, the governments of their home countries and the host countries, and multinationals and the different groups in the host countries' societies.

Leaving aside the radical position of those who claim that multinational corporations represent the extension of the imperialist power of the major advanced capitalist countries, there is a growing body of evidence that multinationals if left to themselves may bring havoc in political, social, and economic terms to most LDCs, that their modus operandi does not represent the efficient way of fostering economic growth and social welfare, and that their claim of providing capital and technology for development of the LDCs is highly exaggerated.

What sort of evidence is available in this respect in the LDCs? First, the large part of affiliates and branches of multinationals in the LDCs has been established by the acquisition of local firms, stifling the growth of domestic entrepreneurial talents and limiting economic opportunities of local enterprises. Second, the concentration of the activities of multinationals in the mining and manufacturing sectors of the LDCs represents a serious obstacle to the implementation by the host countries of their economic policies in such important fields as industrialization, foreign trade, and monetary and fiscal management. Third, the multinationals' ability to play the individual LDCs against each other in the name of the "good climate" for foreign private investment feeds the intra-LDCs' conflicts and results in the excessive concessions granted to multinationals by those LDCs that badly need foreign capital and technology. Fourth, the positive capital contribution of the multinationals to the LDCs is open to doubt. Not only does the multinationals' strategy call for the maximum mobilization of local financial resources by their affiliates and branches in the LDCs (as well as in the DCs), but total profits from their operations when correctly accounted for are as a rule extremely high, and much higher because of their monopolistic and oligopolistic position in the relatively small market than in the home countries. Fifth, the technological contribution of the multinationals to the LDCs is very limited, if present at all, because of the concentration of the research and development (R and D) in the home countries and the widespread practice of exporting technological inputs with little adaptation to the needs of LDCs. Sixth, multinationals are a powerful mechanism for the transfer of patterns of consumption prevailing in the high-income, advanced countries to the LDCs through control of information and publicity media.

To these serious drawbacks for the LDCs arising from the spread of multinationals in their national territories one must add political complications. While it is true that in their home countries multinationals try to keep at arm's length from their governments if they cannot influence the governmental policies and actions in their favor, they do their best to use their home governments on their behalf when conflicts arise between their branches and affiliates in the LDCs and the LDC governments. Such conflicts spill over into intergovernmental conflicts with particularly high frequency in Latin America, where on one hand the large majority of multinationals are of U.S. origin and on the other the region as a whole is considered on political and other grounds as the area of "special interest" for the United States. In Latin America, as a matter of fact, very few people are willing or able to disassociate the U.S. conflict with Cuba, U.S. direct or indirect military interventions in Central America and the Dominican Republic, and the fall of the Allende government in Chile from the powerful presence in all these countries of U.S.-based multinationals. Many people in Latin America who are not necessarily radicals point out, for example, that the deterioration in U.S.-Cuban relations after the Castro revolution reached the point of no return shortly after Fidel Castro's policies affected directly the interests of the giant oil multinationals. The political conflicts involving Standard Oil in Peru and International Telephone and Telegraph (ITT) in Chile are too recent to have to be recalled here.

Until some years ago, Latin America's left-of-center hostility toward multinational corporations (for different reasons, the Latin American extreme right very often has not been friendly to multinationals either) was part and parcel of the ideological anti-U.S. attitudes. This hostility has not declined, as indicated by recent serious research started in the region on the behavior of these giant foreign corporate bodies. The results of this research, carried out by people who hardly can be considered "professional anti-Americans," provide evidence to the effect that multinationals engage in many activities and practices in Latin America that would be considered illegal in their home countries. These practices do not limit themselves to the oligo-polistic division of markets or price-fixing collusion but aim at tax evasion and profit maximization of multinational corporate systems at considerable cost to the host countries. These last practices are known in the jargon of economics as transfer-pricing and reverse transfer-pricing. Transfer-pricing involves fixing artificially above the international level the prices of goods and services (including tech-nology) imported from headquarters by the foreign branches and af-filiates of multinationals. Reverse transfer-pricing, on the other hand, involves fixing unilaterally below the international level the prices of goods exported by the same branches and affiliates in the LDCs to the headquarters and the third markets. The tax havens in Panama, the Bahamas, and other parts of the Caribbean are of particular value for this type of quasilegal transactions. Their frequency and intensity ex-plain the extreme reluctance of multinationals to disclose any infor-mation about their accounting procedures at the foreign-branch or af-filiate level and the paucity of any information in this respect in the annual consolidated profit-and-loss statements, issued as a rule in the home countries only.

Arbitrary and quasilegal practices of the multinationals in respect to technological transactions within individual multinational corporate systems have been discovered lately in a number of Latin American countries that introduced technology transfer-control systems. The evidence in this field, together with the findings about transfer- and reverse-transfer-pricing practices of multinationals, led to the re-jection of the validity of the U.S. Department of Commerce statistics on the profitability of foreign investment in Latin America. It may be worth noting that the most recent UN study on the role of multinational corporations in the world economy, released in early August 1973, studiously avoids presenting many statistical data compiled by the U.S. Department of Commerce on the basis of periodical reports by U.S. investors abroad, data that in the past were widely used in defense of the position that foreign direct investment represents the best if not the only way of helping the development of LDCs.

While very few people in Latin America outside of the radical left believe that multinationals can be "wished away" and many assume that these relatively new corporate forms will continue to grow rapidly, there is a growing consensus in the region about the urgent need of in-troducing some international mechanisms aimed at controlling and, if necessary, policing multinationals. Moreover, it is felt in Latin America that such international control will be forthcoming during the 1970s. Such expectations do not arise exclusively from legitimate grievances against multinational corporations in the LDCs but from the growing realization that conflicts between multinationals and the nation states extend to relations between these corporate structures and the developed countries as well, as suggested by the voices of trade unions and consumer organizations in the advanced countries.

TWO CONFLICTING PERSPECTIVES: NATIONALISM AND DEPENDENCIA
Theodore H. Moran

My background is in analyzing the politics of economic nationalism in Latin America. I suppose I was invited here as an expert on left-handed screws and right-handed screws, which in fact is the subject I'm going to talk about in trying to put the two preceding presentations into perspective. I think very interestingly they illustrate two broad and widely accepted approaches to relations between foreign investors and host countries in Latin America, two broad ways of conceptualizing the evolution of the relationship between foreign investors and host countries.

I want to discuss these two approaches and then add just a brief comment of my own on the specific theme of the possibilities for the international conciliation of international conflicts, of international accords for governing the relationship between foreign investors and host countries.

I think that the first broad approach is generally characterized by the term dependencia, or some kind of dependence. I won't try to pin this just on Professor Wionczek—that is, I'm drawing on other sources, and he may want to disagree with some of my characterizations—but I think that his statements fit into that mold on the whole. Very briefly, at each stage of the possibility of a Latin American breakthrough to some kind of development—whether it was supplying the raw materials and agricultural products to industrial metropolises, or the painful process of import-substituting industrialization, or later the attempt to broaden export markets to the Latin American Free Trade Area (LAFTA), or, finally, through the process of trying to export manufactured products to the developed countries—at each of these crucial stages in the potential for Latin American development, Latin Americans found that they were in some sense dependent upon foreign technology, foreign investments, and foreign corporations, dependent in the sense that they needed these scarce and valuable resources, capital, management, experience, marketing expertise, research and development, and so on. Or they were dependent in the sense that as soon as they set up their own facilities, then foreign investors moved in and either bought up the existing companies or somehow came to dominate these markets. The general thrust of this perspective on what is going on in foreign investment in Latin

20

America is that, as Professor Wionczek said, the crucial centers—
either the most valuable growing industries, the most technologically
advanced industries, the industries that were crucial in the process
of development—were dominated by foreign investors at each stage
in Latin American development.

Now why was this? This was because in fact the foreign investors
did have expertise the Latins lacked. In some cases, in many cases,
it was because foreign investors were more efficient, although, as
we all know, efficiency can take two different forms: It can be realized
either through better products and lower prices for consumers or
through higher profits to be shipped back to the parent company.

I think that probably Professor Wionczek would say that because
of intersubsidiary transactions, transfer-pricing, intersubsidiary
debt, and other kinds of manipulation, the benefits were less great
than we had generally been led to expect. Nevertheless I think that
it is fair to say that most dependentistas here do believe that this is
a non-zero-sum game, that is, there are benefits accruing to both
sides in this process. But even within this non-zero-sum situation
you still have this continuing dependence, this continuing domination
by foreign investors (in particular North American investors) over
the process of development.

For example, if you look at the problem of the transfer of technology, what the dependencia perspective argues is that there really
isn't any transfer of technology. I mean that the control over technology is what gives the foreign corporations the basis for exacting
their high profit rates. In the case of Dow Chemical in Chile, for
example, the crucial issue was not the fact that Dow Chemical wanted
to go there and that Chile wanted Dow Chemical to come there. Nor
was the crucial issue that Dow wanted to keep 80 percent, or maybe
51 percent, control. The important point is that the foreign corporation doesn't want to let go of its technology. In fact all it's doing is
setting up a subsidiary in which it would simply be educating nationals
to be good workers or good engineers or good participants in a process
essentially dominated by a foreign corporation. There is no real
transfer of technology.

So I think that that is one of the broad perspectives on foreign
investors' host country relations: It pictures host countries as
fundamentally dependent on foreign controls; it is the scenario of
dependencia. If you think it is sad, I think it is matched by the opposite
picture, which is what we got from the case study of Mr. Gerstacker.
I would subsume this under the heading "economic nationalism," that
is, seeing the relations between foreign investors and host countries
in Latin America as one of increasing challenges by economic nationalists. I think that Dow Chemical in Chile probably got the squeeze
process in a compressed form that many companies in many industries

(including the mining, manufacturing, and financial sectors) have had generally over a longer period of years in Latin America. I myself don't think that it has much to do with Dr. Allende or Marxism or Communism. I think it is more properly identified with populism, the desire for national autonomy, sovereign control—in short, economic nationalism.

Now, this scenario is looking at the evolution of the relations between the investor in the country from a perspective opposite to that of the dependencia perspective. Here is a company doing what it does very well, being invited by a government to come and contribute to Chilean development—and it could have been Brazilian or Argentinian or Mexican development. Even the Chileans were sensitive enough to perceive that Dow Chemical was not the American Red Cross. They said, "You come in, of course you are going to make a profit, of course you want to keep the possibility of earning your profits, and we recognize this. Come on in, we'll sign the contracts more or less in a form acceptable to you." And then the concessions are signed, the contracts are signed, the financial agreements are signed.

What happens—and, as I say, it happened to Dow in compressed form—is that over a period of five or six years, after the installations are in place, after the operation is a success, after this large stream of profits is either overtly or covertly flowing back to the parent corporation, there suddenly begins a process of squeeze, and all of you are probably better experts than I am on what forms this can take: renegotiations, fiddling around with exchange rates, complete rearrangement of the basic contracts, breaking of old contracts, and so on. In any case, there is this squeezing process that goes on.

Since my experience in Latin America has mostly to do with mine and mineral concessions and with some petroleum concessions and manufacturing, let me tell you just briefly what happens there. Somebody, say Anaconda or Kennecott, points to a mountain and says to the minister of Mining, "We think that there is copper or zinc or tin in there, and we're willing to put in $150 million to see. We really won't have any idea of the extent to which it is there or, more precisely, of the operating costs of bringing it out until we've sunk all this money. If you want us to go in and take these huge risks, sign on the dotted line." And then the government hems and haws, but generally, whether they are nationalists or not, they end up signing on the dotted line because at that point the uncertainty is very great and they want the foreign investment to come in.

I've had some experience in groups I've been associated with in looking over these initial concessions agreements (the one I have in mind was a Japanese company), and the kinds of concessions they demanded in this initial agreement included the likes of which have not been seen since the days of Teddy Roosevelt! Well, we took out some of the obvious nonsense, but pretty much we advised them to sign the generous contract.

Once the money is sunk and the thing comes on line, it turns out to be something slightly short of a bonanza. And five or six years later somebody comes back and says, "Look, it's time to tighten things up." Then this process of squeezing begins. It may take the form of reducing foreign control from 100 percent to 80 percent, or from 80 percent to 51 percent, or from 51 percent to 49 percent, whatever the crucial issue is. It may be limited to renegotiating taxes. In all of these things, again, some of you have more experience than I. But nevertheless the squeeze process goes on. Each time the host country wants more from the foreign corporation. First they get the mine, and then they say, "Look, we also would like to have you refine the stuff here instead of shipping it out as ore." Then the company says, "O.K., let's start all over again," and they sign on the dotted line again. This back-and-forth process goes on and on. In many cases, especially in large crucial issues, it may in fact lead to nationalization, but not always. It is often just a kind of continuing dialectic.

These I think are the two broad perspectives that were presented in the preceding sections. I would like to comment first of all by saying that there is evidence for both of these conceptions, and secondly by addressing the question I said at the beginning I would address: What are the prospects for some kind of international conciliation, international rules of the game, given the dynamics of these two perspectives?

First, the evidence. To make any sense of the evidence I think you have to break foreign investors' host country relations down into different sectors and different industries. Twenty years ago most underdeveloped countries wanted to build steel mills and take control of their own petroleum industry. And everybody said, "No, there is no possibility, steel is a very involved process, you will never be as efficient as U.S. Steel, and you will never be able to produce and refine crude oil." Well, as the situation now stands, you can drop a postcard to a post office box in Houston, Texas, and they will fly down and build the refinery for you, teach you how to run it, and turn it over to you. It is not such a big thing any more to refine crude oil. Mexico, Brazil, and Chile to a certain extent have moderately efficient steel industries, which is no more than we can say for the United States. So that if you look at these two sectors you will find that the economic nationalism is the correct perspective. There has been a process of squeeze, and the host countries have gained from it.

What about industries on the cutting edge of technology today? If you look at IBM, for example or some of the manufacturers of automobiles, you would have to look at this with the perspective of dependencia in the sense that there has been a long tradition of the foreign investor's being fairly invulnerable, being able to control operations fairly tightly. Now I would imagine, not knowing much about it, that this is changing in automobiles. I don't think it will change very fast in IBM. Ten years from now we may find that Bob Bennett will be sitting here looking worried because he is afraid they are going to close in on them at IBM, and Al De Rosso of Exxon will long since be gone or will be working for Sheik Yamani in Saudi Arabia, if he has a job at all! At the same time there will be other people with laser technology or biomedical chemistry or some such thing sitting around the table smiling because they feel invulnerable.

So it seems to me that the most technologically advanced industries have given support to this broad aura of dependencia. At the same time I think that you do have this underlying process of economic national- ism, of pushing, pushing, pushing one industry after another by Latin American countries struggling to take control of the sectors that are crucial to their own growth.

If this is correct—that there are really two broad perspectives of what is going on and that both of them are correct and that both of them are going on at the same time—what does this tell us about the possi- bilities of international rules of the game?

Now if you talk to businessmen, they say, "Look, we can adjust our behavior. You tell us what the rules of the game are, we'll go in and we'll play. It is this damn changing of the rules that we can't quite take. These Latins are always breaking their contracts." But what is happening is that power relations change and are being renegotiated when the balance of power shifts in favor of the host country. That does involve breaking contracts, but that basically is what business and political groups do all the time.

I realize that my point of view is not accepted by everybody. I was asked to give a paper for the American Society of International Law, discussing nationalism and the dissolution of contracts in Latin America, and I asked as a rhetorical question, "Why is it that these contracts are so controversial and so unstable? Is it because Latin Americans are less trustworthy and less morally sound than the rest of us?" And I glanced up to find there were 250 heads that were about to nod agreement in unison, so there are some people for whom that is not a rhetorical question. To me however it is.

When businessmen talk about international standards of conduct, or international rules of the game, they have the dependencia syndrome in mind. They don't want to be challenged in their control over tech- nology, in their ability to control and appropriate to themselves these oligopoly rents. So they are willing to work within any system that allows them some way of keeping that control.

When you talk to host country representatives, they say that we need the UN to devise some international standard of conduct so that nation states have a sovereign right to autonomous development or some phrase like that. Essentially what they have in mind too is some international rules of the game. But these are international rules of the game that correspond to the economic nationalism model. These are the rules of the game that permit them to readjust when the balance of power shifts in their favor. When they need the technology, foreign investors are invited in on terms acceptable to the foreigners. But when the balance of power shifts, they want the right to renegotiate.

This is what makes me basically pessimistic about these discussions on international regulation. Because the two groups have different scenarios in mind, they also have different Gestalts about what rules of the game will mean.

2

CONFLICT OF INTERESTS
AND SHIFTING POWER RELATIONS:
OPEN DISCUSSION OF THE GAINS
AND LOSSES

ACCELERATION OF CHANGE: WHO HAS THE POWER?

William J. Barnds: Ted, you said that the host countries would like to have rules of the game that would permit them at a given point of time, when they feel that the power balance has shifted, to renegotiate a change. I'm not sure that I agree with that. I think that they want to change the rules of the game so as to give them the right to have foreign investment on the basis on which they want it today, not when the balance has shifted. I think that is the problem. Because they are in fact, and have been for quite some time, renegotiating changes in contracts, and so on. What they want now is the technology.

Theodore H. Moran: Well, I think that is true, but part of what you are arguing comes from the fact that there is a great speedup in this play back and forth. The lessons that Libya has learned about renegotiating and pushing against oil companies, and it took 10 years to learn, Ecuador has learned in six months. Ecuador goes through more renegotiations of contracts every few months than Libya has gone through in the last decade. So they start very much near the edge of what other countries get.

Alphonse De Rosso: But that is true for oil, it is not true for manufacturing. You have to make a distinction. Countries that have natural resources can in fact demand their own rules of the game. But countries without resources cannot.

Mr. Moran: I would agree with you, but I do think that this process of inviting in generously and then squeezing after things are established does go on in fields other than extraction industries.

26

Ronald E. Muller: The resentment about initial generous terms can be felt by the foreign corporation, too. When a corporation has to enter a new foreign market, many times, particularly in the manufacturing sector, it sets up a contract with an independent foreign distributor, the independent foreign distributor develops the market for it, and then the corporation sits back and says, "Um, the terms are much too generous, now why don't I start a subsidiary or branch office there?" The contract is then renegotiated, or ended, and a new phase is started. In fact, this whole process is very familiar to your businessman. When you put a new product into the market, initially you have to test it, which takes time, but then there is an exponential demonstration effect, with people learning about it rapidly. Now countries and bureaucracies are no different from bureaucracies in the marketing divisions of multinational corporations. And I think that is what we're dealing with here: We are dealing with the rate of change, which is accelerating on both sides.

Mr. Barnds: Can I ask a question at this point? Do you think the rate of change is increasing because you now have not only U.S. but also European and Japanese corporations?

Mr. Muller: Very much. I think this is part of the changing bargaining power. In 1955 and 1960, when these people went into Latin America, you didn't have too much to worry about because you knew the Germans and the Japanese were just getting off the ground. Today it is a much different ballgame. The competition to you in terms of initial investment process is much rougher, and a host country that doesn't take advantage of this oligopic situation and play the oligopic competitive game with you is rather ignorant. So there are all new parameters in today's world that are forcing this so-called squeeze effect to accelerate, in my opinion.

Mr. Moran: Just to add to that briefly. Suddenly, if you talk to many representatives of Latin American countries, you find they are not even sure they want any rules of the game, because for the first time in 150 years they are starting to benefit themselves from the pulling, pushing, and squeezing. With natural resources they can pretty much write their own ticket. And I agree that international competitive factors enable them to gain more benefits in the financial sector and the manufacturing sector as well. They can take advantage of this process more than they have ever been able to in the past.

DOES THE LDC NEED THE MNC?
DOES THE MNC NEED THE LDC?

Victor G. Reuther: I don't know why LDCs shouldn't be able to negotiate investment arrangements with multinational firms somewhat more in keeping with what their own set of terms and possibilities are. Because all of the developing countries of the world are at one hell of a disadvantage in any negotiations, and always will be, in negotiating with multinational firms whose resources, whose strength, dwarf that of many combined nations. What kind of negotiations can they be except terribly lopsided and unfair?

Obviously a set of circumstances has to be created wherein the great multinational firms who have orated so much about competition and its benefits will have a little more competition from the area of the availability of public funds for investment. The more the area of public funds for investment becomes readily available on more equitable and more satisfactory terms, the less the developing world will be looked upon by multinational firms as just another area for economic exploitation.

I don't care how much Dow Chemical Company may try to be sympathetic to changing economic and political circumstances in the country, you will never be able to escape the onus of all of your fellow multinational firms who have left so deep an imprint on the mentality of people in emerging countries that this has now become a great motor generating this new sense of economic nationalism that seems to worry so many people.

We are confronted with not just the need to demonstrate that the multinational corporations are more efficient in their investments and their managerial talents. Those statistics, impressive as they may sound and appear on paper, are not providing the real answer to the groundswell of a determination on the part of people in emerging countries of the world that they not only make economic progress but that they make simultaneous progress in terms of winning that kind of economic democracy that gives them mastery and control over their own lives, which they do not have today.

The U.S. corporation is supposed to be committed to reinforcing and strengthening the democratic processes, but I would be so bold as to say that the curve of the growth and the influence of multinational corporate forces in Latin America parallels the downward curve of democratic influences in South America. As the influence of the multinational corporations has grown, they have sought to encourage the kind of political climate that is easier to operate from within. I can understand that mentality, but we ought to know the price people are being asked to pay for it.

Allende's greatest error (and I assume he committed many) was that he did not move ruthlessly in acquiring complete dictatorial control of the armed forces. Had he been successful in doing that, he would have won the respect of the multinational firms who now go hat in hand to the most powerful and ruthless communist powers in the world. What is there that permits a multinational corporation to look upon the Soviet Union and China as stable centers for potential economic growth and as potential collaborators in the economic sphere, but to look upon a small weak nation like Chile, headed by a man far less committed to extremist views than the Soviets and the Chinese ever were, as a threat?

It is no secret that the multinational firms in Chile, as in most Latin American countries where they still have a choice between democracy and military dictatorship, through their support during the electoral campaigns stood behind those who would favor a more centralized form of government. That can be documented throughout the history of the multinational firms in Latin America.

And of course multinational firms in Chile played a very active role during the campaign. I salute Dow Chemical in that it did not. Allende did win the elections, and the elections were conducted in the arena of free and open debate, which is damned scarce in Latin America these days. And instead of accepting and recognizing that democratic decision, intervention against it continued through the withholding of terms that multinationals would have offered to a military junta. The same terms were not offered to Allende. And this is a form of economic intervention.

The multinational corporations are in a position to get pretty much the kind of political climate they are willing to pay for at this moment. But I would insert a word of caution. The more times Allendes are crushed, the less options you have open between the choice of an outright military dictatorship and an outright communist dictatorship. The democratic alternative has now been destroyed in Chile. And I don't see much of a democratic alternative in Brazil, where an elected government was overthrown with the support of multinational corporations.

I don't mean to imply that multinational corporations are wild devils that have no sense of morality. Our own people in the United States were treated precisely the same way by the multinational firms before some of them became multinational. And why should one be surprised by certain practices undertaken in South America by multinational firms, whether Japanese or American or German or Italian, when most of these firms had to be brought kicking and screaming into the 20th century? It took enormous social pressures in those countries to get them to put into practice the most simple elemental things that recognize the rights of people to live as human beings who have some voice and some say over the control of their own destiny.

There has been no mention to date of the impact of the growth of multinational corporations on labor relations. Let me just say that when General Motors went worldwide, and Dow Chemical and International Harvester and ITT—that by doing so you did more than Karl Marx ever achieved or ever hoped to achieve in his lifetime in creating an awareness and international consciousness on the part of those employed by your firms, because you still insist on tearing out collective bargaining within the confines of national boundaries and national borders but reserve the right to make decisions as a multinational organization at the world level, free to shift operations across national boundaries, decisions that have an enormous bearing on the established legal collective bargaining rights of workers. But no serious thought has been given by the multinational corporation to a structure that would give the workers within all of these industries where they operate in all of these nations machinery through which they can have their problems heard and resolved.

Now you can ignore that at your peril also. But these problems will find a solution. And I think thus far we have not really faced up to what the real problems are that have arisen as a result of the expansion of the multinational corporation.

Carl A. Gerstacker: Dow performed as well as it could in our opinion in that Chile plastic plant. We didn't force our way into Chile; we were invited. Chile picked us out of 17 companies of many nationalities. We don't think we misled the Chileans in our profit desires, or in the control of our technology, which we wished to have. And we feel that no one forced them to choose us; certainly we did not. In addition, something I haven't said: We had written into the agreement that we would sell part of our stock and the government would sell part of its stock to the Chilean public as soon as the company was operating reasonably well.

I'd like to ask you people to suggest what we did wrong or what we could do better in the future in a similar type of investment. Should we not have accepted Chile's choice of us in 1965? Should we have stayed out of this? If we should be asked, should we not go back into Chile? What should we do if the Chilean Government now asks us to go back and put this plant in running shape? It is not running, it hasn't produced lately, it is a mess. Should we go back and fix it up? On what terms should we go back in if we should? Should we invest in any Latin country? If this operation was wrong, at least for now we don't know how to do it properly.

If we refuse to invest any more in Latin countries, we'll get along, but I think it will be a real loss to the less developed countries if they don't have companies investing in their countries. So I'd like some help.

Terrance Hanold: Is the first question that ought to be considered whether multinationals should withdraw from South America? We have heard some opinions that would suggest these corporate structures do no good in the countries in which they operate, are detrimental to people who work for them, and are destructive of the societies in which they function. Is that the opinion of the speakers on this point?

Miguel Wionczek: I think that is a very good question. I don't believe that at this stage, at this point of history, the less developed countries would subscribe to the proposition that MNCs should withdraw from LDCs. I tried in my paper to present a list of conflicts of different sorts that are arising between the transnationals and the host countries. I do believe that in most Latin American countries, including my own, the intention is not so much to squeeze out transnationals, as Ted Moran said, but rather to introduce at least practices that force the transnationals to practice in their host countries what they are forced to practice in their home countries.

I give you one example. I believe that some kind of myth is being perpetuated, although there is considerable evidence to the contrary, that capital control is absolutely necessary to control a large manufacturing or mining firm. What is important is not capital control in the sense of 100 percent or 51 percent. The real factor of control is technological control, not capital control. The one who controls the access to technology controls the company. If the host country controls 51 percent of the stock but does not have control over the technology, then it does not control the company.

(Mr. Hanold commented in connection with the issue of control that the cause of many problems between MNCs and LDCs was that Latin Americans were operating with a "concept of sovereignty that is as dead as a dodo." In the following interchange he was asked to clarify this. Editor's note.)

James Finn: I would like to ask Terrance Hanold a question. You made the comment, I think, that the Latin American concept of sovereignty was "dead as a dodo." I really wasn't sure whether you meant that it was a Latin American concept, or just a concept that other people had, or whether the concept itself is dead, or what.

Mr. Hanold: Well, all of those things are true. We've conducted this thing with a splendid mixture of mythological terms that are contradicted by statements of fact. For example, the Dow case shows that these countries have choices now. Dow was only one of 17 candidates, and that indicates that discussion in terms of simple ultimatums ought to be foreign to the whole thing. It is no longer an issue. When we get around to the sovereignty thing, Latin America, to the degree that I have become involved with it (and I have never been south of Venezuela), has endowed sovereignty with a kind of mystical and reverential and spiritual quality that does deal in absolutes. So also this discussion has dealt in absolutes, either a colonial dependency or an arbitrary, overriding autocratic nationalism. And in Latin America there has been a swing from one type of mind to the other, and it is this type of mind, which says either we rule or are ruined, that makes it essentially a difficult area for international firms to deal with.

My own judgment of sovereignty is that it is a perfectly amoral concept. The concept of a government is de jure; if it has the power to govern, it does. That's all. We may withhold recognition from it if it is using that power to govern to offend us, but otherwise it is the government of the country.

Now this amorality extends through much of what it does, and any intelligent multinational will approach any government that follows this absolute sovereignty concept with this thought in mind, that an amoral government will regard a commitment as a matter of convenience. It exists because it is in power, its first objective is to remain in power, it will shift whatever commitments have been made by it in the interests of maintaining itself in power. There is no real substantive concept of contract that effectively operates in this area.

Now I don't think that any more in this world any government can take the position that it is unresponsive to any other force outside its own borders. But that is the way I read the attitude of most Latin American governments. They proceed from an absolute premise that the sovereign has total power and the prince is above the law.

Now I feel that if this discussion gets anywhere, it has got to get beyond the concept of dependencia, or colonialism, on the one hand, and absolute unbridled nationalism, on the other hand, and recognize that there is in this world a factor of interdependence. And this is a complicated world, where governments do not possess the total powers they did in the days of Henry VIII. They have—and any intelligent corporation must recognize it—the last word in declaring the policy of the area. But they are dependent in considerable degree on private enterprise for execution in effective terms of those policies. A corporation is simply there to carry through a function of benefit to the society on terms acceptable to society. Every operative corporation has recognized that fact, any that has endured for any length of time. Now these governments must recognize a responsibility to forces outside themselves. They must recognize in different terms, in different spirit, the character of the services they seek.

The whole world is not built on one-on-top-of-the-other, one-up-and-the-other-down. That is where my quarrel lies with the premises on which this discussion has proceeded so far, and that, I think, is the premise on which the concept of sovereignty in Latin America is based. It is supreme, and everything else must be shaped to its own particular design.

Mr. Moran: The idea of Latin American sovereignty may be as out-dated and as dead as a dodo, but it still motivates people to great things. Erroneously or not, it is still a very live concept. It seems to me that foreign investors don't have much choice but to learn some-how to live with it.

You put your finger on, I think, the most crucial question: Why not just pull out? And if everybody is going to cuss you out all the time, you know you have other things to do. Well, why don't you? The reason why is because there is money to be made. Dow's encapsulated five-year experience in Chile was exceptional, but in Mexico people have been playing this game of negotiation and re-negotiation for 20, 30 years and have been making good money in the process. And this goes for chemicals and plastics and other things too. Both sides want to have their cake and eat it too.

Latin Americans want and need more foreign investment. They want to get it there, but when they get it there, they want to squeeze it. North Americans want to go into there because there are good profits, and they go in there even though they realize that the balance of power is going to shift. Anyway, it seems that that kind of dialectic is what we are going to have to live with because these are the facts of life.

THE POSSIBILITIES AND LIMITATIONS OF PHASED WITHDRAWAL AND THE RENEGOTIATION OF CONTRACTS

Stanley H. Ruttenberg: I know it has been discussed in theory, and I'm no theoretician at all, but some academicians have advanced the notion of gradual withdrawal. Would the problem of Dow in Chile have been more easily resolved had Dow, instead of taking the position that they were going to maintain majority control of the corporation, taken the position that over time they were committed to withdraw and gradually turn over the corporation and/or its facilities and/or its technology to the indigenous ownership of the host country? Isn't it possible to look at the transnational or multinational corporation as a structure that is designed to provide the technical assistance, provide the original capital and/or technology, but then have a policy to turn over and withdraw from the country? I am really posing the problem.

Howard Schomer: Moving somewhat in the same direction, I don't find it hard at all to understand the sense of aggrieved righteousness on the part of Dow or any other company that has signed some contracts, gone ahead with an operation, and then found that the rules of the game were changed by the government. But I don't find it at all hard to understand, either, the resentment of the mass of people who see that company as just one of a total group of investors who, all the figures show, have exported much more from than they have imported into that country over the years. So they negotiated, out of weakness, a contract they had to have in order to get a thing started. I can understand Ted Moran's point that just as soon as they feel equal to it and have the leadership that calls for it, they will turn the screw.

My question is, is there a stimulating new model for business, such as the way people are now going about getting into the USSR? A big corporation tells me that they are in the process of difficult negotiations with the USSR to build a $50 million or $100 million food-processing plant. It is quite clear in negotiations that this U.S. corporation will not have title to that plant. It will not be there indefinitely; it has to regard both the technology it brings and the capital it invests and the expertise of management in getting the thing going and the training of the people as a service industry. It is a service that is being bought by the USSR.

Suppose independencia was offered by the U.S. corporation invited to start a plastic company in Chile rather than a particularly advantageous form of dependencia. Suppose we were creative enough to come up with calculations by which we could regard the whole ball of wax, the capital, the technology, and the business training and the education of the people to run the shop as a new kind of enterprise that our conglomerate intended to turn over to the host country and still calculate how to get a reasonable return. It won't be as big as some of the other returns have been, but it could be adequate.

Mr. Reuther: May I just break in to add that 35 years ago those were the terms on which the Ford Motor Company built the first automobile plant in the Soviet Union. I was privileged to spend two years helping in the planning of that factory. Yet in these past years we apparently haven't learned that it is possible to develop a business relationship on terms where you do not have control.

Mr. Hanold: I think that is an excellent point to take off on. Thirty-five years ago you gave them the technology for making automobiles.

And within the last 10 years they had to buy it all over again from
Fiat. And that, I think, goes to your problem. This is a nice little
package that you can all dream up and then mail it down there. Well,
we mailed it over to Russia, and they didn't have it. Peter Drucker
(and of course a good many other people) says that this isn't a world
of technology but a world of information, and information is constantly
being generated and regenerated. Dow can give them everything they
know of at this moment, and two years from now that plant is out-of-
date. It is the connection with the world that counts. That is what an
international corporation does: It connects itself to the world.

Luis Escobar: I would like to say first of all that the choice we are
confronted with is not a choice of take it or leave it. I think we are
fully aware that in our part of the world we are going to need transfer
of capital, transfer of technology; we are going to need a lot of help
in management and technical know-how.

So the real question in my view is that if we will have to face a
form of receiving these types of foreign investors, we must do so in
a manner that assures that we can believe and cooperate together for
the development of our economies. But it seems to me that there are
difficulties with plans suggested by Mr. Ruttenberg and Mr. Schomer.
It is not possible to establish from the very outset a period after which
the corporation agrees to relinquish its controls, because we cannot
foresee all the changes in the world, and we cannot foresee the nature
of those changes. So we have to look instead at how the power changes,
how the country and the company are going to look five years from
now. So we say, "These are the conditions under which you are going
to start out your business in this country, but five, ten years from
now, we agree that we are going to sit down and review the situation
and see what are the conditions under which we can continue cooper-
ating."

Suppose that five years from now we are not any longer the less
developed country; we can finance the capital that is needed for expansion, even though we may still need technology, we may still need
the know-how of the marketing so we can build this company. So we
will say, "Look, we don't need your capital, but we do need your
technological know-how, and we do need your cooperation in marketing."

The problem, it seems to me, has been that in the past all these
negotiations or renegotiations have been done in a static market form
because the original contract was made in cultures where we believed
that marriage is forever. If we have a divorce, it is traumatic, and
there is no easy way out of that situation. Now we are trying to
change our divorce laws, and at the same time we're trying to change
the law for private foreign investors.

Mr. Barnds: I would be interested if some of the people involved in business operations in Latin America would care to comment on how it would affect their profit strategies if the contract was subject to renegotiations in 10 years. Does this give you a feeling of more confidence that nothing would happen before that? Would you feel you would have to have a higher rate of profit in the interim because you don't know what is going to happen after 10 years?

Mr. Gerstacker: I'll comment on that. In our case, renegotiation occurred five years after our basic agreement, but that was only one year after the plant started, so I think that you have to take some of that lead time into account. Five or ten years from what? Taking that into account I think most companies would say that if we understand we have to renegotiate, we'll accept that, and either we don't become a party to it or we do become a party to it. If we are going to become a party to it under those circumstances, I think most companies would want to try to recover their capital in that period, whatever it was, because they would feel that they would not be in an equal negotiation situation when that time came.

Charles W. Powers: Is there any way out of that situation? Is there any way money can be put in escrow or put under control of a third party that would protect against that?

Mr. Gerstacker: I don't know. I haven't thought that far.

Mr. Moran: It seems to me that this will be the direction that foreign investment agreements will tend to take. What about some kind of escrow scheme? I think there are going to be more and more kinds of projects with phase-outs, systematic divestment, or whatever you want to call it. I have been studying, and am very interested in, the financing of the pipeline that runs along part of the Suez Canal, which the investors, Kidder-Peabody, has just won, and they realize that this is a very risky business. They are going to create $200 million for this pipeline in Egypt in the oil business, and if you can think of a more risky situation—well, I can't.
　　What they did was to have payments for the oil go into international banks outside of Egypt precisely because both sides know that the accounts can be blocked (and these are not Swiss banks incidentally; I don't know whether they are French or German or what). They know that if 10 years from now, after the pipeline gets built and the $200 million has not been recovered, somebody tries to disturb this relationship, they can mess things up sufficiently for both sides, and it won't be worthwhile. By placing money in a form of escrow, they can try to maintain stability in a situation with great risk on both sides.

Robert A. Bennett: I think one of the assumptions is that after the company phases out, the local company will then be self-sufficient and be able to carry on. In an industry where the technology moves fast and where very large investments and very large risks are involved, I think the tendency might be, as the period gets toward the end, not to make those investments and not to take those risks, but rather to let it phase out. What you would be left with then is a company that just wasn't competitive.

Mr. Ruttenberg: The phase-out doesn't necessarily have to mean that IBM or any other corporation has got to move completely out of the country. They can still retain x percent of the corporation in a minority position and still provide technical assistance.

Mr. Moran: And most of the phase-outs are not absolute phase-outs, but they are the option to phase out.

Burke Marshall: I just want to point out, in addition to what has already been said, that financing and industrial operation are often interdependent with each other, so that it isn't as if you were just making one thing and then you could phase out and somebody else would take over that one thing and market it in other ways. It may involve components or pieces of something that are put together with something that is made somewhere else. It is a total manufacturing operation, involving a number of interdependent plants, and that is what complicates this kind of situation.

I may also say that this whole notion of what you're talking about, which is essentially drawing those turn-key contracts, is not a new notion at all. Those are being negotiated all the time, negotiated inside the United States as well as outside the United States, and it is a perfectly possible kind of business dealing. But the notion that it is more ethical or involves a greater degree of conscience than other kinds of business dealings is strange to me.

Paul M. Neuhauser: It seems to me that rather than get into a discussion on the details of a blueprint, we ought to try to see if we can come up with some approach toward methods of institutionalizing power relationships. The problem within nation groups is one that has happened many, many times before, going back to relations between the king and the lords, between the government and the individual, the labor problems of the 1930s. What kinds of approaches can there be to institutionalize these powerful relationships so that they don't rupture periodically? It doesn't seem to me that you are going to have a blueprint that is going to work the same way in every industry. What you need is a structure to handle power relations.

Mr. Bennett: This is one of the problems I see with the blueprints that attempt to set rules that apply to everybody, all types of companies in all countries and various environments. I can understand why the attempt is made, but it is difficult to do that, and one of the problems we have in Latin America is that all the country operations are quite different, as Burke Marshall says. In our operation a plant in Latin America is just a piece of the worldwide manufacturing concept. For example, printers from Argentina are shipped all over the world, to European countries as well as Latin American, and also to many countries in Southeast Asia, for use in their computing systems. Our model is completely different from the Dow model or the General Motors or the G.E. or any other, and the problem is to get a set of rules flexible enough to address all the various models.

Mr. Gerstacker: Let me try to answer a couple of specific questions. Mr. Ruttenberg asked, Should companies agree gradually to withdraw their ownership? Well, in our formation agreement we had agreed to that. The Allende government hailed our agreement as a model of progressive investment, and yet one year after we started to operate we were expropriated.

Now Mr. Schomer's question is, Why aren't the relations with the USSR a model that could be followed in Latin America? Well, many companies, and we're one of them, would just not sell our technology. What might be done is to sell at a very high price. In the case of the USSR, I think they are paying far too much today because the people who deal with them feel that they do not have control over what will occur. So the Russians are not getting very good deals as compared to a country that is willing to make commitments for the long pull.

It seems to me that Mr. Moran's view is a very pessimistic one. If you are told that the multinational companies will not trust national countries, then I think we are going to demand very high returns. It is the normal thing to do. If you feel that you're not going to last very long, you are going to try and get all you can while you can. If the national countries don't trust the multinational companies, it seems to me that they are going to try and renegotiate as quickly as they can from the strongest power position that they can. This is a very costly, inefficient way to do business. It seems to me that this says to us that we need a code of conduct for both multinational companies and for the nations themselves to get back to a more efficient basis so that both won't try to hold back and try to make sure that they are going to get everything they can. I can tell you that in the United States, if we don't trust another company that is a supplier or a purchaser, our relations will be very inefficient. We try not to deal with people we can't trust because it is a very bad way to do business.

LEGAL AND POLITICAL DIMENSIONS OF MULTINATIONAL AND NATION-STATE RELATIONS

Many of the problems surrounding the multinational corporation and its relation to nation-states converge on legal and political issues. Thus a good portion of the discussion centered on attempts to define the legal constraints and responsibilities of the MNC in relation to various political bodies and vice versa. But the discussion did not stop at delineation of present or hoped-for legal and political structures. There was also clear recognition that the absence of an overarching legal and political structure to cover the operations of the MNCs created serious problems for analysis.

The nature of this latter problem tended to divide the conference into two groups. Those in one group seemed to say that the absence of international legal structures requires us to look beyond legal and quasilegal analysis in determining appropriate conduct for a multinational corporation. The views of this group are heard more fully in Part III, although their voices are heard in this part too. The second group tended to say that the absence of an overarching legal framework requires even closer attention to the political and legal structures that do exist in spite of their limitations. This group did not deny the existence or importance of other factors. Rather, they insisted that any attempts to deal with economic and ethical issues without attention to existing legal and political realities would hand over even more power to the multinationals and engage them in illegitimate projects, with consequent increase in conflict and misunderstanding on one hand and a dilution of corporate goals and efficiency on the other. These contentions lie behind most of the discussion in this part.

The issues are joined quickly and incisively by Burke Marshall, professor of law and deputy dean at Yale Law School. His presentation outlines the kinds of legal and quasilegal lines of responsibility and constraint that already exist for an MNC and then makes a further point: Once a corporation is "present" in a host country, any attempt to impose standards of conduct from outside the legal structures of that country amounts to ethical and cultural arrogance. These points provoked lively discussion about the nature of arrogance, the search for social and ethical standards that transcend positive law, and the problem of defining the "constituencies" of a corporation.

Charles Powers, associate professor of Social Ethics at Yale Divinity School, develops and clarifies the theme of interdependence (a recurring phrase in the debate) and then proposes a model for

41

corporate decision-making that takes seriously the legal model of the corporation (by defining its constituencies) but tries to open up within this structure a "space" for ethical and social considerations that would not be subject to the "arrogance" charge. Key to this analysis is Mr. Powers's insistence that the neat division between economic and moral issues cannot be maintained, that economic decisions have evaluative dimensions in their impact on the social order. In doing this analysis, Professor Powers anticipates and reaches toward some of the key issues dealt with in Part III. His presentation is answered by several corporate managers.

A third section of this part includes discussion of the relationship between the MNCs and the home country (in this case the United States) and the host countries. A central question raised with respect to host countries is whether a particular political and legal system can always be said to represent the people.

Part II closes with a summary statement by Anthony Wiener of the Hudson Institute on bargaining, shifting power, and the way in which corporate and political actors perceive questions of ethics and self-interest.

(Professor Marshall's presentation originally followed a case study on Gulf Oil in Venezuela presented by Luis Alcala Sucre, included in the Appendix at the end of this book. Although Mr. Marshall's arguments stand independently, the reader may wish to consult the Appendix. Editor's note.)

3

STANDARDS AND
CONSTITUENCIES:
AN ATTEMPT TO DEFINE
ACCOUNTABILITY

THE LEGAL LIMITATIONS ON MNC ACTIVITY
AND THE PROBLEM OF ARROGANCE
Burke Marshall

It seems to me that there are two questions that are floating
around in our discussion. One is a very big question that we have
been talking about around here a good bit, and that is the question of
economics, the inevitable effect of foreign ownership of natural
resources, for example, oil. What might have happened if these oil
resources had not been developed by foreigners but by Venezuela,
and what effect would that have had on the people of Venezuela? Now
that is a very "iffy" question and takes a lot of history, and I frankly
can't answer it except to say that no discussion of the details of how
the international companies generally have conducted their operations
in Venezuela is going to answer it. It seems to me obvious that,
whatever group or company had come into Venezuela, the Venezuelan
people in some sense would have been better off now if they had from
the beginning been able to develop and market these resources themselves.

So that is one question. Now the second question is the one that
I was going to address more specifically and that is found in the part
of the paper [see Appendix A] that deals with the question, Has this
particular company been a good citizen in some sense in Venezuela,
and has it been as good a citizen as it would have been if it had not
been owned by foreign interests but rather was owned by Venezuelan
interests? I accept the statement in the paper that it has been a good
citizen and that it has been as good if not a better citizen than it would
have been if it had been owned, as well as managed, at least recently,
by Venezuelan nationals.

I take it that many of the objections raised about multinationals have not to do with the particular conduct of the company but with the fact that the basic decisions that are made and that go into making up a contract are made by people sitting up in New York or Chicago or somewhere else. These decisions are essentially outside the control of Venezuela, and that includes the decisions they make as good citizens.

Now it is this fact (that decisions are made outside of a particular country) that is critical for questions of corporate social responsibility and what it means to be a good citizen and what factors control it. This is going to be very simple stuff, but being a lawyer I'd like to deal with the question of corporate social responsibility in a few specific terms. When I talk about responsibility I like to think of it in terms of, first, to whom you are responsible and to what extent this responsibility is enforceable, and, second, what standards are applied in relation to the groups to whom you are responsible.

Let's look at that in terms of foreign ownership of petroleum companies in Venezuela. We will find, I suppose, that foreign ownership makes a difference and that there is a responsibility to constituencies involving standards different from what they would be if the company were locally owned and locally controlled. In this connection the thrust of the conversation here has been as if the only responsibility that these companies have, or should have, in some ethical or moral sense, or perhaps even an economic sense, is to the countries in which they are located. If that is the assumption, it is inconsistent with the legal system in which these corporations operate and inconsistent with the reality of the world in which they operate. And here I want briefly to address these realities. I will be talking not only about American companies—although most of the moral objections seem to be aimed at American multinationals—but a good number of the things I say would also apply to Japanese companies, or Italian companies, or French companies, or British companies, or German companies.

In the first place there is a responsibility to shareholders. It is popular in legal circles as well as other circles to treat shareholders now as if they didn't exist because they are an unidentifiable group and just hold a piece of paper and have no ownership interest in the normal sense of the word in the corporation. But the fact is that the management of a corporation does have a responsibility to shareholders who are not Venezuelan and that responsibility is basically not to waste the assets of the corporation. Not to waste the assets of the corporation means not to give them away and to some extent not to invest them in things that would be less profitable than something else they could invest in that would be more profitable. That is not a new or vague statement; that is something that can be litigated; it can be, and has been, the subject of lawsuits. It is an enforceable right that is defined in the U.S. law and corporate charters.

There are also less concrete but just as real ways in which real control flows from the shareholders to the management of the company on the decisions they make. One is that there have been a lot of takeovers of U.S. corporations. This is a common thing and is based mainly on what I just mentioned—that is, a wasting of assets and mismanagement in the sense of pursuing less profitable courses of action. The other technique that is also used, although it is not very common, is simply throwing out the management. Any management has got to be aware of these possibilities and threats in its decision-making. There is some movement in the United States toward the use of this shareholders' right in such a way as to affect decisions in a fashion that a group of the shareholders believes is morally or socially desirable. I will return to this point in a minute.

Second, the corporation has responsibilities to its employees. And I think guilds or labor unions in the United States have a responsibility to those employees. We must remember that the most immediate effect of a decision to build a plant in Latin America by an American company is to deprive the American citizen of the jobs that are going to be taken up in that plant. That is true of any site construction decision. If you decide to have your plant in the South instead of the North, then the people in the North are not going to get the jobs that are in the South. That is a fact of business life. And of course there is also a responsibility to the employees in Venezuela once the company is located there.

Then, third, there are clearly identifiable responsibilities to the government of the United States, and part of those are describable in terms of law. These laws apply to some extent to operations in other countries, including antitrust laws, tax laws, and the laws governing the movement of money in Latin countries that would affect the balance of payments. All of those are rules imposed by the United States on decisions by management based in the United States. At the same time, there is also a responsibility by the management to the laws of Venezuela or the host country. So the corporate manager assumes obligations to two governments simultaneously. This does not exhaust the list, but it does give the principal constituencies to which a corporation is responsible.

Now is there any one ethical or social standard that runs through these various groups? I spoke of a movement in this country that imposes a standard that certain groups believe essential for social responsibility. I have a position about that, and my position generally is that the way we tell what society wants and how to be responsible to it is through obedience to its laws. And the imposition by Americans of some other standard on another country is arrogant. The attempt by any American group to determine what is socially desirable in another country beyond obedience to that country's laws is arrogant. Now that, I realize, is not a very popular position, but that is what I wanted to state and get it out on the table.

I have just one final comment, and that is on the question of the formation of some international set of standards to deal with problems of relationships between multinational companies and the governments of the countries in which they are located. It seems to me that the problem of international rules is not going to be that prevalent. Instead we are going to have to deal with the problem of interdependence. That is, I have addressed myself to responsibilities to the United States and to people in the United States that exist side by side with responsibilities to the government of Venezuela and to citizens of Venezuela in this case. These dual responsibilities are usually complicated by, for instance, the requirement of production in many places, by import and quota systems in many places, and by those interdependences and conflicts between governments and national interests that are going to be very difficult for the companies that operate in more than one country to deal with. But there is at least one structure, a set of laws—not enforceable law but at least a law—that applies to those kinds of relationships, the relationships among governments.

There is also a set of laws that deal with relationships among business enterprises. But there is no structure I know of, no body and no institution, that can on an international basis establish rules between governments and business enterprises that are normally considered by everyone to be binding. So that concludes my comments.

OPEN DISCUSSION ON MORAL ARROGANCE, LEGAL
CONSTRAINTS, AND THE SEARCH FOR
HIGHER STANDARDS

Paul M. Neuhauser: Doesn't your limitation, that the only obligation is to follow what is required by law, contradict the notion that there can be anything known as interdependence?

Mr. Marshall: The interdependence exists in fact, but there is no mechanism for dealing with it, and that is why you get a great deal of conflict among the states—they want the MNC to do this, you want them to do that, someone else wants you to do this, and there are conflicting demands on the same set of practices—we simply have no mechanism to deal with that.

William J. Barnds: Well, suppose you are a corporation operating in a foreign country, and that country has certain laws having to do with safety of the employees, and you don't think these laws are really adequate in terms of your own responsibility to protect your employees. Now you certainly would not have any problem in thinking, would you, that there was an ethical requirement on your corporation to introduce safety standards into its factory, even if they were not required by law? I think there is some confusion as to what you mean.

Mr. Marshall: I think that is not as easy a question as you think it is. Safety is a good thing, and there are strong safety laws in the United States. But if you consider it as a possible good act (I am not talking about what you consider to be good personnel policies or anything like that), what you are doing is taking some sort of an ethic from somewhere and saying, "I must do this because it is ethical," without consideration for what that does to other companies in that country, to the labor unions in that country, or to the labor unions of the United States, or to all these other constituencies that a business must deal with.

I don't have any objection to a company's putting in safety measures that are beyond those required by law, but I think they will do it for reasons of good business. What I am particularly arguing against is the arrogance of imposing U.S. standards on places just because you happen to have a plant there.

A.A. Jordan: I was going to pursue that a little. This raises a question of input: To what extent should a multinational be held to, or itself attempt to establish, higher standards with regard to a whole range of social services, or even wages or working conditions generally, than those prevailing in the country concerned? And by what right would a country move in that direction, recognizing that establishing higher standards can in fact increase its costs and thereby may impair efficiency, resulting in lower profits and return to shareholders? I think it sort of brings us fully up against the question Burke Marshall is raising about the multiple obligations of the corporation. Although everybody recognizes that safety in the abstract is a good thing, how much safety, or how much of anything else in the way of pushing conditions beyond the prevailing standards should be done? And on what criteria do you base these judgments?

Thomas E. Quigley: I want to address the same issue from a very different perspective. Burke Marshall raised the question of arrogance in connection with the concern of groups in North America. But the most important ethical issues about the role and function of multinational corporations in Latin America I hear raised largely within

Latin America, not by the multinational corporations, but by other groups—basically by those who raise these kinds of questions in any society. And these very same questions are being raised constantly in Latin America much more vigorously than they are in the United States.

It seems to me that the crux of the problem lies not in the content of ethical issues—whether they have to do with the environment or safety—but rather in the manner in which the issues get raised. Does the raising of ethical issues constitute an arrogance from outside, or is it something demanded by people who are very directly involved with multinational corporations in less developed countries?

Mr. Marshall: Well, my comments would not deal with the raising of standards of safety or environment or anything else by Venezuelans with respect to the operation of a company. My objection goes to the raising of standards in those areas by Americans. The whole point was that the foreign ownership, U.S. ownership, does involve obligations different from what they would be if it were owned and controlled as well as operated solely by Venezuelans. My comments all concern the effect of foreign ownership of an organization.

In the United States some companies have raised their safety standards because they didn't want to be unionized. Some companies have raised their safety standards because the unions demand it. Some have raised their safety standards because they were making a lot of money and could afford to do so when other people couldn't. There are all sorts of reasons.

Charles W. Powers: It seems to me that the question of arrogance arises only when a standard is adopted that goes beyond, or is different from, that of the host country, a standard that in some way affects the people adversely or in some way is contrary to the mores or customs of that country.

Mr. Marshall: Excuse me, but I don't agree with that. I think it is arrogant when people in New York decide to change the safety standards in Venezuela. The problem is the location of the decision.

Carl A. Gerstacker: We have many cases where we are able to improve the safe operation of plants in less developed countries because of things that we have learned here in America. I can give an example of a company that had a record of 80 accidents per million man-hours, and the record is now about one accident per million man-hours. We accomplished this by bringing to this company the things we had learned. We have accomplished this without raising the cost to the company—in fact it has reduced the cost of our operation. It has not

48

only been good for the workmen, who otherwise would have been injured, but it has also lowered the cost of our operation. If someone is saying that we should not do this, then I simply can't understand it.

We are doing the same thing with pollution. We have set global pollution guidelines, and even where the country in which we operate does not require this high standard, our plants have those standards. We think also that in this case we are lowering our costs because for the most part, at least in our business, pollutants are materials that are being wasted, raw materials not properly used or end products being thrown away. We think that better, more efficient operation cuts the cost, so we are doing good in two ways. I don't see what the problem is if we attempt to improve operations in other countries.

James Joseph: I'd like to address these issues in terms of what I've seen and heard of General Motors in Latin America. Much of the General Motors philosophy is admirable, particularly the point that GM is a local institution in each country rather than a foreign concern doing business in that country. But this obliterates the distinction between host country and home country. For them every country is a home country. Now that sounds good in the abstract, but I'm confused by the view that this is accomplished by recognizing the customs of the country and harmonizing the corporation's procedures and policies with such customs. The question this raises for men, then, is what happens when the customs of the host country or home country are at odds with the basic human values of the corporation regarding the dignity, worth, and individuality of each person? Would GM refuse to invest, or desire to withdraw, because the customs of a country require violation of the corporate conscience?

James Finn: I'd like to follow up on that point. When anyone says that a corporation should be a good citizen of whatever country it operates in, I do think that does blur the line between the terms we've been using previously of home country and host country. In the previous discussion Burke Marshall said that it was a kind of arrogance for someone operating out of a home country to import or impose upon the host country values, customs, and mores not indigenous to the host country, and keeping those terms, home and host, that would make a certain kind of sense. One could argue about that. But you say you are a good citizen of the country in which you operate, that distinction is blurred. Maybe that's a metaphor that carries more weight than is intended, because one could regard oneself, I suppose, as a good citizen of the United States simply as an individual if one goes about one's business and refrains from clubbing one's neighbor over the head or unduly polluting the area in which one lives and ignoring in a sense the social ills of the community of which one is a part. But you could have another sense of what it means to be a good citizen, and that is an awareness of some of those social ills and do your best to remedy them to some degree. Does that mean you could be blind then to the conditions that are brought about by race, color, creed, class distinctions, poverty lines? You would have to become involved in that to some degree. So what does it mean to say you want to be a good citizen of a particular country and at the same time try in your business to remain indifferent to or just ignore those conditions that are brought about by that country, conditions based on distinctions of race, color, creed, class? Or again, to move away from what is most obvious, what happens if you operate, say, in Brazil and the president of Brazil says, We want our share of pollution too, we want modern industrialization—but you have learned that pollution in itself may be bad? Sao Paulo, for example, is a heavily polluted city, and people there are suffering because of that pollution—even Rio is increasing in pollution. Is there an obligation as a good citizen operating in that country to try to remedy that, even though it might reduce your competitive advantage in relation to other companies, other transnationals that do not seek to be as responsible? What I'm trying to find out is what is the content of being a good citizen? Because it does seem to me to fit badly with the distinction we've been making between being a home country and a host country.

Harlow W. Gage: I think the answer to your question "What is it that makes a good citizen?" is simple. It is not whether you think you are a good citizen, it's whether the people in that country think you are a good citizen. And I think you'd have to conduct yourself in such a way as to have them look upon you as a good citizen of that country. We have to remember that we're a guest in that country, and we want them to look upon us as a good citizen. We don't want to go in there and do what we think will make us a good citizen. What we try to do is the things that will cause them to look upon us and say, "Well, there is a good citizen of this country." To talk about that one particular point you mentioned, pollution: We go to great lengths to try and combat that as far as our plants are concerned. All around the world, for that matter. And in many instances we do go beyond the local requirement in pollution control as far as plant emission is concerned.

Terrance Hanold: In a sense the question asked was, Do you feel that, when you enter another country, you come with a superior social ethic because you come from the United States?

Mr. Barnds: Or with a distinct set of obligations, or both?

Mr. Hanold: Does the fact that you have a home country base impose on you the obligation to translate the superior standards of your home country to other countries?

Mr. Gage: If they don't conflict with the local conditions.

Mr. Joseph: First of all, if you are indigenous to the country, there seems to be a contradiction in saying that you're a guest there. One is only a guest of a host. I think that contradiction is what led to the question just asked. But the other thing is that it's not a question of having superior standards from the United States—it's a question of whether you have some transnational standards that transcend any particular nation-state and that impose upon you some obligations wherever you operate. How do you relate to the local situation when the customs and values of the local situation are in conflict with the transnational values you bring to that situation? And certainly it's not a question of bringing superior values in the sense that you've got something superior that comes from the United States. If it's anything superior, it transcends the United States, because some of these countries may have values superior to those of the United States.

Victor G. Reuther: Mr. Chairman, Burke Marshall spoke of the social responsibility of corporations. Generally speaking, that social policy, to the extent it exists, reflects acts in the legislative field, and it reflects decisions reached through the processes of collective bargaining. We've got a new situation now where we have multinational corporate units; but there is not a recognition at the same time by these multinational firms of an obligation to deal with a comparable structure at the trade union level. If this is the problem with our neighbors to the north in Canada—and it is—you can imagine how difficult it is when you're dealing with small, economically weak nations in Latin America. In the automotive field the same corporations that dominate the U.S. market are the dominant employers in Canada. Although the two nation-states signed an agreement establishing a common market, had there not been a single union that spoke for the automotive workers in both countries, there would have been no structure to have established a common wage policy, although the same firms making the same vehicles that sell for a higher price in Canada were paying 50 cents less to Canadian workers than our workers received. They sought economic justice, but the only machinery that existed was the fact that a trade union was on the scene that embraced membership in both countries.

There is an international confederation of petroleum workers. There is for automotive workers a world council for Ford workers, for General Motors workers, for Chrysler, Simca, Fiat, all of which are tied together, and one for the Japanese workers.

What I'm saying is that if the processes of collective bargaining make sense within a country (and I am impressed that our colleague from Venezuela speaks of his friendly relations with the petroleum workers in Venezuela, which I know is a fact) and if it makes sense within a corporation, it is that much more urgent when you start operating across national boundaries. If ever there was an example of corporate arrogance it was in the incident of the visit of one Henry Ford recently to London. When there was a dispute of Ford workers in a Ford plant, Henry Ford met with the prime minister and served notice on the head of that sovereign state that unless the dispute were settled in accordance with the terms the Ford Motor Company had offered, Ford would move its operations to Cologne, Germany.

How do you resolve that? Where do you turn to discuss a problem of that kind? It was resolved because the German workers, who were part of a world trade union organization, said we won't work on that. But there was no machinery through which formal discussions could take place.

And I will conclude with this thought, that unless the private sector represented by the multinational corporate units comes forward voluntarily with a structure that is workable, that will bring not only a greater measure of economic and social justice but also a substitute for corporate paternalism, where the people themselves help generate the policy under which they're going to work and live—unless you do this voluntarily and do it soon, you will see the sovereign states joining in creating their own set of rules under which multinational corporate units will function. They've already done that to some extent. It would not now be before the United Nations if it had been left just to the corporate units and the trade unions. They'd be debating it in the International Labor Organization (ILO), but it is now before the United Nations because the sovereign states are concerned. Long before the Common Market existed in Europe, there was a common agreement among employers and six governments operating transport on the Rhine River that governed wages, sick benefits, unemployment compensation, a host of other things.

If I went back 35 or 40 years to a Ford example in the Soviet Union, it was not to herald that type of relationship as an example but merely to indicate that the door was open 40 years ago to capital investment without raising the question of corporate control in terms of ownership, and it is significant that that same Ford Motor Company was the first to respond at the end of the cold war to new offers from the Soviet Union to build a truck plant. Had the U.S. Government not blocked it, Ford would have built that plant.

Luis Alcala Sucre: I'm not going to try to expand on my talk, which I had to curtail because of the limitations in time, nor am I going to address myself at length to this word that has been repeated so often, arrogance, and the imposition of standards. I don't think that any multinational company has an obligation, as I believe I heard somebody say, because of its relations with the parent country, the United States, to impose the standards of the home country. I don't see where it has an obligation to any of the shareholders to do this. I think it would be arrogant, were the standards of the host country higher than the standards of the United States, to take one example, for the multinational company to come in and say, "Look, your standards are higher than ours, but we're not going to be bound by them, we're going to put in our own standards." But so long as the standards held in the United States are higher, I don't see anything wrong with the multinational companies applying them, be they in safety or in other social areas. What is wrong with that? What is the argument about that? Enough of that.

Now just briefly on Victor Reuther's comments. I believe he said that the multinational companies refuse to negotiate in collective bargaining within international unions. Now it is true that in the case of petroleum, there is an international federation of petroleum, chemical, and atomic workers. As a matter of fact, its headquarters are very close to us. They are headquartered in Denver, Colorado. It is also interesting to note that one of our good mutual friends, a Venezuelan, was the president of that international federation. Senator Luis Tovar, a member of the legislature of Venezuela, was the first president of Fedepetrol, which is a federation of petroleum unions in Venezuela, which is affiliated with the international federation. And the Fedepetrol does call on the international federation for advice in collective bargaining situations. But I would suggest that before the Oil, Chemical, and Atomic Workers International Union tries to convince the multinational company that it would be fair and equitable for them to bargain collectively with that international federation, their even harder job would be to convince the local trade unions, to convince the local federation, that they should abrogate their bargaining privileges to an international company. I think the first job in my own opinion, Victor, is not to convince the multinationals that they should negotiate with the international union but to convince the local union and the local federation that they should allow an international federation headquarters here in the United States of America to do the collective bargaining.

4

INTERDEPENDENCE
AND CORPORATE DECISION-
MAKING: THREE KINDS OF
INTERDEPENDENCE AND THE
SPACE FOR ETHICAL CHOICE
Charles W. Powers

ɛ

I want to make just one quick point about interdependence before moving into my extended and primary comment. Ted Moran has said that the perceptions of multinational corporate activity are split between interpreters who see that activity as leading to dependence and those who see that activity as taking place in a situation of economic nationalism. Terry Hanold argues that, in fact, neither dependence nor economic nationalism is the real interpretation of what's going on, since we live in an interdependent world. Most of us agree that that is probably true. But why then do the Latin Americans and corporate managers keep interpreting developments and approaches to corporate activity in Latin America in terms of one of Ted's two approaches? I think we can see why by looking at three possible meanings we can give to interdependence. First, we can mean by interdependence that parties are trying to achieve a freely chosen common goal by engaging in cooperative activity. Second, we can mean that two parties involve themselves in cooperative activity to achieve compatible goals. One wants one thing; the other wants another. But these differing, yet compatible, goals can't be achieved by either party alone. That's why the two parties engage in cooperative activity. But the third type of interdependence is quite different. In order to achieve part of its goal, one party is forced into cooperative activity with another party who is going to get all of his goal, or at least is perceived as getting all his goal. Now if that is in fact what happens, or is perceived to be happening by either the multinational corporations or by the Latin

Americans, we haven't made much of a gain by talking about inter-dependence. In types one or two, interdependence is without strife, and perceptions that fall into one or another of Ted's approaches will soon give way to harmonious cooperation. But if interdependence of the third type is operating, resentment continues. The party carries resentment and frequently sees itself forced into cooperative activity, because it has, or thinks it has, no alternative. That's why we go back and forth on what's taking place. Miguel Wionczek, who talked the other day very strongly in terms of dependency theory, came back the next day and talked about the need for more MNC activity in Latin America. It was this third kind of interdependence he was recognizing, resenting, but still seeking.

Luis Alcala Sucre: I would like to ask, Isn't there room for a fourth category, namely, where neither party achieves its full goal but one party achieves part of its goal and the other party achieves part of its goal?

Mr. Powers: I grant that. But my point was to try to figure out why it was we tend to have these two different interpretations of what is happening as a result of multinational activity. Somehow the idea is abroad that if we get interdependence going, the problems will solve themselves—that if we talk about interdependence, we won't have to talk about economic nationalism or dependency. And I think once you've got the third meaning going, it's fully explainable why you still have conflicting interpretations of what's happening. The term interdependence does not solve that problem, because one or the other party thinks it is getting the short end of the stick. Perhaps the optimum we can expect in this world is the possibility Mr. Alcala Sucre has just mentioned—where both sides recognize that neither side can have everything it wants but that the benefits are about equal.

I want now to move from this analysis of why tension persists between host countries and MNCs to a discussion of whether MNCs themselves can do anything to lessen these tensions. The issue ultimately is whether corporate managers have the freedom to make decisions that will benefit host countries more—and whether they should do so even if they have the freedom.

Let me start off with the model of the corporation that Burke Marshall has given us. This, it seems to me, is basically the legal model of the U.S. corporation. The responsibility of corporate managements is to the shareholder, but there are constraints upon the manager, not only from the U.S. shareholder but from the U.S. Government, the American employees, and the host country employees and the host country government. You could add other constituencies

55

to this list but those are the five we have used most frequently in discussions. Burke's model could be put into a diagram like Figure 1.

FIGURE 1

Model 1

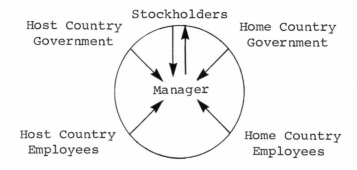

Now the difference between this "legal" model Burke gave us and the one some other participants have used is this: Others assume that managers are not simply constrained by all these other constituents but in fact are responsible to them, for example, to the U.S. Government, to the American employees, to the host country employees, to the host country government. In diagram form there is a line of responsibility for each line representing a constraint. The diagram for the second model would be as shown in Figure 2.

If other constituents represent only constraints, responsibility to the shareholders means that the manager takes into account all these other kinds of restraints and tries to work out the best possible thing for the shareholder alone. As soon as you acknowledge that managers have a _responsibility_ to other constituents, then it seems to me something very different happens. The corporate manager is then seen as one who has options as to which of those constituencies he has to be responsive, and responsible, to in any particular context. Once discretionary space is cleared, once that room to act is opened up, you can argue about its restrictedness or its expansiveness. But

56

FIGURE 2

Model 2

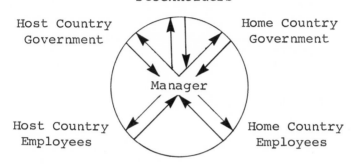

once it's there, once you recognize you're responsible to more than one constituency, you have to talk about some freedom of action for the corporate manager. Most of us here have recognized that some such freedom exists.

Why was it then that once this freedom of action was recognized, Burke Marshall and various others here at the conference were hesitant to say that managers ought to be deciding what it means to be responsible to host country employees or the host government or the American employees? The thing that made us pull back was not lack of power or lack of personal responsibility. It was a fear of arrogance. I'd like to look at the concept of arrogance for just a few minutes.

There's been an assumption that a company's presence and pursuit or its interests in a country is one thing, but that self-consciously responsible conduct by a corporation is another thing—indeed an arrogant thing. It seems to me, however, that the validity of a charge of arrogance hinges on there being a real, ethically significant distinction between impacts of a corporation's presence and its normal business decisions on one hand and its self-consciously ethical or unethical conduct on the other. Let me put that another way. We seem to have been saying that no matter what impact a corporation has on people's lives, in terms of their income or their safety or whatever, there is an increment in arrogance if criteria for your decision are in part

57

ethical rather than wholly economic or technological. And I'm willing to say that I don't think that's true. If you have similar impacts, or in fact are affecting people's lives in highly significant ways, then the fact that you are self-consciously using ethical factors in your judgment rather than economic ones does not lead to any ethical difference at all. When we began to think about why it was not arrogant to make an economically determined choice that adversely affected the host-country employee, our justification was that it was done for the economic benefit of, and because of, an obligation to the U.S. shareholder. Somehow because the one constituency to which the manager is responsible in Model 1 had dictated profit maximization, actions that damaged other constituents were permissible, especially since it would have been arrogant to have decided what the best interests of employees in host countries really were. But if Model 2 portrays the manager's role more adequately, then the single-minded appeal to stockholders won't do. Freedom to choose creates responsibility. It is surely just as arrogant to hide behind an outmoded interpretation of the manager's role and responsibilities as it is to face the decision squarely and exercise appropriate restraint.

Burke Marshall: What I was addressing myself to was the effect of foreign leadership on the conduct of an enterprise in Venezuela. As you said, part of that effect is due just to presence. The question of who should develop the oil and whether it is fair to Venezuelans is there, no matter how a company is managed, whether it be developed by Americans and Europeans, the Japanese, or whomever. And that's a great big economic question that I didn't address. The other thing is the conduct of the company. I said, and I'll use the word ethics if you want, that as long as the decision is made by some ethical code that is American, that seems to me to be arrogant, even arbitrary, from the point of view of the host country, whether it's good or bad in terms of the employees of the host country. That's all I meant.

Mr. Powers: But you were adding something else—that there is in fact no ethic discernible in the host country except as found in the positive law of that country. I don't think that that's right.

Mr. Marshall: Excuse me, I was addressing myself not to that but to the question about who made the decision. If there is an instrumentality, a method of procedure whereby the ethics or the social desires of the host country are brought into the decision-making process, as might for example be true for bargaining with a representative of a labor union there, then I could call that appropriate. But at least that would reflect conditions there. What I was calling arrogant was a group of people looking at flip charts in New York or Chicago or Tokyo or Frankfurt or Paris or London and saying that this is what we think is good for these workers in Venezuela.

Mr. Powers: My point is that I don't see what difference it makes whether or not the factors determining your decision are ethical ones or economic ones if in fact the impact on the people is the same. And I'm saying an economically motivated decision is not more neutral in terms of arrogance than an ethically motivated one.

Mr. Marshall: You and I agree on that. But then all that does is put us on the same side that says there is an effect of foreign ownership on these operations, whatever the motivation for the decision.

Mr. Powers: I just want us to be aware that we will not avoid ethical problems by making decisions on economic grounds. I want to leave aside for the moment altruistically motivated school-building and all that sort of thing and talk only about the kinds of operations a corporation undertakes in the normal pursuit of its business. I'm concerned, therefore, about the impacts of a corporation in its normal business activity and want to try to determine whether there aren't some instances in which a corporate manager does have a choice as to which activity he will undertake. I hope I've persuaded you so far that in fact managers can choose either to ignore choices they have, or to try to find standards to use in making their choices.

Now we move to Burke's question, What standards are appropriate? The term that was most often used around this room yesterday was "justice," or some variant of it. We talked about "fairness" or "equity" or "meeting needs," and so forth. Many conflicting definitions have been given for "justice" in this world. I'd like to suggest that all a corporate manager needs to think about is this very minimal one: that justice requires that people have at least a minimal level of material sustenance and a chance to live in a culture that has some continuity, that is, is not radically distorted by outside influences. We live in a world where most people do not have a minimal level of material sustenance at this point. So we don't need to get into a long discussion about whether justice ultimately requires equal distribution or distribution according to effort. I'd like to propose, therefore, a principle for decision for a corporate manager when he realizes that there is an ethically significant choice to be made and he can make it. It's exceedingly abstract, but it can, I think, guide decisions in specific contexts. The principle is this: A manager should attempt within the limited sphere of choice available (taking into account the constraints of all corporate constituencies) to help persons affected directly or indirectly by the firm's activity to attain a minimal level of material sustenance while minimizing the distortion of culturally specific mores and customs.

Let me try to show how that could actually become something more than a Yale professor's irrelevant rumination. Professor Ron Muller has suggested that the net impacts of a corporation's activity could be sorted out into five different types: employment effects, price-of-product effects, balance-of-payment effects, cost-of-technology effects, and effects on sovereignty. The thrust of the issue now is how in a particular situation these several types of impact relate to raising minimal sustenance standards without cultural disruption or distortion. Let me take just one example of a place where I think my principle could help.

A management is planning to establish a labor-intensive manufacturing operation in a foreign country. It has two countries into which it could go. Country A has a good social security system; country B has a very poor one. Now usually the constraints on a corporation in particular circumstances will force it to go into A or B because one is clearly much more attractive. But let's for the purposes of this discussion say it could go into either A or B because the costs and benefits are nearly equal. How could you use my principle to decide which you should choose? My principle would say, "Take country B, the one with the less adequate social security system," because in going into that country with a labor-intensive industry you would be doing the only thing a corporation could be doing to help that country's people achieve adequate levels of sustenance. The only near-term way they can do it is to have jobs, and therefore a labor-intensive industry is in fact going to help. A labor-intensive industry might not be so important in country A, where you have a very good social security system, since a high-technology operation would yield profits that would feed the tax structure, and people would thereby obtain their basic needs from public sources.

William J. Barnds: Isn't this line of reasoning based on the assumption that oil companies, for instance, are the Red Cross when they make it very clear they are not?

Mr. Powers: No. In the case I am proposing there really isn't very much to choose between the countries in terms of economic factors. You have two countries, about equal in terms of economic opportunity. Now which one do you go into? I'm saying that if you've got room for ethically motivated choice between those two countries, and if you use my principle, you'd go into B, because employment is going to give those people more needed food than an operation in country A. I'm not asking corporations to be the Red Cross; I'm assuming the same projected return on investment and all that sort of thing.

Alphonse De Rosso: Isn't it possible that the introduction of industry will cause distortion of cultural values in country B? That may well be why the social security system isn't well developed.

Mr. Powers: But isn't that an exciting discussion to have, rather than simply assuming that economic activity, economic growth generally, is always going to work for the better. Won't this principle help clarify some of those approaches?

Mr. De Rosso: It would be an exciting principle if we knew how to measure it.

Mr. Powers: I'm saying there are some places where you can weigh minimal sustenance against cultural value distortion. Indeed, since you have a choice, you have the obligation to weigh those two factors.

Ronald E. Muller: I think you're also making it too difficult, because I don't know any culture in the world that doesn't have as one of its prime values minimum material sustenance for people in its society.

Mr. De Rosso: Yes, except that once the corporation goes in and doesn't achieve that, then the social economists and anthropologists scream bloody murder against the corporation.

Mr. Muller: No, I'm sorry but I think the weight of the factors being discussed in this world about the multinational corporations falls more heavily upon material types of impacts, for instance on sustenance of the majority of the population, than it does on the rhetoric that comes at the end of speeches by economic nationalists about cultural distortion.

Mr. De Rosso: Where do you put the criticism against the multinational for paying above-average wages in a particular economy and consequently creating all kinds of distortions?

Mr. Muller: I think social economics can give you an answer that illuminates the fact that you can pay workers a higher wage while bringing about less material sustenance for the majority of people in the country.

Mr. Marshall: If you want a scenario of arrogance, or economic imperialism, it is one where the question "Where shall we do good in the world?" is decided in the boardroom of the poorly controlled, unregulated enterprise.

Mr. Powers: That was not the question for the corporation in my example. It was not "Where can we go in the world?" It was "Which of two countries do we go into when, after all the economic factors are laid out, it comes so close to even that I have an ethical choice to make willy-nilly?" This is very different from saying, "Where can we do good in the world?" It's saying, "When those choices come down the pike and we're looking for them, we can make a significant ethically differentiated determination."

Mr. De Rosso: Don't you get involved in circular reasoning here? The fact is, any operation of a foreigner in any site if going to have an impact, a disturbing impact.

Mr. Powers: And I'm saying that some of those impacts will relate more directly than others to questions of distribution of services at a minimal level.

Mr. De Rosso: Now you're switching from the culture to the economics.

Mr. Powers: Presumably if you came out saying that country B would have more of an impact on the material sustenance side but you'd have an even greater distorting impact on cultural values, then from an ethical point of view you'd go to country A. But at least ask that question.

Miguel Wionczek: I think you are mixed up altogether. You can dispose completely of the problem of employment effects. In answer to Chuck Powers's question, you can, in theory, and there is literature on this subject. If you compare technologies being used by transnationals of one country and transnationals of another, for example, U.S. transnationals versus European transnationals, then you see that there are different strategies. Americans will tend to use capital-intensive technologies. It is not only because they are the best. There are a number of very complicated reasons to explain this. It's a problem of technological horizon; it's a problem of the speed of the technological development. The Europeans, for some reason, in the same developing countries would use technologies that are more labor-intensive, because they were used, say, 15, 20 years ago. Why? Because of their technology horizon. I mean that speed of technology change is different, and many other things are different. So when you have the problem where you can talk about all these things and find out some way of choosing a technology that will not result in producing obsolescent goods, but that will increase employment effect on the country, you have to do so if you don't want to have any friction. But you can go from one point to another and see that you can get agreement on different sorts of goals and different styles of action, which are also related to many, many problems.

Mr. Powers: It seems to me what you've basically been saying the last few minutes, Miguel, is that businessmen will never make decisions on anything else than sheer economic grounds, and you'd like to be in the position of a host country governmental official who chooses the technology most needed, attracts it, and strikes the best bargain. I agree with you; I wish you well and hope other countries develop similar capabilities. But none of that relates to the example I proposed. I was trying to suggest that even when countries have operative the mechanisms you are discussing, a businessman will still have ethically significant choices to make about where he goes, because he can't go everywhere. Perhaps I should just state the assumptions I have made and let others react. My assumptions are that my Model 2 for the manager and the corporations constituencies is correct; that arrogance does not necessarily flow from ethical motivation, since the ethically significant impacts are the same, whether or not ethical motivation or economic motivation is at work; that our talk about justice, equity, fairness, and so forth, could for the purposes of actual decision-making legitimately be reduced to my principle concerning minimal material sustenance and cultural distortion; that the criteria that constitute the net effect of MNCs given by Ron are substantially correct, and that the type of situation I hypothesized could, and does in fact, occur in the world in which we live.

Mr. Muller: I'd like to make a point for clarification in response to Miguel. I think we all know that he's quite right, and that every businessman in here knows there are problems between corporate goals and development goals. What I really would like to get to is the following: "Development goals" is a very nebulous term when you're dealing with 120 nations, as a businessman now or as a consultant to business corporations. But there is some commonality in development goals in all those countries, and this is what in my opinion Chuck is getting to. He's getting to the minimum principle of social justice, which is also the minimum definition of what makes for a feasible continuation of a political regime. That principle is a minimum level of material sustenance for a majority of a country's people. Any regime has to have this, not because it may necessarily be ethical, but because it's the one kind of goal that I hope everybody in here sees as something that a corporation has to consider. If a single company doesn't contribute to it all the time, the sum total of all corporations in the country have to, or else they can't continue to exist in those countries. I think you have focused on the ethical

aspects of development goals, which Mr. Wionczek never defined.
I would also call them the minimum political pragmatic goals for both
the countries and the corporations. If a specific company cannot contribute directly to that goal, that doesn't mean that it has to leave
but it has to be aware of whether the sum total of all corporations in
that society, foreign and domestic, are meeting that goal—because,
if not, none of them is going to be there very long. And in this sense
I think we're beginning to focus on the real issues raised by multinational corporations, and I don't think Messrs. Wionczek and Powers
are that far apart.

H. P. Nicholson: I was going to make that comment myself. The
businessman has to take the long view, has to be conscious of the
national interests of the country he's working in. He must contribute
to those national interests in an economic way. I thought I heard it
implied that a businessman wouldn't be interested in balance of payments. I think the businessman often is interested in balance of payments. He should be, and it's important for him to be. If he's not,
his business opportunities in a given market may be cut off. I know
of instances in my own company and others where in a given country
an adverse balance of payments was so severe that there was a threat
of the business being cut off. I know of a place where my company
set up an agricultural undertaking primarily to produce foreign exchange. That's not peculiar to my company; it's done in others.

Mr. Powers: I think every businessman is, and should be, concerned
about balance of payments in the countries in which he operates. My
point is that it becomes more ethically significant in terms of my
minimal principle in a country that, because of balance-of-payments
problems or whatever, is not able to provide material sustenance
for its people because it can't get the food to feed its people. In a
wealthier nation like France, for example, where the food can largely
be indigenously produced, balance-of-payments problems that reduce
currency for imports may not be so important ethically. What I'm
trying to get people to look at for a minute is that all the factors they
normally consider can be of very great ethical as well as economic
significance in some contexts.

Mr. Barnds: I think we should have some comments from some of
the other business executives.

Robert A. Bennett: In a market in which you are operating long-term
you must conduct yourself in a way in which you will be a good corporate citizen and thereby have a lasting relationship with the government and with your customers and with society. As Ron Muller was

saying, ethical conduct is a prerequisite for economic survival. Most companies have defined the principles on which they operate. When I first entered my company, the principles on which the company was founded were made very clear to me. They have to do with the way the business conducts itself and have an ethical basis. But they make good business and economic sense. They form the basis of the way you must operate if you are going to be successful long-term. I also believe there is a personal element involved and that the way managers conduct themselves is very much based on what they personally feel to be the right ethical conduct. I don't think the example you give is realistic. I can't remember a decision where all of the economic factors were equal and where I had an ethical choice whether to go to country A or country B.

Mr. Powers: I never said equal. I said the range of difference was not so significant that you are not free to make a choice. But can you imagine that if you demanded a little bit more profit margin here, a little better tax break there, you could make the options comparable?

Mr. Bennett: It seems to me that usually the economic things are clearer than that.

Mr. Barnds: Bob, could I come in with a question here? To what extent are business executives reluctant to make explicitly ethical or moral or humanitarian decisions simply because they are, particularly multinational corporations, involved in two cultures? Don't you feel on much more solid ground if you can reduce it to economic considerations rather than get into something that looks rather nebulous in the ethical humanitarian field?

Mr. Bennett: Certainly you feel on more solid ground.

Mr. Barnds: But I think sometimes we try in many cases to be as hardheaded and as quantitative as we can when we do have other considerations in mind, just as we sometimes try to put a very fancy humanitarian gloss on what we do when we're really doing it for reasons of our own self-interest.

Mr. Bennett: What I'm trying to say is that self-interest and ethical conduct are not inconsistent. As a matter of fact they are really consistent. You have to be ethical. You have to conduct yourself in the right way if you are to survive long-term.

Mr. Hanold: I don't think the decision is ever splintered down this fine into its pieces, or that you can decide the economic without having the ethical clearly involved, or that you can make it alone. The first thing you're going to have to confront is an official like Mr. Wionczek, who's going to advise the Mexican Central Bank whether it ought to give you a license to import capital or import machinery or establish the business. For us to say we think we should go into a labor-intensive area because it would create more jobs is fine, but the economic section of the Central Bank may have determined that a capital-intensive industry will fill a great big hole in their economy on which the labor-intensive industries are dependent. And that's his decision; it isn't ours. It's our job to see whether the kind of an enterprise we could offer to establish in that country will in our judgment be of interest to the Central Bank; but it's certainly not our prerogative or our ethical obligation to go there and advise them that this is the way they ought to go.

We make food products, so our range of technologies goes from the simple basics of grains and food stuffs to convenience foods of all kinds. Our approach to foreign investment during the time I was making the decisions was the following: We took something like W. W. Rostow's classification from the early 1960s. He classified countries as (1) traditional economies (where the average annual income ranged perhaps to $200 a year); (2) transitional economies (where the economies were beginning to industrialize in some small degree, but were totally capital absorptive, and where the annual income might run up to $500 a year); (3) takeoff economies; and finally (4) the maturing industrial countries and (5) the advanced economies. We needed a kind of "safe conduct" theory. We did not invest in traditional economies, partly because they were socially uninterested in investment. In a transitional economy a flour mill would represent somewhere between a $5 million and $10 million investment. In our judgment, for a foreign company in that kind of an economy to own it would place it much too high on the economic horizon. However much sense it made economically, it did not make much sense to us politically, so we have interests in countries of that kind of 10, 15, 20 percent in flour mills that are locally owned for the most part. In the take off areas we would take a majority position and at that point begin to move into convenience foods and more sophisticated products. In the maturing industrial economies or the advanced countries, we would take 100 percent because there is no particular impact on the community by reason of a foreign investment that size.

Mr. Alcala Sucre: Listening here to Chuck's exposition, I think there are two aspects. The first is the decision whether or not you're going to a country, or into which of several countries you go when you have the opportunity to be selective. And the second aspect is, once you have made that decision, what should the conduct be of the corporation in that country in order to stay there? Now I agreed with Bob that, at least from my experience, the first decision—where do you go—is based largely on economics. Certainly once you go in there, you have to apply all these principles, these ethical principles, in order to be able to survive. But they're based on economics.

Yet there are certain less obvious factors that do enter into that economic evaluation. It could be stability of government, balance of payments, and so on. And the different weights that one corporation may assign to each of those will certainly vary from the weights that another corporation may assign to the same factors.

5

THE MULTINATIONAL CORPORATION, GOVERNMENTS, AND THE PEOPLE

MNCs AND THE U.S. GOVERNMENT:
DOMESTIC NEEDS AND FOREIGN POLICY

Elizabeth Jager: I would like to suggest that the multinational firms seem to be conceptualized in much of our discussion in a way that the organized labor groups in the United States do not see them. The labor groups are under the impression that they live in a country called the United States of America and that that country has to deal with other countries. They also are working in corporations that are not necessarily primarily direct investors in other countries and are not necessarily involved primarily in transfers to any single country. What I am saying is that we seem to need a study of the institution, since at the moment the word multinational means different things to different people. At times the Soviet Union seems to be a sovereign state that functions as a multinational firm. Meanwhile I have heard from a variety of totally different institutions—Dow Chemical, Pillsbury, IBM—with different structures and different systems, operating as if they were a sovereign entity making arrangements with individual sovereign states. In all this conversation there is, incidentally, no United States—it doesn't exist. Another confusion is added when a comparison is made between the Japanese firms and their shareholders, and U.S. firms, when these are as a matter of fact simply different structurally—the structure of Japanese firms is totally different from that of American firms.

I don't think that any idealistic international codes or any other rules will make sense until people start talking about what is going on in the 1970s. The extraction industries are not the dominant multinationals in the 1970s. The United States does not have the

dominant firms in the 1970s when you consider that the sovereign
state of the Soviet Union acts as a multinational, that states like Brazil
are beginning to operate as a kind of Japanese multinational. You are
using yesterday's terminology as you try to look toward tomorrow.

I would hope that the corporate leadership would begin to think in
terms of sovereign states, because I can assure you that the United
States is not going to go away tomorrow; it is a sovereign government.
Neither are other individual sovereign governments. But when you
compare a country the size of Chile with a country the size of the
United States in economic terms and then try to understand the power
relationship between an individual corporate structure in the United
States and the government of another country, you are talking about
unlike quantities. You can't make rules, and you can't even have a
rational discussion about problems that are simply not related to one
another.

I thought Mr. Gerstacker's most interesting point was that Dow
Chemical Company became a joint owner, not with a Chilean corporation, but with the Chilean Government. A corporation is not a government, and consequently until there is some attempt even to look at
what is going on in the 1970s, it is going to be very difficult to do
much except try and make either a whipping boy or a beneficent god
out of the multinational firms.

Theodore H. Moran: I want to follow up on an earlier comment about
there probably being thematic changes in the kinds of standards that
corporations have to judge themselves by in the past and what they'll
have to do in the future, and I'll also bring up a point that I think will
warm Elizabeth Jager's heart, because it will bring the U.S. Government into the discussion.

I was asked to do a study for the Senate Foreign Relations Committee of the Overseas Private Investment Corporation (OPIC) and
its equity guarantee program, and I was making the argument, not
very profound, that the way the programs worked in the past is that
corporations go in, get investment guarantees, and go about their
business any way they see fit. The only time the U.S. Government
is asked to come in to their defense is when they get in a tight position
because they've been bad, but my opinion based on my own analysis
is that it happens simply because of the pulling, pushing, and shoving
process I described earlier. In any case the U.S. Government is
only brought in at the last minute and never asks what the history had
been in the past 20 years, how many profits were made, what their
return was on equity 20 years ago, or 50 years ago when the dictators
were in power in Venezuela, and so on.

I was formulating this argument and OPIC found out about it. I've
never been treated so cordially in my life. They got in touch with me

and said, "Oh no, you're talking about the old OPIC or the old aid guarantee program," and showed me a list of requirements that foreign investment must live up to. The questions they had formulated included the quantifying of all kinds of issues of social responsibility, including employment and every dimension we've discussed.

The simple point I want to make is that if corporations want the support of government insurance, they're going to have to start trying to think in these terms and to quantify their effects in these dimensions. That's really the only point I want to make. Mike Kennedy and I have talked about this, and he has some follow-up comments about whether or not the U.S. Government can in fact get into the business of trying to tell corporations socially, economically, and ethically what they should or should not do.

Moorhead C. Kennedy: I'd like to speak generally about what the role of the U.S. Government should be, of which insurance is only one aspect. What has worried me about some of the discussion so far was the assumption that a firm, a microeconomic entity, can make some of these macroeconomic determinations: the employment effects, the balance-of-payment effects, and others. It is, after all, the host government that handles such questions, and what the firm may decide is good for the country in which it's going to invest may not exactly correspond to what that country feels is good for it. Similarly, if a firm cannot really make macroeconomic decisions it's extremely difficult for a government to make microeconomic decisions. OPIC and the Department of State are governmental entities and cannot substitute for the board of directors or for the executive committee of the firm. So you really have two very discrete groups, two different elements of decision-making here. And what has worried me about this discussion is that the role of the U.S. Government, which is in a sense the representative of the American people and has the power and the authority to enforce some of these ethical judgments on firms, has been somewhat left out of the discussion until now.

In doing that we reach a very difficult decision here. When a firm comes to the United States and asks for insurance or financing, and OPIC offers both types of programs, the U.S. Government can put a price tag on the extension of the insurance or the granting of the financing by insisting on adherence to a list of standards—and that list is fairly extensive. The development impact (and this is something OPIC inherited from the Agency for International Development—AID) of the investment has to be very particularly justified, the host country's permission has to be granted, and this has to accord with the national planning of the host government.

The problem is that it's not always easy for a firm in a competitive situation to make a decision anticipating what the host government might desire. It is difficult to increase the labor intensity of the investment if there's competition elsewhere that is not going to practice what may be a somewhat less profitable way of doing business. In those circumstances such a requirement can only be levied by government, and by the host government in particular.

But also we mustn't forget that foreign investment is a tool of foreign policy. It is necessarily so in part because the U.S. Government has an obligation, a responsibility, to intervene on behalf of firms that get involved in investment disputes. It is a responsibility we can get out of only with difficulty, possibly on a showing that the firm is really behaving very badly indeed. The presumption is that we must stand by our investors abroad. At the same time we have certain foreign policy goals for investment abroad. Increasingly, these goals are going to be the development of the least developed countries, say, in traditional societies that have very low GNPs and market potential. I think it's legitimate from the standpoint of the development of these countries that we should give incentives and that we should give corporations encouragement of all kinds and set goals.

But it is also true that the issue of how early we can get into some of these decisions is really one of the more difficult problems of our foreign economic policy today. It is far more difficult for the U.S. Government to talk to a firm at an early stage and say, "Are you sure that you're hiring enough indigenous people, are you sure you are bringing in enough capital?"

We have talked about this in the government extensively, about whether we need an SEC for investment, whether we need some kind of screening process from our point of view.

Well, that's another problem. Do you want a bunch of middle-level bureaucrats substituting their thinking for a bunch of middle-level managers? There's no easy answer to this.

Government, for example, can reflect ethical considerations. Consider the great many investment opportunities in the Soviet Union that may be foregone by the concern expressed by the American people through the Congress about the emigration policies of the Soviet Government. A firm, on the other hand, cannot really decide not to do business with the Soviet Union, it seems to me, because it doesn't approve of how the Soviet Union is treating its minorities that want to emigrate.

William J. Barnds: You say cannot or should not?

Mr. Kennedy: I suggest that, in its own interest, it should not. Because if it doesn't, other firms will, with whom it is in competition in the marketplace—and they may not be U.S. firms.

71

Victor G. Reuther: Can a government preclude the right of a private firm from engaging in a contractual relationship, such as when the Ford Motor Company was quite prepared to assist in the building of a truck plant, the Soviet Government invited them to do so, and the U.S. Government blocked it? This "should or could" ought to apply to government as well as to private industry.

Mr. Kennedy: I mean that the U.S. Government has reflected and should on appropriate occasions reflect ethical considerations. The Ford Motor Company, the truck plant problem, was of course decided on what the Department of Defense viewed in those days as possible security grounds.

Stanley H. Ruttenberg: What I want to say is along the same line. The thing that has bothered me about the discussion up to this point is this issue of the host country's making some of the decisions in terms of the kinds of investments it wants, the kinds of companies it wants, and dealing with a totally autonomous U.S. or foreign company that has no obligation other than very modest kinds of restrictions in terms of the United States. Mr. Kennedy says that the U.S. Government must stand by U.S. investors and that somehow the U.S. Government can't waive its responsibilities for corporate involvement overseas; and he then went on to make the point that foreign investment is a tool of foreign policy. I want to address this problem in a slightly different context.

I think the time has come, whether we like it or not, when the multinational corporation in the United States is going to have more constraints—not responsibilities—more constraints placed upon it by U.S. law. And I think the time has come when that's important. We're already, interestingly enough, touching this problem in terms of the most-favored-nation treatment in the trade bill before the House Ways and Means Committee and in fact imposing upon U.S. corporations an obligation to do business with the Soviet Union only if the Soviet Union meets certain kinds of conditions vis-a-vis its emigration policy. I'm not particularly concerned about that issue. I'm more concerned about the fact that no Japanese company makes a decision to invest overseas without very direct, positive, specific authorization of the Japanese Government.

Now one can deal with the ethical or economic issues of what our policy of the multinational should be as it invests in Chile or in Peru or in Mexico. But, important as those problems are, we must begin to focus upon what the U.S. Government and the Congress of the United States are going to have to do with respect to domestic requirements. More and more legal constraints are going to be imposed on the operation of a multinational, not in terms of foreign investment versus foreign policy, but in terms of the multinational's impact upon the U.S. domestic economy.

MNCs AND HOST COUNTRIES:
WHAT ARE THE INTERESTS OF THE PEOPLE?

Howard F. Schomer: Moving somewhat in that direction, I've been
hearing some voices, perhaps particularly Luis Escobar and Miguel
Wionczek, putting heavy accent on the developmental needs of host
countries. I've heard that the struggle to see how the goals and profitable interests of corporations can best be negotiated into the support
of the developmental needs of host countries. Then others have come
along to insist that foreign investment seen from the U.S. side really
has to be an arm of foreign policy, and that like the Japanese we
should be moving much more along that line. It seems to me we're
going down two roads there that will end up in an impasse. I wondered
if a little more critical ethical thought about the concept of "host country" and "investing country" isn't called for. "Host country" covers
a multitude of evils. So does "investing country." We all remember
the Japanese experiences of the 1930s. I wonder if we're moving in
that direction in the 1970s once again.

With respect to host countries, Burke Marshall spoke of the positive laws of host countries as about the only standards you could turn
to in terms of measuring the impact of an investment and its desira-
bility. But I would submit it's worth remembering that most host
countries probably have unrepresentative governments today, especially in the less developed countries, where the investments are expanding. I wonder if the positive laws of most host countries, whose
governments probably do not reflect the deepest and broadest desires
of the masses of their people, can be accepted as standards for investment either by corporations or by investing countries, if there is
a closer relationship between country and corporation.

Secondly, I wonder if the positive laws of host countries that
sometimes are in direct conflict with international agreements,
whether the ILO type or the Universal Declaration of Human Rights,
should be accepted uncritically as standards by which investments
should be made or not made. But you could say the same thing about
a number of investing countries. If you move around the Eastern
European sphere and see how Soviet investment operates in East
European countries, you can raise some of the same questions. So I
am asking myself and asking my friends around the table if you aren't
inevitably forced to that third level of the argument to which we are
headed, I'm sure, in our whole conference—namely, the development
of international standards.

The enforceability is another question with respect to international
standards. It is very difficult for either the host countries, mixed lot
that they are, and behind them the corporations, mixed lot that they

are, to conform to one reality. Some of us have been very close to that Universal Declaration of Human Rights that took so many years to hammer out. When the nation-states comprising international bodies work together, they create standards that are far above their own practices, any one of them, and far above the practices of their component parts, be they trade unions or corporations or the state investment apparatus of the Soviet Union. Maybe that is the place to begin. Maybe that's what the UN is currently doing, trying to establish those standards by which the decisions of the corporations, the investing countries, the host countries, and the domestic development bureaucracies in the host countries can at least measure what they're doing, see in what measure it corresponds to the best thinking of mankind at the international level.

My final point is that when you think in these terms, isn't the distinction between an area of economic decisions, probably rather big, and an area alongside of it of ethical decisions, probably very small, a false distinction? Economics is a part of culture and cannot be set over against it. I would argue that economics, l'economie politique in classic 18th-century French thought, is a part of ethics, which is a part of philosophy, and some would say of theology. It's a phony distinction to ask, as some have tried to do at several points, "Businessmen, when you've got the economic decisions all in order, and all other things are about equal, what can you do about ethics?" The economic decisions are either unethical or ethical, but there are no neutral economic decisions. And then I would say we come to the level of the international definition of standards by which those economic decisions have to be judged by honest minds.

Carl A. Gerstacker: I've been desperately trying to listen to all the suggestions this morning and relate them to past and present and future experience. Let me start with Howard Schomer's point about whether people should deal with nonrepresentative governments, in other words, governments that don't represent the majority of the people in these countries—and there are many such cases today. Brazil I suppose might be one. It's a very interesting problem. There's a very large minority, I think, in the United States that disagree with many of the actions of the U.S. Government over a number of years, and so the people are changing. Often what is a minority becomes a majority, and this poses a problem. In Malaysia you have a very interesting situation. Malaysia has minorities, but Chinese have moved into Malaysia and they have multiplied more rapidly than the Malayans have, so that actually the majority of Malaysia's population is now Chinese, not Malayans, but Malayans control the government. Now who is the majority in Malaysia? On the purely democratic basis it would be the Chinese people, but it's the Malay country, and the Malayans are in charge, and should you deal with the Malayan government or not? It poses quite an interesting problem, at least to me.

Let me give you a specific example there. The Malayans have palm oil, and they have rubber. They have to weed. They used people to pull the weeds, a very laborious job, but later on they decided they would use chemical weed killers, in accord with proper wisdom or not. I don't know whether you should have more people laboriously pulling weeds or whether you should do it with weed killer. They imported the pesticides from a number of countries. Then they decided they wanted their own plant to produce them and so they went around and asked various companies to put in the weed-killer plant. The plant was built. In this case it helps both the U.S. balance of payments and employment, and it helps Malaysia, because raw materials are shipped from the United States, and if the plant were a U.S.-located plant there would not be just the raw materials coming from here.

But one of their local customs specified that at least half of the employees have to be Malayans, and so you cannot hire people in that country as you perhaps normally would—you have to make sure half of them are Malayans. Now is that fair to the Chinese majority, who thereby are discriminated against in a country that really isn't theirs but where they are the majority? These are some of the confusing problems that companies face.

Let me make just a point on Charles Powers's point earlier of deciding between countries. It seems to me in the practical world that you seldom get into that situation. In the Andean countries they tried to divide up production because they couldn't all produce everything, and they decided that perhaps Peru would make polyethylene, and Colombia maybe would make polyvinyl chloride. In the real world this hasn't worked out too well. They keep negotiating and theorizing on this, but usually each country then wants the plant, and so the outside company rarely can really make the decision. It's the local governments that say, "We want this; will you produce this in our country or won't you?"

Let me get back just a moment to the problem of a multinational company imposing its customs or mores or standards on other countries. I don't like that. I think it's very human not to like that. Sometimes it's the host government that forces its wishes through the company on the other country. But there are certain areas where I don't mind being arrogant and where I will continue to be arrogant, if that's the term, and one of those areas includes human safety and pollution. No matter how much people may decry it, if we know a way to run the plant more safely to hurt people less, to have less human life hurt, I'm going to be that arrogant whether anyone likes it or not. And it seems to me that if a multinational company, whether it's Japanese, European, or American, can show good standards of production that are good for people, this will upgrade the other local manufacturers, who will by comparison be forced to improve their safety action, and that I think should be done.

We have another problem here that has been brought up: Should you put in primitive plants or sophisticated plants? If you put in a primitive plant, you'll employ more local people. However, it may well not be competitive internationally. Therefore it may not survive if it wants to export, or even be able to survive against imports coming into the country, unless the local country then puts on high tariffs or quotas or some sort of protection. I've never been able to sort this out completely in my mind as to what's best for the people in the receiving country. Is an inefficient plant that uses a lot of people better than an efficient plant? I think probably the host country must make the decision, and I hope they make it with a great deal of wisdom, because it's not an easy decision.

One last comment, and there are many more I could make. India is a nation that obviously needs a lot of help, a lot of help in food, a lot of help in employment, a lot of help in a lot of things. We have tried, and I'm sure other companies have tried, to do things that India said it needed, but I think India is suffering greatly because of the difficulty of companies working with the Indian Government. The Indian Government is simply a very difficult government to work with. I think this is a tragedy, because whether it be a European company or a Japanese or a U.S. or whatever nationality, India does need a lot of help for its people. On the other hand, I think India's government must make the decisions. Perhaps it's happy with things the way they are.

6

A CONCLUDING STATEMENT ON INTERDEPENDENCE, BARGAINING, AND THE SELF-INTERESTS OF ACTORS

<u>Anthony Wiener</u>: I'd like to return to the interdependence issue. I think that one of the things we've run into at several points in the course of the discussion has been the danger of an abstraction, and I think we saw it clearly this morning when the word economic was used in two different senses.

There was the notion, I think, in what Charles Powers was saying, that businessmen make decisions on narrow economic grounds, perhaps quantifiably, and that after that there is a noneconomic criterion that may come in for consideration. That's a very unrealistic model of what businessmen do, because, although they are motivated by self-interest, their concept of self-interest is one of being a good businessman, and that means that a lot of unquantifiable and intangible considerations enter into a decision, and there are considerations of styling and many unconscious criteria for business decisions. Is this the kind of business we want to be? Are we operating in the way we like to operate? And although businessmen like to think of themselves as maximizing their self-interests, and in one sense they are doing so for the most part, some of that is ideology too. It makes a businessman feel better to think he's maximizing his self-interests and his return on investment. He likes to talk about the bottom line. He thinks that's just business, but very often he's behaving in a way he likes, and if he's a good businessman, the way he likes to behave is also the way that yields him at least good returns—he's learned through long experience that this is the way he behaves as a businessman. And it's quite different from the way he would behave if he maximized narrow economic considerations. So the whole model of economic considerations being equal, when you then take a look at noneconomic issues, it is apt to appear a rather unrealistic one.

Charles W. Powers: Could I say just one thing here as a point of clarification? When I said that after economic considerations were judged
to be equal in making a business choice, the businessman should then
look at noneconomic issues, I did talk as if it were a chronological
kind of sequence. I didn't mean to do that. My point is that it seems
to me worthwhile to get a kind of precision about ethical issues and
concepts that begins to compare in decision-making with the kinds of
statistics that businessmen use in weighing economic matters. I completely agree that a narrow definition of economic considerations is
completely unrealistic. It is true that noneconomic factors do operate
in economic decisions, but I think getting precision on these noneconomic factors and seeing them in relief against other kinds of factors
is very, very important if we're going to talk about this at all.

Mr. Wiener: Right. No, I agree and I think it's important to make
some of the ethical considerations as explicit as we can, and I'm sympathetic to that. I mentioned this point about abstractions only as an
introduction to what I want to say, because I want to use an abstraction,
and I want to make the point that there are great dangers in using them.
    Let's go back to this interdependence, because I think that Carl
Gerstacker raised a very important issue having to do with interdependence and the continuity of expectations and with the ethical considerations surrounding the making of contracts and under what conditions certain governments will gain investment from the outside and
under what conditions they will not. A whole range of issues of this
kind is in danger of being slighted because I don't think we were looking
sufficiently at what kind of interdependence exists. Ted Moran mentioned something in connection with this at the beginning of the discussion, but unfortunately he didn't pursue it. He said it wasn't a
zero-sum game, and that's perfectly true. And what that means is
that the sum of the gains and losses of the parties is not necessarily
zero. In other words, both sides may win, and it's also true that both
sides may lose. And in the expropriation situation, we had a case
where both sides lost.
    Now there are a couple of things to bear in mind. One is that in
the typical case, and most of these foreign investment decisions are
typical cases, it does not happen that what is best for both sides added
together is best for either side alone. It is a very unusual situation
when optimizing gains for both parties is the same as the maximum
gain for either side alone. That creates a dilemma, and this dilemma
has been studied by game theorists in the abstract. It exists in a great
many situations and in most international dealings, whether between
nations or between companies and nations, and in many other bargaining situations. The problem is that the temptation for each side
is to maximize his advantage at the expense of the other, even though,

if he succeeded in maximizing his advantage, the net outcome for both would <u>not</u> be better, and even though he creates a risk in his bargaining that the outcome for both is actually worse.

Two points follow from this. One is that from the international point of view, allowing this bargaining to proceed in an unregulated way does not maximize the gains for the world. If there were international mechanisms to prevent expropriations without compensation or to insure against such losses or in some other way to prevent that particular kind of loss from taking place, the gains for the world would be maximized. It might be true that in some cases particular countries would lose, because they may now be in a position to extract maximum gains for themselves, but that is not the same as maximum gains for everyone.

There's a second point, and that is that in this kind of situation it can often seem rational to a particular actor to use threats, and yet he would lose if he were to carry out those threats. Expropriation is a typical example of that kind of situation, where the threat of expropriation is the major bargaining lever the host country has after a capital investment has been made and has become hostage, and yet the host country doesn't really want to carry out that threat. Nevertheless, it remains an important bargaining tool. So there has to be some explicit recognition of the fact that the bargaining position changes, that the multinational company has the maximum bargaining power at the time before entry, when it is in a position to make a certain kind of contract. But once capital investment has begun and a commitment has been made, that bargaining position is changed, and it ought to be foreseeable that that change will occur. At that point, temptations will be presented to the host country to maximize its advantage very narrowly conceived or to threaten certain acts that would hurt the company if they were carried out. But it does this in order to gain advantages.

III

ECONOMIC FACTORS IN MULTINATIONAL AND NATION-STATE RELATIONS

Many participants in the conference insisted that the key to understanding the MNC is economic analysis. The central thrust of their contention, beginning with the section by Miguel Wionczek in Chapter 1, is that MNCs as giant microactors are having profound impact, frequently disruptive, on macroactors (nation-states) and on the structures of international financial processes. Furthermore, they argue that traditional tools of economic analysis are not adequate to deal with this new economic pattern and plead for new modes of information-gathering and analysis in order to permit macroactors to understand what is happening to their economies and to help microactors see the effects of their own activities. In relation to the kinds of issues discussed in Part II, the voices in this group contend that no adequate legal controls can be devised without going through critical macroeconomic analysis and that issues such as national sovereignty and moral accountability are best understood when translated into economic terms.

Ronald Muller, Assistant Professor of Economics at American University, prepares ground for the first half of this part with a paper outlining the changes in international economic structures occasioned by the development of the MNCs. His views are debated in two rounds of discussion, the first focusing on the home country (the United States) and the second on host countries.

The second half of this part is devoted to the question of information and disclosure: Who has the information needed for an adequate understanding of the new economic processes, what kind of information is needed, and who should take the lead in generating, collecting, and regulating the information? It is interesting to note that here again the contention is made that even in this matter political structures must initiate and control whatever processes are devised for this economic analysis. The discussion moves full circle.

CHAPTER

7

THE ECONOMICS
OF THE MNC

THE GLOBAL CORPORATION AND
PRIVATE-SECTOR TRANSFORMATION:
INSTABILITY AND THE PUBLIC-SECTOR LAG
Ronald Muller

This consultation has shown once again what students of the interdependent relationships of global corporate operations between poor
and rich countries have often experienced in similar meetings held in
the United States and Europe: that only now are people in the developed countries beginning to understand the uniqueness of global corporations as compared to national business enterprises. In this regard, the less developed countries (LDCs) have, because of their
experiences, a much firmer comprehension of the distinguishing characteristics of the global corporation's impacts on the individual nation-
state. How and why these impacts in LDCs occur and why they appear
to be changing since the early 1970s, compared to the previous 20
years, I have detailed elsewhere.[1] Here these impacts and their

This paper is based on the author's oral presentation at the
Council on Religion and International Affairs' Corporate Consultation I,
Aspen, Colorado, September 1973. It represents an updating and
summary of the author's writings that have appeared in various jour-
nals and in his book, coauthored with Richard Barnet, Global Reach:
The Power of the Multinational Corporations (New York: Simon and
Schuster, 1975). The latter was serialized in the New Yorker in
December 1974. Dr. Muller is a member of the Faculty of Economics,
American University, Washington, D. C.

changing nature in LDCs are summarized, particularly as they illuminate the specific problem of the U.S. Government's ability to implement its regulatory prerogatives over the private sector, more specifically over U.S.-based global corporations as compared to U.S. nonglobal business enterprises.

Thus in this chapter I have attempted to bring much more detail to bear on the uniqueness of global corporations, how their emergence has transformed the manner in which our own and the world political economy behaves and in turn has brought to governmental policy-makers new dimensions in carrying out their public-sector charge. A fundamental conclusion of this work is that the public sector lags far behind in understanding the realities of what is now a transformed private sector. For the many aspects of social and economic policy-making involved a timely and appropriate correction to overcoming this lag will be forthcoming only after the public sector has a detailed comprehension of how global corporations operate and what the impacts of these new operations are. A second conclusion hopefully made clear by this chapter is that, in a world that has achieved a historic degree of interdependence through the rise of the global corporation, policies adopted in more developed nations will affect people in the less developed areas and vice versa.

The Global Vision

By 1970 the advanced industrialized nations of North America, Europe, and the Pacific Basin had witnessed the rapid evolution of the newest form of the private economic institutions that characterized their societies. The largest and most dynamic domestic enterprises of these countries' industrial, financial, and communications sectors had transformed themselves into global corporations. As the 1970s proceeded, there was a flourishing recognition of this corporate transformation. Business magazines rushed to add additional columns to their annual statistical surveys of the nation's Top 500, showing that more and more of the giants were becoming truly "globalized" as the ratios of their foreign-to-domestic assets, sales, and profits began surpassing the 30 percent and in many cases the 50 percent mark. The globalization wave was led by industrial firms but was quickly followed overseas by banks, advertising, and public relations agencies determined to serve their industrial clients on a worldwide basis. With increasing frequency the head managers of these corporations began referring to themselves as "the new globalists," the "advance men" of "economic one-worldism," wearing "the robes of diplomats," to use the words of First National City Bank President William I. Spencer.

Writers began coining such terms as the "World Managers" or "Earth Managers." The political reaction to this new fact of transnational economic life was inevitably varied, depending on where the viewer fell on the political and geographic spectrum of Right to Left, resident of a rich North country or a poor South country. The Right refrained from speculation, while European analysts worried over the "American Challenge" and promoted action to counter it by spurring the globalization of their own firms. The radical Left largely ignored the institutional uniqueness of the global corporation, treating it as a traditional instrument of the state imperialism of rich nations over poor nations. Starting in the mid-1960s only the academicians, technicians, and business consultants of the liberal-center, in rich and poor countries alike, took the transformation of the corporation into a global entity seriously. In poor countries the focus was on how and why the impacts on their local economies would differ as between global versus national corporations. In the United States, although economists continued to pay it little heed, business schools and consulting firms studied how the corporation could capitalize on its worldwide network of subsidiaries to gain further profits relative to a strictly domestic operation.

By the late 1960s these studies identified the unique characteristic of the global corporation as its ability to bring together and coordinate resources from many different countries for production in still another nation and then for marketing in as many national markets as possible. In essence the uniqueness of the global corporation is the transnational mobility and control of its three most vital resources, its mechanical and managerial technology, its finance capital, and its advertising-communication techniques. This mobility has led to the dramatic increase of its importance in the world political economy. For all sectors of the world political economy, MNCs number about 1,000, with more than half coming from the United States. In the industrial sector, where statistical information is more refined, the UN counts some 650; between them they control over 50 percent of total world nonagricultural trade, with many of them registering gross annual sales in excess of the national incomes of the numerous countries in which they operate. With regard to the world's money supply, global corporations control somewhere between $160 billion to $270 billion in liquid assets—from 1.5 to two times the total world reserves in the hands of governments. U.S.-based global corporations alone account for more than 70 percent of this nation's exports and some 40 percent of its imports.

This rapid rise of the global corporation into its current position of dominance in the economic affairs of nations was made possible by a number of technological and institutional innovations occurring shortly after World War II. In the private sector breakthroughs were made in the technology of management, accounting, and communications, thereby making feasible the control from parent headquarters of a global network of expanding and diverse subsidiaries. In the public sector individual nation-states were able to create the international institutions that gave the globalization process legitimacy. The international monetary system of Bretton Woods guaranteed the relatively free movement of finance capital and exchange rate stability, an essential prerequisite of the early internationalization of business, while a second necessary condition, that of relatively "free trade" among nations, was promoted by the General Agreement on Trade and Tariffs (GATT).

Although national governments had provided the institutional framework for taking much of the risk out of global business mobility, their decision would begin to come back to haunt them some 20 years later. For where the corporation has achieved global mobility and control over resources, the nation-state government is more restricted, the immobility of its sovereignty being defined by the concept of territoriality. Does not the juxtaposition of global corporate mobility with the immobility of nation-state sovereignty threaten a government's ability to control the way in which resources are used for the development of the national economy? It was in this general and unspecified form that liberal academics raised the sovereignty question in the late 1960s. As we shall examine shortly, it was the first in a series of what I call "systemic" problems to be identified with the transformation process of the global corporation.

The response to the sovereignty question is what the Brookings Institution's Fred Bergston and Theodore Moran have termed the "liberal vision." The cornerstone of this vision is the assumption that the global corporation is the most efficient productive institution yet devised and therefore holds out the best chance for solving the world poverty problem. After 200 years it epitomizes Adam Smith's dream of a world political economy based on a perfect global division of labor. Because of its size and experience, which permit it to achieve mobility, it can combine resources from various global sources for production at the cheapest location and then distribute this output worldwide. True, sovereignty is a problem, but it is a transitional problem on the way to a new world order. The global corporation, by definition, accelerates global interdependence between nations. The increased national income resulting from the new global efficiency will assure that nations become, as Princeton's Robert Gilpin has noted, "enmeshed in a web of economic interdependence from which they cannot easily escape."

No nation will give up the resulting economic benefits for such vague goals as greater sovereignty and national autonomy. In short, nation-states will accept, if at times reluctantly, greater dependency

on the outside world and eventually give their full support to what the
global visionaries would call heightened "interstate cooperation" or
the "new internationalism." Thus the visionaries point to the thrust
into Eastern Europe and the Soviet Union as direct evidence of how the
global corporation can become an engine for world peace, "the most
powerful agent for the internationalization of human society," to quote
Aurelio Peccei, a Fiat director and promoter of the Club of Rome.

The global visionaries therefore admit that the "cosmocorps," as
George Ball has written, "do have the power to affect the lives of people and nations in a manner that challenges the prerogatives and responsibilities of political authority." Yet "the logical and eventual development of this possibility," in the opinion of John Diebold, "would
be the end of nationality and national governments as we know them."
This is a necessary outcome, according to Jacques Maisonrouge, head
of IBM's World Trade Corporation, because "the world's political
structures are completely obsolete. They have not changed in at least
a hundred years and are woefully out of tune with technological progress." Global interdependence will require the harmonization of national economic goals and policies to achieve the irresistible goal of
greater and greater amounts of the goods and services that global
corporations are currently producing. As the web of this interdependence increases, so too will the degree of necessary international harmonization. Thus, concludes a 1967 consulting report of Business
International, "the nation-state is becoming obsolete: tomorrow . . .
it will in any meaningful sense be dead—and so will the corporation
that remains essentially national."

This then was the visionary response to the sovereignty issue as
orchestrated by the globalists of the late 1960s and early 1970s, a
vision equaling "the prologue to a new World symphony," as a dean
of the Columbia Business School once phrased it. But the world of
1974 is far different than the vision of the globalists would have it.
Internationalism is faltering, and in its place nationalism is on the
rise. Close and distant neighbors, once considered the best of U.S.
allies, are now taking a new look at the meaning of global interdependence in a world rocked by resource scarcities and double-digit
inflation. The international monetary system of Bretton Woods is
dead, with disagreement on what replaces it adding a further rupture
to an Atlantic Alliance (including Japan), the members of which are
increasingly looking at the development of regional economic blocs
and bilateral swaps rather than adhering to the principle of worldwide
"free trade" as espoused by another currently faltering international
institution, the GATT. What is beginning to emerge in this situation
is a change in the foreign policy of many nation-states, a "new geopolitics" bluntly asking the question of whether the post-World War II
system of international economic and political relations can maintain

itself so as to assure the individual nation continuing access to foreign resources and export markets. (For example, a burning question of the so-called energy crisis asked by politicians in the oil-consuming nations was why national authorities had so little influence over the global energy companies' decisions governing the worldwide allocation of the oil shortfalls resulting from the OPEC embargo.

The international transmission of economic disturbances, however, does not limit itself to only the natural resource question. It encompasses a potentially even greater threat to stability, namely, the interdependence of world money markets (more accurately the interdependence between one nation's money supply to that of others). This interdependency is best symbolized by the $100 billion Eurodollar market, a vast transnational pool of dollars and other currencies coming under the institutional control of no one government. Given the web of worldwide financing engaged in by global firms and banks, a major default or sudden large withdrawal of deposits in the unregulated Eurodollar market can trigger liquidity crises in many different countries. Such financial collapses, in turn, carry with them the danger of a heavy recession or depression. In reviewing these current international problems Brookings President Kermit Gordan concluded before the December 1973 American Economic Association meetings that "the present situation is clearly unstable. The United States has lost. . . effective leadership in the creation of new institutions and arrangements, and other sources of leadership have not yet appeared."

If the nation-state is globally interdependent, then instability in the international arena will be mirrored by instability at home. Since the late 1960s the U.S. economy has been suffering the worsening strain of "stagflation," persistent unemployment coupled with increasing inflation. National policy-makers have met frustration in their efforts to control it, and the economic theory of the Keynesian Revolution upon which they rely cannot explain it. Also starting in the late 1960s, the constancy in income distribution, a cherished hallmark of the U.S. economy since World War II, turned toward instability, with a significant shift toward growing income concentration reported by most recent studies on the topic. Unemployment, inflation, and income concentration have combined to bring about a decline in the real income of a significant majority of U.S. families over the past two years. Meanwhile, consumers and business alike continue to accelerate their use of credit as measured by the ratio of total credit increases to increases in real GNP, a ratio that has been on an exponential upswing since the 1960s. Thus accelerating credit requirements meet head on with growing liquidity problems at a time when a liquidity crisis overseas can be quickly transmitted back to the home country. Another instability issue is the government's fiscal crisis. It is becoming increasingly difficult for an administration to avoid deficit spending unless it chooses to neglect further the nation's social infrastructure. The fiscal crisis is due in part to a steady erosion in the corporate tax base as a source of federal revenues. This erosion is occurring at a time when expenditure needs are greater than ever for the nation's transportation system, alternative energy sources and other environmental areas, the refurbishing of its cities, and welfare payments to accommodate the problems of unemployment and income concentration. Finally, the instability of the U.S. balance of trade is reminiscent of a Latin American nation's. U.S. trade swings within the four years 1969-73 have been oscillating between record deficits, surpluses, and are currently back into the red.

These then are some of the issues of nation-state instability that face the United States at home and abroad. The keynote characteristic of this instability is the interrelatedness of the issues that define it, the dovetailing or overlapping nature of the various "crises" that have plagued the nation increasingly over the recent past. The OPEC phenomenon, for example, highlights not only the vulnerabilities of global interdependence in terms of resource supplies but further feeds the volatility of international money flows and their relation to inflation and liquidity crunches while running head on into the needs of conservation and the maintenance of an ecological balance. Thus the current situation is in stark contrast to the global visionaries' projection of increasing international harmony, stability, and prosperity. What was wrong with this projection, and how does the globalization of the nation's largest private enterprises relate to these issues of instability?

The answers to these questions can be explored only after a brief examination of what was overlooked in the analyses of the global visionaries. In turn, these oversights can be related to the manner in which global corporations operate and how those operations escape the coverage of the various policy tools currently used by governments to regulate their economies. To preview our discussion, there are three aspects that we can highlight here. First, the globalists based their visionary projection on only one part of economic theory while overlooking other parts. Second, they did not foresee the scope and intensity of the structural transformation process the globalization of the firm represented. Finally, they did not account for the changing international geopolitical power relations this transformation would in part help bring about.

Flaws in the Vision

The global vision was based on the foundations of modern orthodox economics, the classic writings of Adam Smith and David Ricardo.

The appeal of Smith and Ricardo has always been their basic conclusion that a world political economy that included the two principles of a global division of labor and free trade would maximize the planet's output and yield a distribution of that output for maintaining a harmony of interests between all actors, nation states and their respective consumers and producers. This was the desirable and overriding systemic impact—that is, inherent result—of the dynamic interaction of the individual actors that constituted such a system of political economy. It was from these two principles that the globalists of course derived their vision. These two principles, however, defined only one aspect of the Smith-Ricardian system, the efficiency aspect. But other principles or conditions have to be adhered to within and between national economies in order to achieve the other aspect of their basic conclusion, the harmonious distribution of benefits resulting from such an efficiently produced output. The most important of these other principles was the condition that the social institution of the market, the allocation and distribution mechanism within and between societies, would be characterized by a large number of small independent, non-affiliated, and competitive producers and consumers. In other words the individual firm, besides being small, had no formal or implicit relations to either other firms with which they bought or sold or to consumers at the point of final retail sale. It was this distributional principle that the globalists overlooked in projecting their vision, and yet where the social institution of the market does not conform to this condition, the harmony of interests aspect of the Smith-Ricardian conclusion does not necessarily follow.

If harmonious impacts do not necessarily follow, what does? Some helpful insights into this question can be gleaned from a quick perusal of the realities of the global corporate world. Both our own and the world political economy today can be classified as largely a "post-Market Economy." For years students of American industrial organization have tried to convince the academic and policy-making community that the vast majority of corporate transactions in the domestic economy in no way go through a Smith-Ricardian market mechanism, with the systemic upshot that the distributional impacts between different regions and income groups have been less than harmonious. The subsidiaries of the 500 largest industrial corporations, which account for around 70 percent of sales, profits, and employment in that sector, typically transact their purchases and sales with other, wholly owned parent subsidiaries around the country. The prices affixed to these intracorporate transactions, so-called transfer prices, are rarely related to competitive market prices of independent firms in the socioeconomic sense intended by Smith and Ricardo. These arbitrarily administered transfer prices follow a principle of parent profit maximization, but again not in the Smith-Ricardian sense of that term. Thus a subsidiary producing in an area of high state and/or city corporate taxes can underprice its sales to a subsidiary located in a lower tax area, resulting in diminished profits in the former and higher profits in the latter subsidiary. For the parent, profits are higher than what they would have been had competitive market prices prevailed. Under the Galbraithian concept of countervailing power, however, this negation of the market's social function can be constrained as regards the extent of the negative distributional impacts experienced by the residents and local government of the higher tax region. On one hand the countervailing power of organized labor maintains wages and has tended to equalize them between regions. On the other, the regional government can tend to rely on various forms of income transfer programs from the federal government to offset local tax losses. While the former's corporate tax base can be eroded by such nonmarket transactions, the federal government's is not, because the higher profits show up in the consolidated tax reports of the parent.

With the globalization of the large domestic enterprise, transfer pricing and other techniques of intracorporate "cross-subsidization" were integrated into what now became the goal of global, not domestic, profit maximization. The most important corporations, which constitute the bulk of global corporate assets, sales, and profits, typically have a network of subsidiaries that span many nations and industries. The majority of export and import transactions of these subsidiaries are between them and their sister units of the same parent's global network. Currently at least one-half of all U.S. exports are intracorporate, nonmarket transactions. Even higher percentages have been recorded for Latin America's total foreign trade. Similar findings are now emerging for Europe and other areas. Obviously the many nations involved in this global intersubsidiary trade have different corporate tax rates. The leading business schools and consulting firms have produced an abundance of technical literature documenting the energy that global controllers devote to the use of transfer prices as a key tool in minimizing their worldwide tax costs. Analysts have been studying this phenomenon much longer in underdeveloped countries, particularly with regard to the social and international distributional impacts of global corporations. Their numerous studies have documented what the dictates of global profit maximization would lead one to expect: underpricing of exports averaging 40 to 60 percent and overpricing of imports ranging anywhere from 20 percent to 8,000 percent.[2](Besides the purpose of tax minimization, such pricing behavior is also found where there is the perceived threat of rapid devaluing and/or appreciating currencies between nations.) The modern accounting technology that makes global corporate cross-subsidization feasible does not stop short of just the two nations representing the origin and final destination of intersubsidiary trade. In many cases the transactions involve a "triangular trade," being routed through a holding subsidiary located in an offshore tax haven such as Panama or Monaco. It is here in the tax haven where the profits from under- and overpricing accrue, not in the country of origin or final destination. From the tax haven these profits are then transferred to the home or any other country of the parent's network, using other forms of cross-subsidization, again bypassing market mechanisms and minimizing tax costs. For example, the tax haven subsidiary can make a 12-month or less short-term "loan" of this finance capital to another subsidiary in the United States. At the end of the specified time the loan is repaid and then "rolled over"—that is, re-lent directly back to the U.S. subsidiary. By using this type of "profit-loan swap" the parent has avoided the U.S. tax on income earned abroad while having the benefit of continuing to use that income.

The Internal Revenue Service is of course aware of these techniques, and in fact has laws such as regulation 482 to control transfer pricing, but effective enforcement of literally millions of transactions is virtually impossible, given current corporate disclosure requirements, existing loopholes, and inadequate IRS resources. These insights into the operations of global corporations, however, outline two important points. First, they demonstrate exactly what is meant by global corporate mobility versus nation-state immobility. Second, these types of operations, called "distortions" by economists, demonstrate how the social function of the market is negated and therefore lead to less than harmonious patterns of income distribution within and between nations. The chief distortion referred to here is that the global corporation is not a small domestic firm but rather a global oligopoly, one of a few firms dominating an industry or industries worldwide. In addition, a further oversight by the global visionaries (and by too many governmental policy-makers) concerns one of the two major breakthroughs in modern neoclassical economics, the General Theory of the Second Best. (The other, the Keynesian Revolution, we shall return to shortly.) For the purpose at hand the most important aspect of this theory is the proof that where distortions to the market mechanism abound, then "first-best" harmonious distribution impacts need not result. Instead some "second-best" outcome occurs, which the tools of neoclassical economics cannot generally predict. Hence each situation must be investigated independently to determine who benefits. To leave the jargon of economic theory behind us, we can see, for example, that in the case where a nation's exports are underpriced by say 40 percent, it will be getting back approximately 40 percent less foreign exchange than the amount of resources it gave up in the form of its exports. The resulting impact on world income distribution is obviously not in the national interests of the exporting nation. Equally important is the negative impact on the tax collection power of the local government; more specifically, it undermines the government's countervailing power to maintain stability in the national economy.

To what extent and when, where, and why do transfer prices deviate from what the market mechanism would dictate? At what point and by how much do global corporations expand their use of transfer pricing, profit-loan swaps, and other cross-subsidization techniques like "leads and lags" in order to transfer their finance capital from what they perceive to be a devaluing currency area to an appreciating one and in the process help make the perception a reality? Do national statistics really reveal the true value of resource exchanges, be that exchange between the United States and Germany or Appalachia and New York? In a world where global corporations are the dominant actors behind the domestic and international economic transactions of nation-states, how has this private-sector revolution affected the public sector's efficacy in using traditional monetary and fiscal policy? The answers to these and similar questions have been the topic of intense inquiry for a number of years in the underdeveloped world. With few exceptions only recently have they become a topic of research in advanced nations. A complete set of answers has yet to emerge. These questions all focus on the validity of the Smith-Ricardian harmony of interests conclusion, which not too many years ago the former head of a global corporation reinterpreted to mean "what's good for GM is good for the nation." Today Charlie Wilson's words are being received with growing skepticism. The above analysis that led to these questions, however, should begin to answer why the projections of the global visionaries need not be true and, more importantly, indicate that there is a relationship between the globalization process of the large corporation and the current instability of the nation-state.

Postwar Structural Changes in the World Economy

The global visionaries not only failed to appreciate fully the realities of a global oligopoly's operations and how they violated the assumptions underlying their projections, they also underestimated the scope and intensity of the structural transformation in the national and world political economy that was to accompany the globalization process. Associated with this transformation was a set of impacts defining the instability issues mentioned earlier. From 1950 to 1970 these issues were almost singularly identified with the impacts of global corporations in underdeveloped countries. Starting around 1970, these issues were increasingly raised by three groups of actors in the advanced industrialized home countries of the global corporations. Organized labor, strictly national business firms, and various components of the federal government became concerned with what can only be termed the erosion of their countervailing power vis-a-vis global corporations. In the United States and other industrialized nations, the specific impacts surrounding the issue of countervailing power include income distribution and employment, increasing industrial and financial concentration, and the behavior of global corporations, particularly as they affect governmental stabilization measures in the interrelated policy areas of balance of payments, inflation, taxes, money, and credit.

To understand these issues it is important to note the post-World War II structural changes in the world political economy. These changes fall into two component parts. The first concerns a pattern of convergence and divergence in the levels and composition of consumption and production worldwide, the second a series of locational changes in where output was being produced. In a recent book Yale's Richard Cooper has made an excellent analysis of the convergence theme. After the war the globalization of U.S. firms brought about a rapid international transfer of technology, shared to greater and lesser extents by most countries. Through the planning efforts of the Japanese Government, the duplication of industrial technology was accomplished largely by licensing from U.S. corporations and laid the basis for the rise of Japan's own global corporations. In Europe large local corporations (subsequently aided by local government) had to compete vigorously with U.S. subsidiaries to share in the postwar industrial reconstruction of that area. Until the mid-1960s attempts at industrialization in the underdeveloped world were almost solely dependent upon the subsidiary operations of U.S.-based global corporations. With this worldwide homogenization of productive technology came an obvious convergence in the composition of consumption, a convergence in the needs and demands for raw materials to feed this technology, and a convergence in the problems accompanying such production, such as pollution and urban congestion. But whereas advanced countries experienced a striking convergence in per capita consumption levels (over the period the ratio of U.S. per capita income to Germany's and Japan's went from 4/1, 6/1 to 1.1/1, 1.6/1 respectively), there was an equally striking divergence in the consumption gap between poor and rich nations.

The success of the planetary enterprise as an "engine of development" for advanced nations led to a second aspect of structural transformation, ironically raising for the first time the issues of global corporate impacts on the home economies. Through the 1950s and early 1960s, U.S. corporations proceeded to expand relatively unimpeded by competitive forces from the large oligopolies of Europe and Japan, which were focusing inward and still recovering from the aftermath of the war. With recovery complete the focus of European and

Japanese firms turned outward. The first target of their globalization process was the rich markets of the U.S. economy. U.S. oligopolists, long conditioned to a stable division of market shares between themselves and a few other U.S. firms, now faced a formidable competitive challenge. The latecomers to the globalization process had learned well from their pioneering U.S. counterparts. In addition to the still relatively lower wage rates enjoyed by foreign-based global corporations in the 1960s, they also benefited from lower production costs by acquiring much of their mechanical technology via licensing from U.S. firms rather than having to make high initial outlays for R and D purposes. As regards marketing, accounting, and other global management techniques, foreign corporations were able to absorb these nonpatentable types of technology through the relatively costless process of learning from the demonstration effects of the U.S. pioneers. "The advantages of the latecomers," as Thorstein Veblen remarked years earlier while studying the nature of international industrial competition, "are many" if they can overcome the momentum of the pioneers' head start. In the European and Japanese cases close business-government cooperation also added significantly to to these firms' ability to catch up. Throughout the 1960s the new global corporations of Europe and Japan increasingly made successive inroads into U.S. markets for metals, textiles, plastics, electronics, and many other product lines.

It was in response to this foreign challenge that the second aspect of structural transformation occurred for the U.S. and world political economy—namely, a rapid change in the location of production. To counter the foreign corporate advantages (intensified since the late 1960s by an overvalued dollar) U.S. global corporations moved their plants and equipment to low-cost locations in underdeveloped countries. From these locations output was exported back to the U.S. and/or to third-country markets formally serviced by their U.S. subsidiaries. Thus emerged the newest and latest phase of the globalization process, the "export platform" function of foreign investment, which gradually became equally important as the earlier two phases, the extraction and processing of raw materials and, in manufacturing, "import substitution" investment for producing goods locally for sale in the host country. Clearly a prime force behind export platform expansion was to overcome European and Japanese inroads by taking advantage of 50 cents an hour (versus $3 per hour in the United States) wage rates in such countries as Brazil, Singapore, Mexico, and Indonesia. Industrial analysts such as former Rand consultant Jack Baranson quickly found, however, that global corporations had other reasons for relocating to the export platform countries. Workers formerly jobless proved quick to learn and equally or more productive than in the home country, while many host governments guaranteed labor force stability through antiunion legislation. Global accounting technology via cross-subsidization techniques realized substantial tax savings. The absence of antipollution controls yielded still further cost savings, particularly in the processing and basic manufacturing sectors, compared to production in the home country. The export platform expansion has been rapid. For example, at present it is difficult for U.S. consumers to purchase TVs, other household appliances, cameras, or cars that have not been partially or totally produced overseas. Even the Pentagon is now finding that many of the key parts in its arsenal of military hardware are now dependent on a foreign supply source.

The demonstration effects of the export platform innovation of U.S. global corporations were not to go unobserved by European and Japanese oligopolists. By the early 1970s the United States and other advanced nations had experienced not only a convergence in the levels and composition of consumption and production but also a corresponding convergence in wage rates, pollution costs, and finally exchange rates. Again the latecomers duplicated the innovation of the pioneers. European and Japanese corporations accelerated their own push toward export platform investments in Latin America, Asia, and Africa. The dynamics of the world political economy were now fully characterized by global oligopoly competition. With the export platform innovation, the global corporation achieved a new dimension of transnational mobility. With it the nation-state has reached a new level of global interdependence, and the transformation of its own economy has become a reality.

The transformation of the U.S. economy has raised in the first instance a set of institutional issues of instability. These institutional issues refer to the question of power. Besides concerning the countervailing power of government, the issues also focus on unions and national (nonglobal) business enterprises. For the institution of organized labor the issue is a question of maintaining its bargaining power, not only to defend wage rates and guard against unemployment but also to voice its legitimate interests as to what will be the future composition of U.S. employment and the adjustment path it will take. For the institution of national business enterprises the multitude of relatively small banks, farms, subcontracting, end processing, and/or distributing firms in the United States, the bargaining power question involves no less than their ability to maintain their existence. All three institutions trace the diminution in their regulatory and political power to the globalization of the large U.S. corporation, namely, its mobility compared to their immobility. The instability in the power base of these three institutions is itself part of our political economy's transformation.

The whole issue of countervailing power revolves around what is now a historical fact. A dominant institution of society, the large corporation, has transformed the way society functions; the other major institutions have yet to make a commensurate change. The result is a series of "structural lags" in the functioning of these other major institutions vis-a-vis the global corporation. The current outcome is a systemic instability in countervailing power, the modicum by which our society has sought to maintain equilibrium in the distribution of economic and political prerogatives as between its various groups.

It is not the first time our political economy has undergone transformation, although the velocity of transformation has accelerated. After the Civil War the United States went from a set of regionally based economies to that of a nationally integrated economy side by side with the transformation of the local-regional firm into the large nationwide corporation. During the Great Depression the "lagging" institution of organized labor was finally given its legitimization while at the same time Keynes transformed the lag in economic theory. The translation of the Keynesian revolution, albeit with a lag, into the new policy-making prerogatives of government represented a basic structural change in that institution. This was the last transformation of the U.S. political economy. We are now in the midst of another.

The mobility-immobility clash between the global firm and the domestic union stems from the former's worldwide "complementary production" facilities. These facilities not only permit the production of parts in one part of the globe for assembly in another but also permit a subsidiary in one country to absorb the production from a sister unit in a different territory where output has stopped because of a strike or other interruptions. In addition, for purposes of wage negotiations the corporation can threaten to close down the U.S. plant and establish an export platform subsidiary (labor calls it "the runaway shop") should the wage demand be considered too high. These types of mobility weapons have been used in numerous negotiations with unions, as documented in university studies conducted in Europe and the United States. The corporations cry "foreign competition"; the unions claim "unfair tactics." Global cross-subsidization techniques also make it difficult for unions to determine the actual profitability of a domestic subsidiary, so that the threat of foreign competition may or may not be true. Thus, one aspect of the union's structural lag is that corporate mobility has made the strike a less effective negotiation weapon. Two other forms of structural lags characterize the erosion of labor's countervailing power. National unions have still to achieve coordination with their foreign counterparts effective enough to counteract transnational corporate mobility by transnational union action. Second, government has failed both to devise new arbitration institutions for resolving the new business-labor issues of the global corporation and to provide adequate adjustment mechanisms for the rapid changes in structural unemployment resulting from the transnational mobility of production.

To understand the decline of small national business enterprises it is important to highlight another unique aspect of the mobility of the global corporation. It is not only a global oligopoly; it is also a global "oligopoly-conglomerate." Besides operating across different national boundaries, almost all of the nation's top industrial and financial corporations operate across more than one product-line industry. GM has its household appliances and finance divisions, ITT its Wonder Bread and Sheraton Hotels, and the largest banks have been transformed into One Bank Holding Companies. The latter, besides engaging in commercial banking, also pursue activities in product lines such as credit cards and the purchasing and leasing of planes and tankers. The large conglomerate captures unique economies of scale by utilizing technology and marketing expertise as well as finance capital developed in one established "profit center" for cross-subsidization into newer operations. In the country and industry of the newer operation smaller national firms find it difficult to compete against the conglomerate's new entry, which is richly endowed via the use of parent cross-subsidization. Ultimately, the single-country, single-industry national enterprises lose much of their market shares and disappear, either through acquisition or bankruptcies. Thus the twin force accompanying globalization is accelerating industrial and financial concentration in the domestic economy, of the host countries and the home country, as reflected in the record-breaking surge in concentration for the United States during the 1960s. This oligopoly-conglomerate expansion process is cumulative and systemic unless institutional innovations are made to the mechanisms for regulating concentration. Thus far the structural lags persist. Domestic business, by definition, functions neither on a transnational nor on a transindustry basis. The governmental institution of corporate disclosure conceals more than it reveals about cross-subsidization. Antitrust laws are designed for times past, when the large corporation was neither global in scope nor objectives.

The twin forces of globalization and increasing domestic concentration have been discussed in terms of how the social function of the market as an institution is negated by the use of intracorporate cross-subsidization techniques. As we shall see below, market negation results not only because of the increasing predominance of intracorporate transactions but also because of the effects of increasing oligopoly-power vis-a-vis consumer prices. The lack of recognition afforded the negation of the market is the chief symptom underlying what is probably the most important of the structural lags characterizing the institutions of government. This lag is reflected in the failure of government to modify and change its economic policy-making tools (and the underlying Keynesian theory upon which they are based) to account for the structural transformation in our political economy. The lag in policy-making tools has a direct bearing on the government's current inability to deal with instabilities in income distribution, inflation, and persistent unemployment.

Before proceeding further, some additional indicators of transformation should be mentioned. Thus far this transformation has been identified in terms of its institutional indicators, namely, the mobility-immobility theme, which gives rise to the instability issues of countervailing power. Here some of the quantitative dimensions of transformation can be highlighted. Because of space constraints and the general familiarity of statistics portraying the cumulative increases in concentration, I shall not dwell on these data. Instead attention will be focused on the globalization indicators of transformation. What the figures show, however, is not surprising given that U.S. global corporations account for the vast majority of this economy's industrial and financial transactions. Nevertheless, while the foreign dependence of specific U.S. corporations is much discussed and documented, the new, overall dependence of the U.S. economy, due to their globalization process, is less well understood and seldom analyzed.

The true extent of the U.S. economy's dependence on foreign operations cannot be gleaned by focusing on exports and imports as a percentage of GNP. In 1960 the proportion of total corporate U.S. profits derived overseas was only 7 percent, commencing exponential increases around the year 1967. Today more than 20 percent of total U.S. corporate profits are derived from overseas investment operations. My own estimate, taking account of exports and imports as well as how cross-subsidization techniques can conceal the true origin of profits, is closer to 30 percent. Another indicator of the new global dependence of the U.S. economy is the amount of total investment by U.S. manufacturing corporations that goes overseas versus here at home. In 1957 foreign investment in new plant equipment was 9 percent of domestic plant and equipment expenditures. By 1970 it had reached a figure of some 25 percent. Again the exponential increases occur starting in the years 1965-67. In 1961 the sales of all U.S. manufacturing abroad represented only 7 percent of total U.S. sales. In 1965 the proportion of foreign to domestic sales crept up to 8.5 percent, but in the late 1960s the picture changed abruptly. By 1970 foreign sales accounted for about 13 percent of total sales of all U.S. manufacturing corporations. As an indicator of changes in our banking sector we find that today the foreign dollar deposits of the nation's largest global banks are estimated at more than 65 percent of their domestic deposit holdings, up from 8.5 percent in 1960.

When so many different indicators register changes in the same period, it strongly suggest that something important has happened. My view is that the U.S. economy experienced a fundamental structural transformation, with a turning point somewhere between 1965 and 1967. But there are other indicators that can be associated with this transformation process. One of these is the dramatic change in total federal tax receipts derived from corporate income taxes. In 1958 the annual corporate tax contribution was 25.2 percent of federal revenues. By 1973 it had declined to less than 15 percent. The acceleration in this decline, as with the other indicators, can be timed between the years 1965 and 1967. In addition, various congressional studies have documented the fact that it is the largest corporations, all global, that pay the lowest effective tax rates and have received the vast majority of benefits derived from the investment tax credit and the accelerated depreciation allowances.

U.S. employment impacts of globalization can be divided into two major categories: short- versus long-term impacts on aggregate employment, due to the transnational mobility of the nation's largest employers, and adjustment to changes in the composition of employment resulting from the worldwide relocations of production that global oligopoly competition necessitates. A reliable answer has yet to emerge about the net short-run employment impacts, although there has been an intense statistical battle between union- and corporation-sponsored studies, with both sides guilty of using inappropriate methodologies combined with inadequate data bases. Long-run trend analyses, however, indicate the possibility of negative impacts. Even here much more work is needed before definitive conclusions can be reached. Adjustment mechanisms are still lacking to assist adequately both the workers of subsidiaries relocated overseas and the owners of subcontracting firms whose orders have been lost to the offshore components of the global corporation's worldwide complementary production system.

Corporate and union lobbyists and various agencies of government have almost singularly debated short-run employment and balance-of-trade impacts of global corporations, to the relative neglect of income distribution. On this issue both the empirical evidence and theory are more conclusive, showing that the twin forces of globalization and increasing oligopoly concentration have made a significant contribution to growing income inequality during the 1960s and 1970s. Thus a 1971 Rand study by the University of Chicago's T. Paul Schultz concluded that income inequality "has apparently increased substantially," while the Library of Congress's Peter Henle, in his 1973 report, found "a slow but persistent trend toward inequality" over the 1958-70 period, with the (Gini coefficient) income concentration measure up by almost 14 percent. Other studies have highlighted a notable aspect of this shift toward greater income inequality. The loss in income shares came not from the poorest 20 percent of American families but from the middle 60 percent. The gain in income shares was registered exclusively among the richest 10 percent of all families. The dovetailing of globalization and concentration provide at least three reasons that have significant bearing in explaining these distributional impacts. The timing and occupational breakdown of changing income shares correlate well with those employees affected most by the acceleration of export platform investment, affecting first workers in labor-intensive and later those in more capital-intensive sectors. The structural lag in organized labor's ability to maintain bargaining power, combined with the threat of worsening unemployment, has reduced union effectiveness in negotiating wage-rate increases. Finally, and perhaps the most important reason for negative impacts on income equality due to globalization, is the distributional difference between foreign versus domestic investment. The income stream generated by domestic investment is distributed to both the "owners" of capital and domestic labor; the income stream returning to the United States from foreign investment, however, goes only to the recipients of profits, not wages. As the ratio of total U.S. foreign to domestic investment accelerates, there will be a corresponding increase in the proportion of total U.S. national income that takes the form of foreign-derived profits. Since the domestic ownership and control of profit-producing capital is highly concentrated, globalization will further promote income inequality unless offset by new government income transfer programs. To date, such programs have not been implemented, and their absence is another indicator of the structural lag in policy-making.

Currently the most important issue surrounding the transformation of the U.S. economy and the impact of its global corporations is the question of economic stability in terms of inflation and international financial movements. It is here that we find a most significant part of the structural lag in orthodox economic theory and policy-making for regulating what is now a globally revolutionized private sector. In the area of international monetary relations, however, some economists are becoming convinced that in a world political economy characterized by global oligopolies neither a free exchange-rate system nor a less-than-free exchange-rate system can guarantee stability in international monetary movements. This conclusion is thus far a theoretical one. But then too our current economic policies are in fact derived from Keynesian-type theory, the assumptions of which stand in stark contradiction to the actual manner in which corporations and therefore national and world political economies behave. In short, both forms of exchange-rate systems are based on the assumption of perfectly competitive markets. If instead that assumption is replaced with the more realistic one of global oligopoly competition and its concomitant growing negation of international markets, then one can only derive an indeterminate solution—that is, the international monetary system may have built-in tendencies toward or away from stable equilibrium. Thus "the predominance of large multinational firms," as Oxford's Thomas Balogh has recently written, "profoundly alters the nature of international trade, payments, and capital movements in a sense wholly ignored by conventional economics . . . orthodox global methods of maintaining international balance has failed."

In Germany studies have documented how another technique of global accounting technology "leads and lags" (an unrecorded transaction for quickly shifting funds between countries) has "rapidly offset. . . within a period of one month" and "by a factor of 80 percent" the intended effects of traditional policies to fight inflation and exchange-rate stability. In a globally interdependent world, what is one nation's instability quickly becomes another's—all the more so since the business cycles of advanced nations are now in-phase, another indicator of transformation in the world political economy.[3] This convergence in national business cycles, occurring after 1970, now makes the fight against inflation even more difficult. In former times in the United States, for example, inflationary pressures were dampened because our major trading partners' downturns in their cycles meant a relative decrease in their demand for U.S. goods. Today business cycle convergence reinforces inflationary or depressionary forces between nations.

In recent years a growing number of econometric studies have found consistent evidence that the use of orthodox Keynesian monetary and/or fiscal policy for stimulating or dampening the economy has led to either ineffective or even perverse results. In the monetary area, for example, recent work has shown how the globalization of U.S. banking carried out by the largest U.S. banks has permitted them to offset the intended effects of certain policy tools. This would appear to have been the case during the tight monetary policies of late 1968 and 1969. In another example from monetary policy—interest rates— the oligopoly-conglomerate power of the largest and most important corporations in the country allows them to pass on to consumers increased financing charges rather than, as in the theoretical solution, lowering corporate investment demands, thereby dampening inflation. There is also substantial evidence that general monetary policy has contributed to further concentration in the financial sector, thus bringing about a vicious circle: Standard policy leads to further concentration, which in turn means further ineffectiveness of the policy itself. In fiscal policy a similar vicious circle has already been mentioned:

Current tax laws relatively subsidize the largest corporations at the expense of the smaller ones, which in turn further increases concentration; and, with the accompaniment of the growing globalization of the largest corporations, there occurs a further diminution of the federal government's tax-collecting capacity.

These are but some of the examples indicating the nature of the structural lag in the public sector, compared to a globalized, nonmarket corporate private sector, and reflecting the continuing use of governmental economic policies designed for times past. More specifically, as in the case of the recent "energy crunch" and the oil companies, the public sector finds itself in a <u>crisis of information.</u>[4] The current legal statutes on corporate disclosure are not adequate to regulate the new global accounting, financing, trade, and technology transfers that characterize the large corporations that make up the most important sectors of our economy. Consolidated balance sheets hide more than they reveal. Data are not available to determine which products and in which country what proportion of total profits and total costs are being generated. Information, however, includes not only data but methods and theories to interpret what that data means; here too there is an obvious dearth. Finally, in a world where corporations can move rapidly and nation-state governments only slowly there is also the timing question of the public sector's ability to respond quickly enough to changes in both the international and domestic economy, given the conflicting goals underlying its pluralistic decision-making processes, compared to a corporate world with the singular goal of profit maximization and a centralized decision-making authority.

It is thus questionable whether the government has sufficient policy-making tools to assure that the private sector's goal of global profit-maximization will not conflict with and/or thwart the nation-state's social goals of stability and equity, which is the public sector's charge.

Conclusion

The transnationalization of the private sector obviously poses a significant challenge to the regulatory powers of government. It is only recently that governments in more developed countries have become aware of how formidable a challenge they face. The efficacy of the economic planning role of government is, to quote the World Bank's Albert Waterston, largely a function of the "lessons of experience." At first glance one may find it ironic that it has been the so-called less developed countries that have thus far been most able to learn from their lessons in dealing with global corporations. As noted earlier, it was in the underdeveloped world where the uniqueness of the global corporation, compared to the national business firm, was first studied and comprehended. These studies also revealed systematic evidence on the negative impacts of global corporate operations on income distribution, employment, balance of payments, and concentration. [5] The absorption of this "new knowledge" by LDC policymakers was one of the prime reasons enabling many of these countries to gain increased bargaining or countervailing power and begin to reverse some of these impacts. [6]

Part of the structural transformation in the world political economy, namely, the emergence of export platform investments by global corporations, provided a further opportunity to increase LDCs' bargaining power. An additional aspect of this transformation is the convergence in consumption and production between advanced nations, which has presented still another force for augmenting LDCs' bargaining power. Export platform operations have more favorable income distribution, employment, and balance-of-payments impacts, providing LDCs can exert sufficient control over transfer pricing and other cross-subsidization techniques; here their new knowledge can prove valuable. This new form of foreign investment has brought with it a growing dependency of global corporations and their home nations on one of the two most abundant resources of the poor countries, their inexpensive labor power. Similarly a historic increase in the dependency of global corporations and their home nations on the underdeveloped world's natural resource abundance has been the result of the convergence aspect of developed countries' transformation. The effects of OPEC are dramatic proof of how well LDCs have learned from their lessons of experience in dealing with global corporations. The demonstration effects of how OPEC has used new knowledge to control global corporations are not going unobserved by other LDCs in natural resource sectors besides petroleum.

The LDCs' new knowledge and the structural transformation in the world political economy have provided the real opportunity for controlling the impacts of global corporations. The political necessity to ensure that this opportunity is fully exploited by LDCs has come from the record-breaking increases in poverty experienced throughout the 1950s and 1960s by these countries. Regardless of where on the political spectrum a host LDC government falls, its own desire to maintain its domestic status-quo power position compels it to implement requisite controls over foreign actors in order to reverse the poverty trend. Since about 1970 this is precisely what the available evidence on host LDC governments indicates is taking place, not only in natural resources, but equally important in the manufacturing and finance sectors. Depending on a host of factors, the timing and approaches differ. [7] There can be little doubt, however, that we have witnessed the beginnings of a notable shift in the power and control capacities of

LDCs over global corporations, in turn, beginning to alter the impacts of the latter on the societies of the former.

With a shift in the "terms of trade" governing the exchange of exports, imports, technology, and finance capital between rich and poor countries, what is to the betterment of one comes at a cost to the other—at least in the initial period of change. This is particularly true in a world as interdependent as ours has now become, given the rise of the global corporation. It is not surprising, therefore, that the timing of the relative increase in LDC bargaining power coincides with the emergence of the first significant objections against global corporations coming from their own home nations. There is not space here to detail the economics of the relationships between LDCs and MDCs that can explain at least a substantial part of these objections. Nevertheless, the point does serve to capture the consequences of global interdependence when there are rapid shifts in the structure of the world political economy. In addition, what is equally relevant for our purposes here is that a thorough study of how LDCs are overcoming their own public-sector lag in regulating the transformed private sector of global corporations may provide some insight to the steps that U.S. and other developed country policy-makers will find themselves taking in the future.

THE EFFECT OF MNCs ON THE U.S. ECONOMY

Stanley H. Ruttenberg: I am impressed with what Ron has done here, because I think it illustrates the one point I have been trying to make on two or three previous occasions when I've interjected my point of view. When one looks at this period from 1970 on, as the Latin American countries move from import substitution industrialization to finding export markets first within a common market area of their own and then later in the developed countries of the world, we see an emerging fundamental problem that I think host countries and multinational corporations based in the United States must face up to. As more and more industrialization takes place around the world, and as more host countries pursue the economic development they think is in their best interest, the United States will have to do one of two things. Either it must accelerate the rate of economic growth in the United States and the rate of per capita income growth in the United States, or it will have to become more restrictive in its import policies. (The latter would force the host countries to face restricted markets in the United States.) As it invests and produces in host countries, the multinational corporation will have to decide from what point it is going to export its product, because the United States will say it can no longer tolerate worldwide exports to the United States from the developing countries of the world.

The same problem is going to confront Japan and the Common Market. We've got to share that around the world. Unless we face up to that, it seems to me the multinational corporations over the decade of the 1970s are going to find serious problems. Instead of defending its current actions around the world, the multinational corporation, along with the labor movement of the United States, ought to face up to the reality of what one does about a market in the United States that can no longer, in my judgment, absorb the large expanding export platforms that are developing around the world.

Elizabeth Jager: I'd like to make two very brief comments about, first, employment, and, second, about concepts like social justice, interspersing with this a few comments about statistics.

It is evident to the people in various kinds of industries in the United States, and it has been evident for many years, that there has been, and continues to be at an accelerating rate, a new form of export of employment in an almost mindless way out of the United States into both developed and developing countries. Recently this phenomenon has been taking place also out of developing countries. Within the last few years it's been very clear that in the developing countries in this hemisphere, in what you all call host countries, there has been an export of jobs from one so-called developing country to another by various conglomerate multinational firms.

We have documented this export of jobs from the United States in two ways. One, we have shown individual movements in a series of seemingly isolated examples that we have presented to the executive branch and to Congress. Because the economic theory does not go along with it and because other people don't agree with it, this material was first discounted as being simply a series of isolated examples. Now, however, we also have evidence that two things have happened across the board in most American industry in the United States. It is true, however; it is measured, whether it's in manufacturing industry or service industry. The first is that, beginning about 1966, studies show there are fewer jobs, that is, in employment figures, in industry after industry, new and old, in the United States; secondly, there are not in the United States enough jobs for a growing work force.

We also have said repeatedly that although we do not consider the multinational firms the only actors in the game, or necessarily guilty and malevolent parties, we do say that it is inaccurate to segment out parts of industry and assume that the fact that any given number of firms surveyed happen to have more jobs in the United States has anything to do with the problem.

The second point I wanted to make is that we have a very difficult problem with value judgments that are totally undefined. The one that I find most offensive is social justice. The more recent studies by the Brookings Institution, the Overseas Development Council, and other groups used the word social justice in terms of development in relation to the improvements in the economies of Korea, Taiwan, and Singapore. As long as people in the intellectual community consider those developments social justice, I don't think there's going to be any fruitful dialogue between the working people of the United States and the intellectual community, because we do not consider that the developments in dictatorial societies, where the labor and working conditions and individual freedom are thoroughly suppressed, represent social, economic, or political justice. The use of this concept of social justice, which is then translated into a series of statistical games, will lead to enormous disaffection both in this country and in other countries. The unions in the United States as well as many Americans not in the unions are increasingly concerned about the interaction between the growth of economic institutions and the loss of liberty both here and abroad. It won't do you any good to continue to try to impose upon any economy, but particularly the economy of the United States, a logical abstraction and tell everybody he's better off because the figures say that he is.

What we have been suggesting is that you look at real people and real facts and real case studies and not move to the abstraction first and then deduce social effect from that. That's really what we're quarreling about with the economics profession. You can't take a series of unrelated universes statistically and put them together. To take one corporation, which hasn't told you or me or anyone else the details of its accounting structure, and put that together with a series of other unknown accounting structures and come up with a new game plan, I suggest, not only is going to cause more confusion but will also lead to the kind of know-nothing reaction in the United States we saw in the latter part of the last century, where they're just going to tell the academics that they don't care what they do because they're not related to anything real that's going on in the world. Where real people are involved there are real employment problems and labor standard problems that cannot wait for game theory or purely abstract arrangements.

Ronald E. Muller: I don't think there is a difference between Elizabeth and myself. If I moved too rapidly and misstated myself, I apologize. What I wish to say about employment is this: There are two sets of surveys, one basically done by people in the labor movement and another basically done by those affiliated with transnational corporations. And one side says that they are creating more jobs than they're losing—

that is, the multinational corporations, and their representatives with the U.S. Government. The other side says not so. In looking at the techniques, the methodology utilized in those studies, I do not believe that either side has gone about the problems correctly.

Now what are my own views in how we have approached it? My basic conclusion about employment is your conclusion, that the employment problem is going to get worse and worse in the United States if these current trends continue. Here I think we agree, all of us, and let's just keep that straight. What I'm saying is that neither the labor movement nor the multinational corporation has come up with a methodology to give us a conclusive piece of evidence about what the job situation will be in 1975 or 1980 due to transnationalization of business. When I come back and try to correct for those methodologies, and then incorporate my corrections, I come to the same conclusion I think you are indicating.

The second point is that if I in any way implied that the development of this problem as I see it is leading to more social justice or less social justice, I think you misinterpret my remarks. I have not said anything about that. All I said was that it is creating a new set of problems much more rapidly than in the past and with much greater dimensions, and my job as I saw it was to try to summarize via that set of constructs what I see has been happening. I did not make any normative conclusions about that.

Mrs. Jager: But the point that's missed, and it is a key one, and I'm sorry but I have to say it, is that you're going to get into more and more mishmash with the multinational firms. What we were saying in making a proposal called the Foreign Trade and Investment Act was that we view the multinational firm not as a separable issue from the United States of America or any other country of the world but part and parcel of each. All the Foreign Trade and Investment Act, the Burke-Hartke bill, says is that we think it's time for the United States to assert its sovereign right to adopt its own laws and policies so that it can engage with other countries in the kinds of arrangements for international negotiation that seem to be the topic for discussion here. We can't wait to do this, because it's very clear that every other nation of the world has about 25 Burke-Hartkes in operation and they're changing every day. If you want a rational conclusion, you have to accept the fact that there are nation states in existence, and the United States is one of them and it has a domestic policy. It has to have domestic policy, and to the extent that we talk about foreign policy exclusively vis-a-vis other countries, we worsen not only the United States but the position of other countries also.

Therefore the Burke-Hartke bill is not an attack on multinational firms; it's a proposal for a framework of looking at the problems of the United States so that it can deal with other countries. It is not an economic model, and it should not be, because the economists are not lawyers. But laws are very important, and the United States has no modern laws on the subject that are integrated. It was in fact the Government of the United States and the firms themselves that dressed this up into this almost unbelievable David-and-Goliath kind of mismatched struggle. Organized labor is not interested in destroying all their national firms. They're not crazy. They know they're here to stay and are the dominant force of business in the world, however defined.

THE EFFECT OF MNCs ON HOST COUNTRIES: A HEATED DEBATE ON TRANSFER-PRICING

Miguel Wionczek: From the point of view of the developing countries, we are living in an nth-dimensional world, where at certain points the interest of many parties in that world come together. Only if you look at one of those points will you be able to find out whether there is a conflict between a transnational and a host LDC. Once a subsidiary is established in an LDC, for the purpose of negotiations with other nation-states that particular subsidiary becomes a part of the local scene, and there is a combination of interests between them. You can fight them on one level, and on another level you join forces. For example, for us the Burke-Hartke bill is just another attack upon our attempts to export to the United States, and here we forget—or it becomes irrelevant—that the company that is going to export is not going to be a Mexican company—that is, even though the exporting is done by subsidiaries of transnational corporations located in Mexico, for our particular purpose—our response to the Burke-Hartke bill—they become part of our family. Here we would join forces with the MNC, while in other situations we would fight them.

What I'm trying to show is that there is an nth-dimensional world, and we are in a tremendous quandary when trying to understand the whole. I'm not going to argue whether economists should take care of it or lawyers or politicians, but as far as the economic trade is concerned, we have a set of obsolete tools, tools that might work for a three-dimensional world but not for this new nth-dimensional world. So we have to work out new tools. Even with all his genius, Karl Marx could not have had any idea of what was going to happen. My quarrel is not only with capitalist economists but also with traditional Marxists and with the extreme left. I say, stop it. You're using concepts that were invented by someone in 1850, 1860. How can you apply that analysis to a world situation that has nothing to do with the world situation of the 1970s? And when I start talking about the problems of balance of payments, I say to my Marxist friends, you are right but for the wrong reasons, and you had better learn more analytical tools—

then you will be able to prove logically what you're proving with tools that are antiquated and absolutely useless on logical grounds.

Now, let's go to this question of economic analysis. I think I can tell you things that would be of interest, how we began to look in new directions, how we started putting into question the assumptions of traditional economics and the statistical games done there. In 1967 in Colombia there had been for several years a growing number of subsidiaries of multinationals that were showing for tax purposes losses but that at the same time were involved in a confused process of acquisition of Colombian manufacturing plants. Now Mr. Yeras, who happened at that time to be president of our country and who is not known for his contributions to economic theory, called his advisers and said to them, "Look, something strange is happening. These people are losing money. At the same time, the same people from outside are buying out all of our firms and they remain an attractive investment. Would you kindly please put it together and explain it to me in somewhat clearer form? Are they mad or is there some game going on which I don't understand?"

This is the way it started. A group of people started working with statistical material, and they started discovering most unusual, most interesting things like transfer-pricing, headquarters charges of 5 percent, sometimes 10 percent, sometimes more, of gross revenue, and so on. And the longer they worked, the more curious it became. There were statistics on jobs that we couldn't find.

Now these statistical games, a sort of Alice-in-Wonderland technique, permitted the MNCs to report losses to us on the one hand while at the same time making great profits from the standpoint of the home country through transfer-pricing, charges for research and development, and so on. And for the first time we began to see why we were losing in the game, and what we had to do to stop it.

Now a question: Why does IBM charge 10 percent of gross revenues for a headquarters fee?

William J. Barnds: You raised two different points here, though, didn't you? One is the problem of the statistical game, of reporting losses and of statistics you can't locate, and the other is the 10 percent of revenue charge. Now there's no statistical dispute on the latter.

Mr. Wionczek: No, I was just giving you examples to show that we are playing some kind of games. Even the 10 percent figure is not critical—it could be 20 percent. The question is, why is it 10 percent.

Robert A. Bennett: Ten percent is approximately what the company spends on research and development and the related activities that that represents. That's why it's not 20 percent; that's why it's not 5.

Mr. Wionczek: We could get together for two hours to discuss our approach to this, and our approach is very simple. It is not that we developing countries have to subsidize 30 percent, 40 percent, 50 percent of your R and D. For us what is interesting is the marginal costs of your R and D from your point of view and the cost of producing that technology by ourselves. Now the cost of reproduction may be $100 million. But your marginal costs of applying technology to a new market is very small. You don't do all of this research for Mexico, or for Argentina—you do all of this research for your worldwide operations, and even you don't know how much of it is being used in West Germany or how much is being used in Mexico.

Mr. Bennett: Then what better way is there than to do it on the basis of the revenue we receive from the products.

Mr. Wionczek: No, it is a problem of negotiating with you, you see. Whether 10 percent is acceptable or whether it's a little bit too much and maybe it should be cut to 6 percent must be determined through negotiations and a clear picture of what we are getting for this 10 percent you transfer to headquarters to pay for technology.

Terrance Hanold: The closing comments are quite interesting. We're going back to my original proposition that governments are fundamentally amoral. They seek only power through the development of national advantage. In private business we call it profit. Now he's saying we're entitled to a special deal. You should sell us these machines cheaper. You should sell to us on an incremental cost rate rather than the fully distributed cost rate. So that would mean that you ought to get this thing 20 percent cheaper than it's sold in the States. Well, I don't want to open the argument to illustrate the mentality of national advantage that permeates the whole thing, and to lead to the point that I hope to get to ultimately, that you can't write the rules for a transnational corporation unless you also write with them rules controlling the area of legitimate advantage that nations may seek through transnational corporations.

I have no competence to follow what you so well described as the Alice-in-Wonderland technique that accountants get into when they extrapolate figures, but this item of transfer price has come up many times. It was pointed out, I think, that 80 percent of agricultural commodities exported from the United States go out on a transfer-price basis. We're in the food business, and I would rather resent any inference anyone drew that we were engaged in a devious, concealed profit sort of enterprise. I wish we were somewhere around the range he was mentioning. But having been brought up in Mr. Schomer's church, that would be emotionally if not intellectually impossible for me to pursue.

Now, how do you go about this kind of a thing? We're shipping this week 17,000 tons of wheat to Venezuela. That's $2.5 million worth at current rates. Well, the Mocama flour mills in Venezuela may buy it from us, they may buy it from Mitsubishi, they may buy it from Cargill, they may buy it from Bunge Born, which is an Argentine transnational. Let's say they buy it from us. Under this definition it would proceed as a transfer sale from Pillsbury to an affiliated firm. Well, we get the bills of lading and the other things together, and we take them to the Venezuelan consulate and say, "We want your consular endorsement on this so that these goods can obtain entry when they get to Venezuela." What does he require? He requires validation of events stated on the invoice. You say, "Well, this is just something that your bookkeeping department makes up." He doesn't really rely on what our bookkeeping department tells him; he relies on the publication in the <u>Wall Street Journal</u> and other official reports of what the market price of those commodities is. When that shipment gets to Venezuela and is unloaded, and we proceed to the banks and they to the Central Bank with their payment for that shipment, what occurs there? The Central Bank verifies the figures stated on those invoices. There is no monkey business, and to suggest otherwise impugns the honor of the consul and of the people at the Central Bank and the other banks. I think it's most unfair to say that public officials in Latin America in general are venal or incompetent or indifferent to their jobs.

Mr. Muller: I made it explicit that I was not suggesting the people were bad or that they were conspiratorially acting to do harm.

Mr. Hanold: If you weren't inferring that the figures were false, then why did you make any comments at all?

Mr. Muller: Let me make the point of what I meant when I stressed, and why I stressed, the transfer-pricing. Transfer price is a neutral term, and I, who am looking at the impacts on the total economy, have to go back to some very basic principles. The transfer price can represent the cost to a society of the resources put into that product; it can export it and get back the resource cost in terms of foreign exchange. Then it comes close to its market value. On the other hand, the transfer price could represent a return in foreign exchange, either less or more. Those are the three possibilities. The problem I'm getting at is not focused on your company. You are one of many, many, many observation points in the universe, and the problem with the nation state is that it has to deal not only with your company but with averages, either by group or across the entire country.

Mr. Hanold: But my point is this: that the firms that are dealing in these commodities in Venezuela are known, they are not all that many, and the people at the ports and in the consular offices do their job, and I don't think it's legitimate without investigation to create an atmosphere of doubt with respect to either the validity of the data or the purposes to which those transfers are put by suggesting a conclusion of the extremity you've advanced.

Mr. Muller: I am saying that the reason this is an important topic to discuss is not to go around and accuse people of being either too honest or dishonest. I am saying that it is extremely important to any nation state to have policy tools that allow it somehow to maintain stability, and that the current manner in which those policy tools are derived— that is, based on recorded statistics—gives information that in many, many cases is incorrect in terms of what the society is gaining or losing. To implement such policies ends up in results that distort the objective they were originally designed for.

Mr. Hanold: I'd like to proceed further on the games nations play and the involved companies that are part of this total scenario. I'd like to offer, just for your thought, two suggestions. One was about 1958 when we were exclusively an exporter of flour. The AID—or I think it was AID—undertook to finance a mill in one of the Central American countries. That had been a market of ours served out of Buffalo for 70 years. I wrote a most admirable letter of protest to Under-Secretary Douglas Dillon outlining the fact that we were able to do this most efficiently—the capital was already invested, the market was there, there was no advantage to the world economy to create a new facility. He wrote back and rather brusquely told me to bury my head somewhere. A year later, having seen that the world was going other than I wished, I wrote him another letter and suggested that we too would like to build a mill in the Central American area and would he forward our application for some financing through AID. He wrote back and said he had a very clear recollection of my letter to him and would look to us to finance our own mill—which we did.

Now this same technique that led to the construction of these mills in Central America was used also in Venezuela. The government there said that instead of importing, it wanted to manufacture. So Venezuela installed a system of licensing, saying that you could import flour only upon license, and the number of licenses would diminish year by year as new construction of mills in that country occurred. The first to go in was an Argentine group, the second was North American, and we came as a lately convinced third. At that point we had a mill fully adequate to the business in Buffalo, which served Central America and Africa. We went into Venezuela with a new mill to protect a market, to protect jobs, at least in the marketing side of the business, that existed there from long commerce. This isn't a matter always, you know, of the company electing where it will do its manufacturing or where it will supply from. There is a contest going on every day in the week between the so-called LDCs and those who have had the export business as to whether that's the arrangement that's going to continue.

That's one—and not at all uncommon—situation, and it's a continuing one. Mexico has a regular program of requiring local manufacture versus imports, and a company faces the prospect either of withdrawing completely from the market or of satisfying the market from a new source of supply.

There's a second thing, and that is the extension through these corporations extraterritorially of the sovereignty of the nation state, which was elegantly phrased this morning as saying that the MNC is a tool for foreign policy of the home country. In 1951 we entered the flour-milling industry in Canada. Canada, I think according to Mr. Schomer's point of view, would be a sufficiently advanced country to say it is proper to do business with them. Canada has been fully recognized diplomatically by the United States. About 1961 President Kennedy had a small difficulty with Cuba, and in consequence it became illegal to export flour or wheat from the United States to Cuba. Now in Canada the sole agency for the sale of wheat is the Canadian Wheat Board. It collects the wheat and sells it for the account of the wheat growers. About 1963 and yearly thereafter the Canadian Wheat Board would sell wheat to Russia, which was also a forbidden transaction for us, although that could be gotten around in the State Department. But the Russians said, "We're subsidizing Cuba to the tune of a million dollars a day and part of that is feeding them, so we don't want to take all of this wheat in the form of wheat. We're going to buy the wheat, but you translate it into flour in Canada and ship it from Canada to Cuba."

Throughout this time Canada had maintained diplomatic relations with Cuba, so the Canadian Wheat Board said to the flour-milling industry, "Negotiate the price of a couple of million hundredweights of flour here with Russia and arrange for the shipment of the flour to Cuba." So the industry did, and they came around and said to us, "Your share, since you've got 15 percent of the milling capacity in the country, is 15 percent of this order." We said, "Thank you, but why don't you handle it?" Our only reason for refusing it (and it was a very profitable business) was that some of us are allergic to indictment. So the consequence has been all these years, to the great displeasure of the Canadian Government, that we will not mill flour at Calgary out of Canadian wheat.

I maintain, and did quite unsuccessfully with people at State, that this certainly was an area where we were bound in all good conscience to follow the rules of the Canadian game. The United States consistently took the position that if we did, we did so at considerable personal peril. I'm a coward. It's more fun to deal with corporations, I suppose, but we're dealing here with the self-interest, sometimes selfish in the most miserable degree, of nations quite as much as the power-profit-hunger of corporations.

H. P. Nicholson: You've made such a large point that I hate to add just a small point, but I too have been astonished at what I hear people get away with in transfer-pricing. From my European experience—and we do relatively little intercompany transfers—I've been repeatedly struck by the vigilance of the national customs services to see that the valuations of imported goods are kept up, and sometimes arbitrarily valued up, in order to safeguard their customs receipt, and on the other side by the knowledge and keenness of the national income tax authorities to keep import valuations down in order to maximize taxable income and therefore their income tax.

Burke Marshall: Victor Reuther, Stan Ruttenberg to a lesser degree, and Ron Muller particularly have all made statements addressed to the representatives of the multinational corporations here that suggested they had some secrets and that if we knew their secrets, we would have answers to these problems. Now I, as some of you know, am not a believer in the notion that foreign policy or basic national economic policy or international economic policy should be made in the boardroom of the corporations. I think that's backwards. But it seems to me it would be fair if you believe that there are data that these corporations have, either individually or collectively, to be more specific about what those data are. What information is it they have that you think is going to answer these problems? That's what I did not understand earlier, and I still do not understand.

Mr. Muller: I included, I believe, in my most basic criteria, employment, income distribution and stability, and for stability I outlined two issues, balance of payments and inflation, to take the current ones most important in this country. And I said that, in my judgment, the balance-of-payments problems and inflation are coming from causes quite different from those that the policies we are using today to correct them are assuming. The policies are not working, and all you have to do is look at the cost-of-living indices and employment. What I said we had to do is to reevaluate what the causes are.

If you come in here and tell me that IBM and Pillsbury and Coca-Cola are doing this kind of transaction and all of the transfer-pricing they do is at market value, I say that I believe you. But somewhere in the universe there are those who somehow get the average statistics skewed away from market value. That's one basic point I'm trying to make. We have to understand that there are different kinds of multinational corporations; they have different kinds of activities; and

we have to learn which kinds are creating, or contributing to, or playing, a role in the kinds of major economic problems this country is
addressing itself to today.

As to your more specific question on disclosure, what I suggested
was that the whole process of managing a national economy today involves information we are not receiving, not because of conspiratorial
design—and I've said this now 20 times—not because these men are
keeping secrets from us but because they are not required to report
that kind of information. The government has not taken a lead to any
extent in updating its legal institutions, or whoever is responsible for
updating legal institutions and reporting departments.

One specific kind of information would be the costs of production.
Costs of production have to be known if we're going to find out whether
our exports are being costed out of this country in any kind of shape
or form that represents the resources we're giving up for them, and
vice versa for imports. That's just one example of the kinds of disclosure. Another kind of disclosure has to do with intracompany loans.
You asked the question "How can the Rand Corporation and the National
Bureau say we have these rates of return when we don't have these
rates of return?" Well, here's one reason, and it has to do with intracompany lending and intracompany loans. There is significant evidence by these organizations, which are not radical organizations, that
says there is increasing use of intracompany loans, not to hide or dis-
guise, but because of new techniques of corporate management to
maximize cash flow. So what we'd consider a profit in 1900 before
transnational accounting now shows up as a cost. In this situation how
is a nation-state economic manager, minister of finance, or other
public official expected to know what's going on in his economy if he
doesn't even know what's happening in rates of return? Those are two
specific examples I can give you.

Mr. Marshall: As I understood you, you are talking about information
that is necessary in your view for the people that make economic policy, macroeconomic policy for a nation. That is, you were talking
about gross statistics about production costs and so forth within a nation, including stuff that goes out and stuff that stays in. The inade-
quacy of that information in gross is what you're talking about. Well,
if that's what you're talking about and if the problem is, to take your
hypothesis, that we don't have enough information to understand what's
going on inside the economy of the United States or on a larger scale
in the international economic community, then it is unfair to treat
that question, as some have here, as if these individual companies
had secrets, that they knew an answer to these questions, and that it
was all withheld, and that all somebody had to do was tug enough at
them and they would disgorge it.

Mr. Muller: I did not say there were secrets.

Mr. Marshall: And I say that because you asked the question, and when I heard the response, I think that they really did not know what you were asking for.

Mr. Barnds: I think, if I may make a comment, that there are two things involved here. One is the question of whether or not the corporations might have an answer in the sense of a broad understanding of this. The other is whether they have the data that, if made available, would make better analysis possible.

Charles W. Powers: It seems to me we're getting back to a fundamental question about the extent and limits of national sovereignty. Does the home country in fact have a legitimate interest in certain kinds of information, either because it can't figure out what's happening to its employment practices or balance of payments? We probably could agree that it does, and then we ought to say, okay, disclosure of that sort is needed. But we're going to be getting into lots of other kinds of issues that go well beyond that one. For example, how far does sovereignty extend to control of production rather than simple disclosure? How far does the nation-state have a right to control labor intensity versus high-technology industrial decisions, and so on?

Theodore H. Moran: I think I can follow along this line and on what Burke was saying. I've been bothered by the repeated statements suggesting that we have a bunch of case studies, and the case studies are all good, and you guys are good, but the aggregate statistics are bad, as if the bad guys aren't here, and we've got only the good guys here. This I think leads to the question of who has the secrets and where are the data. If we were having a conference on population explosion, somebody would come up with the bad story they tell in Brazil. Someone says, "You know, a baby is born every ten seconds," and somebody else says, "We'd better find that woman and stop her." It's the kind of approach we've taken here.

Thinking about that, I was drawing up a list of what kinds of sectors and what kinds of industries do use transfer-pricing and what kinds don't. My guess is that in the shipping of grain and in some kinds of processing they don't use transfer prices. And I could go through the other industries, especially minerals and petroleum, to show which ones do use transfer-pricing, but I think it would just take too much of our time. I have a more optimistic point to make and one that leads to the question of international organization. More and more companies are beginning to come to us and say, "My God, we sat down, we had sharp pencils, we figured all of this out, and we never called it transfer-pricing, but it looked good to us, since it allowed us to use our funds the way we want to. Now we've got the IRS on our backs, and we've got other governments on our backs, and we've got labor on our backs, and we don't know what to do. We're confused—can you guys sort it out for us?" In fact, one proposal they frequently come up with is that we have some kind of global standard of taxation: Let somebody else tax us at a standard rate and then let the governments divvy it up and fight it out. That might at least get them off our backs. Well, it's possible that that might be a solution to the transfer-pricing problem and could be handled by some kind of international standards.

I'd like to conclude by backing up the point that Stan Ruttenberg and some other people have made. It's precisely because the corporations are under these kinds of pressures that they're so worried. The Burke-Hartke bill is one thing, and I happen to think that economic nationalism is another contributing factor. It's precisely because of these and similar pressures that they're being forced to worry about the moral questions. And I would agree with some of you here that we couldn't talk for even 30 seconds without getting into moral concerns. But that doesn't mean that for international harmony we can depend in the least on the moral consciousness of the top-dog corporate executives. I still think that the basic considerations are shifting balance-of-power considerations, and the reason why corporate officials are concerned is because suddenly they find they may not be the top dog. They worry about this, and for the first time they're having their power challenged.

NOTES

1. The facts, mode of analysis, conclusions, and opinions presented in this section draw on my work published elsewhere, in which I have given extensive sources and bibliographic references. I have avoided footnoting here except where elaboration of a particular statement or conclusion was omitted because of space constraints. In such cases I have given reference to where the elaboration can be found. Those aspects of my work relevant to this section include: The Political Economy of Direct Foreign Investment: A Policy Appraisal for Latin America (Washington, D.C.: Inter-American Development Bank, 1970); "The Multinational Corporation and the Underdevelopment of the Third World," in C.K. Wilber (ed.), The Political Economy of Development and Underdevelopment (New York: Random House, 1973); "Poverty Is the Product," Foreign Policy, Winter 1973-74; and a comment to Raymond Vernon in Foreign Policy, Summer 1974; "Foreign Investment in the United States," Testimony before the Subcommittee on Foreign Economic Policy of the House Committee on Foreign Affairs on February 21, 1974; "The Underdeveloped and the Developed:

Geopolitics, Power, and the Potential for Change," World Congress of Sociology, Papers and Proceedings, Toronto, August 1974; with R.D. Morgenstern, "Multinational Corporations and Balance of Payments Impacts in LDCs: An Econometric Analysis of Export Pricing Behavior," KYKLOS, April 1974 (a more detailed version can be found in "Effectos de las corporaciones multinacionales sobre la balanza de pagos de los paises subdesarrollados: un analisis econometrico de la determinacion de los precios de las exportaciones," El Trimestre Economico, Mexico, July-September 1974); with R.J. Barnet, Global Reach: The Power of the Multinational Corporations (New York: Simon and Schuster, 1975); "Nation-State Instability and the Global Corporation," Business and Society Review, Fall 1974; and "Nation-State Instability and the Global Corporation: The Impacts of Transformation," in David Apter and Louis Goodman (eds.), The Multinational Corporation as an Instrument of Development: A Yale University International Symposium (New Haven, Conn.: Yale University Press, 1975).

2. See Muller, KYKLOS and El Trimestre Economico, op. cit.; and with R.J. Barnet, chapter 10, op. cit.

3. For why global corporations' operations significantly caused business cycle convergence see Muller with Barnet, op. cit.

4. See Muller testimony, op. cit., for a review.

5. See Muller, in Wilber (ed.), op. cit.; and Foreign Policy, op. cit.

6. See Ronald Muller, World Congress of Sociology, op. cit., section 3.

7. Ibid.

8

THE PROBLEM OF INFORMATION AND DISCLOSURE

WHO HAS THE INFORMATION?

William J. Barnds: Several suggestions have been made here, by corporate representatives and economists, that multinational corporations have the greatest fund of knowledge.

Robert A. Bennett: They probably have as much as any other segment of society.

Mr. Barnds: I wonder if they have more knowledge in the sense of knowing the raw facts and the raw data of the various transactions or more knowledge of the economic and social impact. I would think they have the former. I would have serious questions as to whether or not a corporation, or certainly the typical corporation, even some of the biggest ones, would really have thought through some of these problems in the very frontiers of knowledge.

Alphonse De Rosso: The interesting fact is that the U.S. Government doesn't have it. It's just beginning to face up to this problem, and I think that's what has happened to all of us. We're just beginning to face up to a problem that has suddenly overwhelmed us. Not only is the present situation new and overwhelming; incredibly rapid changes are taking place at the same time. It's difficult enough for us to cope with what's happening today, let alone try to anticipate what's going to happen tomorrow. The other problem is that the social sciences, which are most relevant to this, have yet to develop the techniques and tools of analysis that would in fact help their governments and multinationals to cope with these problems.

Ronald E. Muller: I'd like for the first time in this meeting to address myself specifically to the multinational corporate executive. I have done personal consulting with different corporations. The book we are going to publish will be printed in two parts in the New Yorker in December 1974—which is not a radical journal, please note. We interviewed over a hundred multinational corporate executives. People like Jacques Maisonrouge, Carl Gerstacker here, and so on; people in the banking sector, in the manufacturing sector, people in the raw materials sector. We interviewed people at the top and in the middle. We interviewed people in U.S. operations, and we interviewed people who were running subsidiaries. And these interviews lasted a long time, particularly with the line people out in the subsidiaries. It is from them that we got the most awareness of the kinds of problems occurring in the less developed countries.

I could quote some of those people and do what Mr. Hanold did in relating specific cases. I could tell you stories about executives and their wives who have broken down and cried about some of the facts they had, but I choose never to use that type of argumentation. We have interviewed IRS people, and they have problems. The IRS people have published studies about their inability to control the new kinds of structural changes, not because they didn't want to, not because they were receiving cash payoffs from corporations, but because their organizations and procedures were set up at a time when they were designed to do other things, and that time has passed. And if you don't believe it, for goodness' sake, hire yourself a bunch of social scientists to go out and tell you confidentially whether or not the kind of statistics I have quoted to you are reliable or not, the kind of statistics Miguel Wionczek quoted to you. The fact that Jacques Maisonrouge is at the UN indicates that even he feels this is something you should find out more about.

We are talking about degrees. No one can deny the kind of trend changes that we see. I believe every word that Bob Bennett put in his paper, as I have told him and I have told this group. I believe Carl Gerstacker. But my own experience in consulting and being paid by multinational corporations as an academic researcher indicates that MNC executives, like everyone of us, have dimensions of experience that are beyond them, and they are therefore what the dictionary terms ignorant, just as I am ignorant about what it takes to get a product onto a production line, out and marketed in a specific industry. If I know something about the drug industry, I don't know something about the automobile industry.

What I'm suggesting, and here I disagree with Chuck Powers, is that we don't start by discussing whether or not morals fit into this or not. We have a number of problems our country and other countries have to deal with. I think the focus should be on international codes of conduct, the problem of disclosure, whether or not you want disclosure, what you feel is unreasonable. What about the problem of getting the Japanese to do what you want to do, getting the Germans to do what you want to do? We have tons of problems, and yet we sit around arguing about statistics because we have a personal experience that contradicts an average.

I don't think this place is going to get anywhere in arriving at a definitive understanding of what our problems are if you keep denying every source, even sources that you yourselves have used in the past.

WHO SHOULD TAKE THE LEAD, GOVERNMENT OR CORPORATIONS?

Mr. Muller: Many people from the corporations have asked the question, what can we do?—tell us. I'm saying that, like any other major group in society, you have influence, and in each society you use that influence in a different way. For instance, in Brazil is it possible that automobile manufacturers could get together on the pollution issue and say that if we continue polluting Sao Paulo— and you know the statistics as well as I do, it's one of the worst cases in the world—in our long-term interests it's going to be detrimental. Maybe we could collectively lobby for the incorporation of pollution standards. Here we've got an issue that affects not only the corporation directly but also the greater community. Isn't it possible—and I'm recognizing your dilemma of international competition—for you to get together and promote what some of us would feel would be progressive social change, even in the context of the Brazilian situation?

Harlow W. Gage: I guess I'd have to say it's possible.

Mr. Muller: Have you taken any efforts in this direction?

Mr. Gage: Not to organize jointly with other companies, no.

Mr. Muller: Do you feel it's a completely naive suggestion? Do you feel it's not feasible? What are the reasons it has not been attempted?

Mr. Gage: I guess basically for competitive reasons.

Mr. Muller: But I'm saying, go to your competitors and say to them that if we all promote the same kind of change, we don't change our respective competitive positions today. To illustrate: When you all go in unison and argue against having differential tariffs on imported parts by a company—there you are asking for uniform treatment as a group of companies, and that doesn't change your competitive position. I'm saying, let's take it out of the realm of real products, real economic cost considerations, and move over to social economics or social concerns. Why can you not organize as a group and promote at least certain kinds of change you think are progressive?

Mr. Gage: I don't know if there would be any restrictions against that or not.

William J. Barnds: You mean antitrust restrictions or policy restrictions?

Mr. Gage: No, I'm talking about local government restrictions. I couldn't answer that question because I don't know whether that would be in the local laws or not.

Mr. Muller: I'm trying to bring out suggestions and find out your viewpoint on the feasibility. Just one more. The question of disclosure is going to become more important over the next 10 years, and I think you recognize that. The key dilemma of disclosure, and we talked about it yesterday, is that if any one home government, such as the United States, forces you into disclosure requirements that are significantly different from those required by Japanese, German, or Swedish law, and makes available public information on your company, this allows your competitors to have information on you that you can't get on them, and it again helps to destroy your competitive position. Thus I would ask, given the kind of social problems that are happening and the new kinds of causes behind them, is it again naive to envisage that corporations could take a progressive stance on recognizing that disclosure requirements are going to have to be changed and that they're going to have to be changed under some type of international harmonization between companies so as not to destroy the competitive rules of the game?

Mr. Gage: That's a big order.

Mr. Muller: I'm asking, is it naive for me, as a social scientist who consults only once in a while inside corporations and doesn't work with them every day, to be asking this question? Is it feasible to envisage that you and the Japanese and the Germans get together and promote a new disclosure system you feel will help the social problems you see in your home countries? And they are very similar in Germany, the United States, and Japan—there's a growing similarity. Now again, is it naive to envisage you could take this kind of action, an aggressive, not a defensive action?

Mr. Gage: I would say it is naive. Anything like that, I think, is a long way off. When you start trying to take people from Germany, Japan, and the United States and put them together and try to come up with one answer, you're going to have one hell of a problem trying to get any agreement at all.

Mr. Muller: So again you feel that the whole disclosure issue will probably be handled nation-state by nation-state, with the corporations in defensive reactions against other groups promoting disclosure. Then you end up having to worry about the crises problems when the United States groups have gotten disclosure laws passed that require you to give information, but the Japanese, of course, haven't got that kind of a disclosure requirement. There goes your competitive position, and that is not in the best interests of the United States.

Mr. Gage: No, it isn't.

Mr. Muller: I'm asking, why aren't you taking progressive steps to try to avoid this kind of dilemma? It's quite clear that, given the nature of German business-government interaction and the nature of the Japanese business-government interaction, it's more likely that a more progressive disclosure law will be passed in this country with its existing social forces than in those two countries.

Terrance Hanold: To me this is abstract. Could you give an example in specific terms of the kind of data dealing with a particular situation that you might get disclosed?

Mr. Muller: Well, let's take certain industries that are now facing real ecological constraints. We must now effectively measure the social cost of the resource usage, given these growing ecological constraints, and this will require that you report new kinds of cost information not currently being reported to the Internal Revenue Service. If that information becomes public record, it gives the Japanese competitors in the same industry certain information and facts about you that you don't have about them. If, for instance, we require on patents a more complete disclosure of the kind of real innovation you did and the kinds of innovation you are attempting on patents already registered, any kind of technical information in the patent realm that might be required by a new patent law in this country would give the Japanese and the Germans a very, very strong competitive advantage over the United States. I think Mr. Gage has admitted this. And isn't that of major concern here when we talk about this kind of national structure that's emerging?

125

Mr. Gage: I would say it is a major concern, but I think we've also got to recognize that the business climate in the various cultures, in the systems of the countries you're talking about and others all around the world, is very diverse. Who is going to be this great international group that's going to pull us all together and get everybody on the same track?

Mr. Muller: I wasn't envisaging international groups. I was envisaging basic nation-states as they exist today, and the corporations within them, getting together.

Mr. Gage: If you want all these groups to get together on something like this, you've got to pull it together on an international basis, haven't you? I don't quite follow how you're going to accomplish this.

Mr. Muller: For example, there is a movement under way in this country to change the board of director compositions of major corporations. Your competitor, Mr. Ford, has just spent X thousands of dollars to go around and find out how strong the move is for bringing in, for instance, consumer advocacy groups, organized labor, and church groups to the board of directors. If that movement gains legal recognition and becomes a legal requirement, but it does not gain legal-requirement status in Japan or Germany, it will force your companies to be operated in a different fashion, reporting different kinds of information than that reported by the Japanese or German competitors. And every day the U.S. economy becomes more and more independent and interdependent on international trade.

Mr. Gage: How do you propose to go about accomplishing this in Japan and in these other countries?

Mr. Muller: One of the things I asked you was whether you do think it's naive to think this is possible.

Mr. Gage: I do think that.

Mr. Muller: So then we sort of see a hopeless situation.

Victor Reuther: Several of you have concluded that it's not up to industry to formulate what you call the public policy without the government, and it's really up to government to tell you what facts are needed.

Let me cite an incident out of my own personal history which relates to relations with the General Motors Corporation. Some years ago, when Mr. C.E. Wilson was president of General Motors Company and Walter Reuther was president of the United Auto

Workers (UAW), we proposed the discussion of a supplemental unemployment benefit program and a supplemental private pension program. The first response from General Motors Corporation was quite expected. They said what most corporations said, "What the hell are you talking to us about that for? That's up to the government." At the same time, they went to Washington to hold the unemployment benefits and social security benefits as low as possible. So, since we couldn't solve it in the public sector, we laid it at the doorstep of industry. Now I come to the problem of getting facts about things that relate to the public policy. When it was laid at the doorstep of General Motors as a practical matter we both had to solve, General Motors and the UAW both but separately and concurrently employed the finest actuarial experts available in the country. It was a damn costly thing to both General Motors and the UAW. And there came out of that a study of actuarial information that the Government of the United States itself did not have, and a collective agreement was signed supplementing public unemployment compensation through private funds and supplementing public pension programs. That had an effect on millions of people never employed by General Motors or ever members of the UAW. You influenced public policy enormously by that, and you contributed facts and figures and statistics and data not available before. And you did it because you had a problem at your doorstep that you had to solve.

You've got a problem now, and if you delay it and procrastinate by saying, "Oh, it's the government's business, it's not mine," you will complicate your own life, and you will leave people less able to make an intelligent and reasonable decision. You will encourage them to make the less reasonable decision.

What I want to say in conclusion is that there is in existence in every industry where multinational corporations exist at the international level a trade union structure. Nobody has ever asked General Motors or IBM or Exxon to sign a worldwide collective bargaining agreement, but will you tell me where workers who are employed by General Motors can discuss with your corporation the problems we're talking about? If we go to Detroit as an American union, we will be told we don't have anything to do with these matters. Why talk to us about balance of payments and international trade? Can workers in Mexico talk with General Motors about imbalance of payments and international trade? You have no forum, and you will spend thousands of dollars to hire social scientists and technocrats to consult with when you're not even talking to your own workers. You had better open a means of communication, and, if you do, we'll find out that many of these problems that seem so global and so difficult to grasp are really manageable. Perhaps by agreement within the private sector in many areas we can open the door to a solution of problems that we consider only up in the public stratosphere.

Reginald Tuggle: I want to ask Mr. Hanold a question that Ron asked earlier, and which in part Harlow Gage indicated it was naive to think about: Why can't the corporation become an initiatory agent in the formation of policy?

Mr. Hanold: Well, I suppose there's the basic human instinct of economy of effort, sometimes known as sloth. That is, no one wants to do a damn thing. The approach that has been suggested is without the focusing effect of a man with responsibility making the demand. It does not narrow the area of exploration or of development to boundaries that in our judgment are economic or useful or productive. For example, I can open a conversation with the dean of the law school of the University of Minnesota on this subject and develop all of the information we have discovered, and presumably it would have no effect except to form the basis of a prolonged and doubtless enjoyable conversation.

There is an obligation to work effectively, and Harlow's comments really bring it home. One of the vain things in life is to extend a tool beyond its useful reach. The MNC in an economic function has a proven value. As an instrument of social ends that well-meaning individuals would like to see advanced, in my judgment it can be a tool of doubtful accomplishment, which may impair the economic function it is obviously designed to perform.

Let me pursue that a bit. One of the participants has stated that he in association with others got the United Nations to approve a Declaration of Human Rights, and I am assuming that in that pursuit they found the concurrence of approved tyrannies a necessary part of the concurrence that he sought. Now what has the UN or the gentlemen who initiated this program or the states that adopted it done to give it effect? I would judge from what he says that they've done very little, because if the primary people responsible for the job who were the sponsors of the effort and felt it was a worthy thing to do have not done it, why should they seek to escape from its accomplishment by in effect shunting it to a secondary function, an economic instrument that obviously does not have the accomplishment of those purposes for its primary objective?

Jon P. Gunnemann: I think some people still read the statements that were made by several people here about the need for disclosure as a charge that corporations are unwilling to give information and that something devious is going on. Now my guess is that there are corporations in which there is something devious going on, but there are also churches in which there is something devious going on. This is not the question. Nor is the question whether the MNC should be used to effect idiosyncratic social goals. Ron Muller and others are suggesting that we need new analytical tools because the structure of

128

international operations has changed, and that this is of paramount importance, not just for governments, but for the future of MNCs. The question is, Does the corporation see a necessity of contributing to the development of new analytical tools and information, for its own sake as well as for society's?

Mr. Hanold: Let me answer that. During the course of a very amiable discussion this afternoon among five of us, there was no shadow of dissent from anyone that the United States needs a better statement of economic policy for the guidance of business as well as the other elements of society than we've now got, and to create such an economic policy, we will probably require more and better information than we've got now, and that the corporations in America, whether they're MNCs or otherwise, would feel the obligation to contribute in proper spirit to the creation of that policy.

Stanley H. Ruttenberg: Let's assume that the U.S. Congress and executive branch said that it was in the national interest for a corporation to provide a breakdown of its consolidated worldwide balance sheet, country by country, and to indicate simultaneously how it allocated costs to each country. Would you disclose that information? If it were on a voluntary basis?

Mr. Gage: Wait a minute. You said on a voluntary basis. Not unless everybody else in the industry did it, no. Why should we give the others the benefit of that sort of competitive information if they didn't reveal the same thing?

Mr. Ruttenberg: All right. I agree with that. Would you then fight a proposal within the Congress that required compulsory reporting?

Mr. Gage: I don't think we'd fight it, no. I think we would express our opinion, perhaps, that we don't see the necessity for it, but I think that if it were on a voluntary basis and everybody is not going to do it, we would not do it. Otherwise we're giving away a competitive advantage to other companies.

Charles W. Powers: There's a funny thing going on here, and it relates to some concepts that functioned in the old U.S. business creed. On the one hand, you're saying responsibility begins only after the fact. First, the policy is formulated by government, then corporations support it. Then there's a very strong element in U.S. business that believes that the incredibly incompetent government isn't doing what it's supposed to be doing.

Mr. Hanold: Is that a matter of debate?

Mr. Powers: It's likely that government in many cases is not going to do the job, and therefore you may have to spend your life paying for incredible legal services to fight off incompetent kinds of government actions. Isn't that less efficient than going into law schools and getting groups of public-spirited law students, maybe even for free, to begin to articulate the kinds of questions and areas that will be helpful in the formulation of an economic policy we all agree is deficient? That's a kind of competency you've got, and you could help the public agencies. It seems to me that efficiency would require you to take the first steps, if you really believe that the government is incompetent.

Mr. Hanold: Well, the point is this. One microactor isn't qualified to do the job. That's us. Multiplying him by two does not make him more capable of doing the job. You've still got to get the macroactor into the act. Now if you're saying that you and your associates propose to go to Congress and say, "We've got a problem here—there's no economic policy to guide the functions of the government as they pertain to international trade, so why don't you create the obligation in one of the agencies of the government to proceed with that job?"— fine. We may join you, and that might do something. But we can create data only of a limited kind, because we people of exuberant good will who are willing to engage in this kind of exercise are not all in agreement by any means and are not going to arrive at a final conclusion—it certainly is not going to be binding on anybody. You have to start by determining who's got the job. We'll work with him. But so far, we're not saying that anybody's got the job. Our government is totally incompetent, but it's the only agency that can do the job.

Although the CRIA conference did not arrive at even a working model for international regulation of MNCs, some patterns of needs and possibilities did begin to emerge. Luis Escobar of the World Bank outlines actual efforts in this direction together with his interpretation of issues raised in the conference.

Anthony Wiener of the Hudson Institute lifts out some of the key problems in international bargaining, using an illustration drawn from game theory. He also articulates two aspects of the MNC that had been latent in many of the earlier debates: that conflicting interests with respect to the MNC exist in both home and host countries, and the extent to which the MNC is the nexus of cultural interaction. Not only does the MNC involve economic and political issues, it also is an institution where a multiplicity of world views come into contact and conflict with each other.

This latter point is taken up by two churchmen, Howard Schomer and Thomas Quigley, who draw on their experience with the peoples of Latin American countries.

CHAPTER

9

SHOULD THERE BE AN INTERNATIONAL REGULATORY AGENCY FOR MNCs?

Luis Escobar

Last January the Institute for International and Foreign Trade Law of Georgetown University—in collaboration with its sister institute of Germany—organized a very well-attended conference in Dusseldorf, on international organization for investment; the papers and conclusions will be published in a book later this year by Praeger. Before and after that conference there has been active debate on the subject, but probably for a long time the papers discussed on that occasion will be the most quoted reference material on the subject.

Among the activities taking place at the moment the most important is the work of the Group of Eminent Persons—appointed by the Secretary General of the UN following a resolution by the UN Economic and Social Council in July, 1972—"to study the role of multinational corporations and their impact on the process of development, especially that of developing countries, and also their implications for international relations; to formulate conclusions which may possibly be used by governments in making their sovereign decisions regarding national policy in this respect, and to submit recommendations for appropriate international action." The report, prepared by the Department of Economic and Social Affairs of the UN Secretariat to facilitate the deliberations of the Group, constitutes a good survey on the subject.

Professor Seymour Rubin, summarizing the Dusseldorf conference, said that "there was consensus against any major attempt at an international organization which would oversee the MNC. But there

---

The author is a member of the staff of the IBRD; however, the opinions expressed in this paper have not been cleared with the Institution, and consequently he is solely responsible for them.

was wide agreement that more ought to be done on the side of gathering and exchange of information, a presumably safe enough subject."

It is interesting to note that the opposition to the idea of international control of investment came, at Dusseldorf, from all sides, that is, from representatives of developed as well as less developed countries, and also from the MNCs themselves (even though everybody participated only "in their personal capacity"). As Professor Rubin said, "The LDCs would seem to fear that the international agency would seek to restrain their activities in regard to the foreign-based MNCs"; and the businessmen seem to be worried "that any international agency would rather fetter than free the MNC."

This view, however, is not unanimous today. I was interested in reading the presentation made here by Mr. Carl A. Gerstacker of Dow Chemical, in which he said that he believes "the multinational companies would welcome standard international rules to work by, together with a code of international standards governing their proper treatment by the host nations—some internationally approved method of governing the relationships between the nation-states and the MNCs and settling their disputes in an impartial court." In my opinion the need for such a set of international rules of the game is becoming clear.

Also, Business Week magazine, in its August 18, 1973, issue, carries an article by W. Michael Blumenthal of Bendix Corporation in which he argues for "a GATT for investments"; he said that "some businessmen have been critical of GATT rules because of their relative ineffectiveness in certain situations. No one, however, has seriously advocated scrapping law and order in trade matters or going back to a world in which every nation is free to do as it pleases. Paradoxically, this is precisely today's situation as regards transnational investment. Although such investment has become much more important than exports alone, there is no predictability as to national behavior, no firm assurance against arbitrary actions, no real inhibitions against competitive discriminatory moves by individual nations. In sum, there is no accepted system of law and order in the growing international investment world." At Dusseldorf, this GATT-for-investment idea was considered to be neither feasible nor desirable at present.

As for the governments of developed countries, I personally do not have a clear impression of what their reactions would be to a concrete proposal to organize some sort of international control of investment. I suspect they would not be enthusiastic, since that might interfere with negotiations in process on several policy questions in which international agreement seems to be extremely difficult, as we are witnessing these days in the monetary and trade fields, for example.

Now, why are we concerned with international regulations of MNCs? Excluding the cases of ideological hostility to private foreign investment (which in some instances goes together with aversion to private investment in general), one can say that opposition—in the host countries—to the activities of multinational corporations is due to the fact that, occasionally, their respective interests may not coincide.

National governments may think that MNCs are effectively outside their control, that they cannot count on them—as they could on domestically controlled firms—to meet certain social and economic goals and, much less, to meet defense, security, or, in general, political goals. In addition the growing relative importance of MNCs in the economies of both developed and less developed countries is a matter of concern; according to some estimates the volume of business done by MNCs will continue expanding at an annual rate higher than that of the world GNP.

Rainer Hellman, a German journalist and specialist on the European Common Market in Brussels, said at Dusseldorf that "the fear is widespread that some 200 or 300 gigantic MNCs will control, in ten or fifteen years, more than half of the world's industrial production, and that they will take their decisions without much respect for regional or national interests. . . . George S. Ball considers the MNC the greatest challenge to the nation-state in the Western world since the decline of the temporal power of the Catholic Church in the fifteenth century."

Hellman sees some countervailing powers to the MNC: the nation states and regional organizations—which want to defend their sovereignty—and the vigorously developing international labor movement. So he says that, in fact, the countervailing power to the growing MNC will not be an international organization. The real and effective countervailing powers are already in operation. They are national regulations, regional organizations, such as the European Community and the Andean Group, and the labor movement, which is starting its multinational counterorganizations. But at least between Europe and North America he favors a permanent system of consultations on mutual problems of direct investment by MNCs on questions of interest rates, fiscal aspects, transfer-pricing, and antitrust surveillance.

In fact, at the Dusseldorf conference many speakers favored a system of increased consultation as being better than setting up a new international regulatory agency for MNCs. As Professor Rubin puts it, "Better consultation may result in some progress toward agreements. . . . There is no forum in which the problems, even those of a regional nature, are systematically examined. It would seem sensible now to establish such a forum, or perhaps such forums, without attempting to formulate GATT-like rules."

I personally agree with the "consultation approach." We need a forum, or series of forums, where consultations could take place. The purposes would be (1) discuss and agree on the facts and (2) if possible, agree on interpretation and hopefully policy implications emanating from those facts. This leads me to repeat here the ideas I presented at the Dusseldorf conference:

Proposals.

1. I do not believe that the world is going to be able to control investments <u>internationally</u>;

2. If any "control" is going to be exercised, it will be done nationally. In fact, today, there are controls on private foreign investments going from simple registration requirements up to much more sophisticated sets of rules to screen foreign investment and about sectors of activities, ownership requirements, and the like. A regional group—like the Andean countries—can agree on a foreign investment code, but the code is nationally implemented. This tendency toward stricter national controls and scrutiny can be also clearly detected in home countries as well, including—and perhaps most conspicuously—the United States.

3. What can be aimed at, it seems to me, is to "monitor" investment internationally. In other words, I think we need a monitoring device and information center, a reference bureau dealing with all aspects of the activities of MNCs, a true data bank on the matter. So I would say there is a need for an <u>international organization</u> to facilitate the <u>national control</u> of foreign investments. This international organization would do research work, would provide information and training facilities, and in addition should be able to provide, on request, advice to governments or private business about their prospective or present activities of an international nature. Some of these activities have already begun in a rather embryonic way.

4. Let us call this international organization simply "the Office." The Office would be established out of the conviction that, first, private foreign investment is needed to speed up the rate of economic growth of LDCs, but that the foreign investors must adjust their activities to the true needs and priorities of the host countries, with due respect to their sovereignty and national goals. In doing this, private foreign investors have the right to fair compensation and fair treatment as true partners in the development process. Second, however, it would be recognized that occasionally the interests of the parties involved may not be the same. The interests of the MNCs may, in fact, be incompatible with those of the host countries. Third, it would be also recognized that, if left alone, the negotiations between MNCs and LDCs do not always end up in the kind of balance conducive to a smooth, friendly, and dynamic partnership. The reasons for this are, on one hand, the impressive financial power of the MNCs compared with that of many LDCs and, on the other, the relative lack of information, organization, and on occasion expertise in LDCs to deal with the highly sophisticated management of the MNCs. The Office would have no power other than that of persuasion if and when its advice is asked for. Also it would be influential by means of its publications, which would enjoy the prestige of being supported by the best information center in the world. The Office would deal with private foreign investment in a broad sense, with both developed and developing

137

country questions, and with both socialist and market economies. This means that it would be interested in investments made in an LDC and also in those made in industrialized countries (for example, U.S. investments in Latin America and U.S. investments in Europe and Canada) and that it would also follow the investments made by an MNC—based on a market-oriented economy—in a socialist country.

From the foregoing it can be readily seen that the Office should be organized very much like a research institution with a well-developed information center. Obviously the information function would be fed by the research activities. Training would also be an important task. And finally, as we have already suggested, the Office would have an advisory department to give services, upon request, to both governments and private foreign investors.

The International Center for the Settlement of Investment Dispute (ICSID) is conducting today one of the most necessary basic researches; it is compiling all legislation of the member countries of ICSID on private foreign investment. This, of course, will provide a first basis for comparative analysis of the actual characteristics (legal, financial, economic) of investments made, the information necessary to move toward the harmonization of local differences in the treatment of MNCs (local legislation, antitrust, pricing, profit repatriation, taxation, and national business practices).

It would be essential, in my opinion, that from its inception the Office invite the confidence of both developed and less developed countries, which can be accomplished only if it is regarded as an independent center and if it is managed by a truly competent and well-balanced international staff. Otherwise the Office would be considered simply as an additional instrument of the rich countries or as a forum for LDCs and without impact on the problems with which we want to deal. The image of the Office at its inception, its organization and management, will in itself be its first contribution toward a better dialogue and understanding between MNCs and host countries.

Since there are a number of institutions that are at present performing one or another of these tasks, obviously the first task is to determine who is doing what and suggest possibilities of coordination or absorption of the related efforts. Most likely the Group of Eminent Persons will undertake this job. The group might also explore possible contributions from regional banks and regional economic organizations on this matter—and of course the possibilities of utilizing ICSID (with or without amendment of the Convention that created it). They should also make suggestions on the procedural questions of what is the best way to go about organizing such an enterprise. Finally, since the financing of this Office would be crucial for its activities and image of independence, the group should also explore this very important aspect of the question.

An International Center, or series of international centers, like the one described—which incidentally would also satisfy the idea of a forum—is not incompatible with proposals that have been put forward for international action in some specific areas. For example, Anthony Solomon, former U.S. Assistant Secretary of State for Economic Affairs, writing on international control of investment in the trade sector (for the Dusseldorf conference), said, "Increasingly we hear the view that the GATT presupposes a model of international trade which has been substantially altered by the MNC, that a large and increasing percentage of trade now is intracompany trade and not trade between independent exporters and importers." After analyzing the statistical evidence Mr. Solomon reached the conclusion that available data do not support that statement. The forms through which competition may be lessened as a result of the growth of the MNC are classified by Mr. Solomon in the following categories:

1. takeovers of existing firms;
2. allocating noncompetitive marketing areas among subsidiaries;
3. limitation on use of technology;
4. international pricing behavior, particularly in the oligopoly-characterized industries, where multinational companies tend to thrive.

Solomon suggests that "a beginning for some form of international surveillance in the trade area could be made in the transnational takeover activities when they result, or threaten to result, in the lessening of competition." In this connection it is also interesting to note that the European community, if my understanding is correct, has made some decisions in the field of rules of competition that will certainly affect MNCs.

Nicholas de B. Katzenbach, among others, has suggested that some areas worth exploring for international agreement include the "harmonization of tax systems as they affect corporations doing business in a number of countries; efforts to apply national laws to foreign subsidiaries of national corporations; balance of payments and intercompany transfers." I understand that in some of these areas the European Community has already taken some action, as for example in the field of harmonization of direct taxation.

Professor Jack Behrman has suggested an Organization of International Industrial Integration (OIII) "to deal with the creation of joint projects and industrial policies. It would be a central coordinating body where rules could be formulated by members applicable to the various situations that would arise. It is within these objectives and under these rules that guidelines for the Multinational Enterprise would be developed."

To finish this paper, I just want to say that two conclusions are clear: first, that decisions are being taken and implemented at the national and regional levels, and, second, that the international community seems to be moving in the direction of seriously discussing the establishment of an international regulatory agency for MNCs. However, the precise nature and jurisdiction of such an agency, or agencies, is still conceived in widely different ways by different authors. It is therefore expected that more light will be thrown on this subject—and that the discussion will be narrowed down—after the work of the Group of Eminent Persons is published. But all the interested parties should have clearly in their minds that in the meantime host countries, home governments, regional groups, the multinational corporations themselves (which have already approved Guidelines for International Investment in the International Chamber of Commerce in Paris in 1972), and the international labor organizations will continue adopting resolutions that—in one way or another—will affect the flow of capital from developed countries to LDCs and the flow of private foreign investment in general and, in particular, will affect the operations of MNCs. And this leads me to say that in this matter the sooner the international community moves, the better.

10

MULTIPLE INTERESTS IN INTERNATIONAL BARGAINING
Anthony Wiener

We have turned, as we must finally, to the question of what should
we do, and because of an accident of the agenda we have approached
the question in the form of what should we do with respect to international organizations. But we might have asked that question about
any number of other areas of policy-making, and we would have raised
the very same issues. What we should do depends very much on one's
view of how the various issues that have been raised by the participants in the consultation ought to come out.

As I listened to the consultation I was reminded very much of the
old story I suppose most of you know, of the country judge who listened to a lawsuit. He listened first to the plaintiff's case, and he
said, "Mr. Plaintiff, I think you're right." And then he listened to
the defendant's case, and he said, "Mr. Defendant, I think you're
right." And then a spectator in the courtroom spoke up and said,
"Your Honor, they can't both be right." And the judge said, "Mr.
Spectator, I guess you're right too." The problem really is that you
cannot discuss complex issues of the kind we have before us in two-
minute intervals. All you can do is make a simple point, which is too
simple, and then is attacked by someone else on some other ground,
which the first speaker would also have probably agreed to if he had
had time.

What goes on in any area of policy formation, just as what goes
on in the legal system, is that there are competing considerations
and policies that intersect. Decisions are made at precisely those
points where competing considerations intersect, defining the boundaries. So its impossible to discuss any of these issues briefly or in
terms of a single consideration. There are some people who are here
primarily as advocates of a particular point of view they don't think
has been sufficiently appreciated. They have a right to stress

141

particular considerations. But when it comes to considering what we should do, we are put in a different role, where stressing any one particular consideration, as an advocate, is no longer appropriate. Now we have the problem of balancing conflicting considerations and delineating their intersection.

It's also very clear that what we come out with depends very much upon the data we assume are valid and upon the analysis we happen to believe. I was very interested in the statistics cited by Ron Muller. I haven't had a chance to look at the primary sources, but if after looking at them I agree with him, that will change my view of many of these issues. I've read a lot of Rand studies, and I don't agree with all of them, so the fact that Ron's data emanated from that particular organization doesn't impress me especially, but it may well be a good study. If it is, it will make a great deal of difference. If there is a 40 percent return on investment from host countries to the MNCs, that makes a great deal of difference. If, on the other hand, there is a sizable loss to a home country due to the operation of MNCs, that presents an entirely different problem. Neither of these is an assumption most people looking at multinational corporations have made.

It seems to me if we ask what we should do with respect to international arrangements, we need to look at the matter from at least four points of view, and there may be four different answers. The four points of view are as follows: What should the host countries do, what should the businesses do, what should the home countries do, and, finally, what should the international community do? And there are different answers from these points of view because there are different interests present, although of course there are some common interests, too. Even this is too simple, since there are conflicting interests, for example, of investors, managers, employees, within each country too.

First, I'm not too concerned at this point about the host countries because I think—barring Ron's statistics on 40 percent return on investments for the moment—there are many indications that host countries within their sovereignties have an enormous amount of power. Nothing could be more irrelevant than to compare the GNP of a host country with the sales of a multinational corporation, as my good friend Lester Brown and others have done. Strictly speaking, if you want to make any such comparison, you ought to compare GNP to value added rather than to sales. But even then that tells you nothing about their relative power. The annual sales of General Motors may be a larger number than the GNP of Switzerland, but GM cannot operate in Switzerland except according to Swiss law. Moreover, once an investment is made by a multinational corporation in a host country, that host country can almost always do very much what it likes with that investment, including injuring itself, and this is a consideration for the international as well as for the host countries, as Carl Gerstacker suggested. The relationship of the regime to the people, and of the leading to the lagging sectors in development, is a complex issue I won't go into now, except to say it can be misleading to speak of the host country's interests as though they were simple. Suppose, for example, by investing in a new plant, you provide new jobs and increase the GNP of the host country but you also increase disparities of wealth in that country. Then you've helped some people and hurt others.

The second important issue we've talked about a great deal has to do with the kinds of action the multinational itself is capable of taking and ought to take. Many people have said, and I agree with this statement, that we can't divorce social responsibility or, as James Joseph said, corporate responsibility from ordinary business practices. It's a mistake to think of social responsibility as consisting of projects that are done in addition to normal business activity. Let's go back to Milton Friedman's well-known position that the only social responsibility of business is to maximize profits. That's clearly misleading by itself, because profits are always maximized within constraints imposed by law and concepts of "good business," and those constraints can change as social expectations change. What we are asking now is how do these constraints change. No businessman makes a decision according to the abstract model that Chuck Powers gave us the other day, by first calculating economic advantage and then asking, if economic advantages are equal, what is my ethical choice? To the extent that they are socially responsible and ethical, have a sense of business style and a sense of what is good business, businessmen intuitively take into consideration ethical considerations as they operate.

The problem is that ethical considerations serve social functions; they don't exist in the abstract, apart from or opposed to business considerations. Someone said they come to us in a cultural tradition. But the cultural tradition is full of competing ethical claims, and the ones that are operative in a given situation depend very much on what's going on and what works and what helps the system operate. One of the reasons good businessmen have a sense of what is good business is that there is the latent understanding, even if not consciously expressed, that the system breaks down if too many people indulge in bad business practices, even if these practices are legal. I want to disagree with what I think Burke Marshall said. I thought he said at one point that the only way you know what is expected of you in any country is through its laws, and I think that's clearly not true. The law sets certain minimum requirements, but there are plenty of other requirements you need to know about how to operate in any country, including the United States.

So the problem is this—and it is the problem that I think Ron Muller was addressing in his cross-examination of Mr. Gage, although it was a little rough on Mr. Gage—Are you sensitive to changing conditions? Do you see that the situation we're in is changing? Whether or not it's changing may be debatable. But if it is changing, there ought to be a sensitivity to the changes, and a sense of what is good business ought to change correspondingly. That's the crux of corporate social responsibility. Just as responsibility must acknowledge the claims of laborers and consumers and environmentalists and other relevant interests in domestic policy, it needs to acknowledge the concerns of the international community about the growing role of the multinational corporation and the possibility for abuse in the limited kinds of accountability that exist with a multinational corporation.

If there is to be social responsibility for the multinational corporation to numerous governments and to the international community as well, there needs to be some sensitivity as to how these conditions are changing, and this sensitivity has to result in an inherent sense of responsibility about how you operate if you're going to stay in business. This turns out to be completely functional in almost every case. Companies that have this sense, that operate in this style, are the companies that are more likely to survive, although they may not survive in every particular case. For example, Dow Chemical may be an exemplary company and yet may have been victimized in the Chilean case. That kind of thing can happen. But on the whole your chances for surviving are a lot better if you know what's going on and what people expect of you.

Third, we have to look at this question of regulation from the point of view of the home country, and here we talked at length about disclosure. Terry Hanold made it very clear that he would disclose to any agency that had the authority to issue regulations, because in that case the disclosure would do some good. So he's willing to disclose to the Securities and Exchange Commission (SEC), but it isn't enough for him that Ron Muller writes a book that says we ought to know more about transfer payments. That isn't going to motivate him to spend money on publishing information about transfer payments. I think that's a perfectly reasonable position.

But there are other things besides requiring more disclosure that the United States could do. It might make sense to codify certain rules of international behavior on which there is broad consensus in the United States. For example, I don't think it is now a criminal offense to interfere in a foreign election or to conspire to interfere in a foreign election, but I think it might be very much worth considering making it a criminal offense for any U.S. citizen to do that. I don't think that could hurt the U.S. business competitive position vis-a-vis West Germans, Japanese, British, and French. I think it could only help. It doesn't follow, because the law is passed, that it will prevent all such acts. We're dealing with violations of law all the time, including violations by some of the highest officials in the country, so we should expect continued violations. But it sometimes helps very much to codify a particular moral standard, to publish the matter abroad, and to try to enforce it enough of the time so that people must at least weigh the risks of violation.

You could add to that list. Besides interfering in foreign elections, what are some of the other things about which there is legitimate concern? Here's one that I think needs a lot more discussion, because this is a difficult one. Should it be a criminal offense to bribe foreign officials? Bribery of officials is an offense if committed in the United States. I never heard of anyone's being prosecuted for doing it extraterritorially. But it's not hard to make it an offense, a U.S. criminal offense. Should you do it? Well, that goes back to the question we discussed of arrogance and Rudyard Kipling and relativism. There are certain countries where it's very hard to get anything done without bribery. You may just have to give money to officials to expedite perfectly legitimate transactions, just to save time, to get your papers walked through the offices or put on the top of the pile. Sometimes you've got to give some money, and that's standard business practice in many countries. It would be unfair, probably, to prosecute a few people, because you wouldn't have evidence against most of the people who did it.

Fourth, there is the point of view of the international community. I think it's clear that the international interest, to the extent that there is one, is different from the interests of either the host or home countries. Luis Escobar raised that question in his talk when he asked the question: "What is the vested interest of a citizen of Chile who works for the World Bank?" In general it's hard to know, because there are no world citizens, there are only citizens of particular nations working for international organizations. The UN is a certain organization that includes one particular group of nations.

Nevertheless, it's perfectly clear, if you make judgments based on the kinds of data most of us have perhaps too uncritically accepted up to now, that the multinational corporation plays a dominant role in international commerce, or a more important role than is now played by trade. It is likely to play an increasing role and is the dominant source from the world point of view of the transfer of capital, technology, management, access to markets, and so forth. So it serves tremendously important social functions for the world. It is the major instrumentality for getting these things done, and it is likely to remain so. It might remain so even if it continued to cause problems for both host and home countries.

So from an international point of view you probably want to foster these institutions, but do something to regulate them. Certainly nobody is doing more to increase gross world product than multinational corporations are doing at this point. They may be doing it in ways that sometimes conflict with host or home country interests, or both.

All right. I agree with Luis that it would be premature to set up international regulations. I think we have to look to data collection, to informing, to all sorts of ancillary functions on the part of these groups. I'm interested in the activities of ICSID, which Luis mentioned in his paper. Unfortunately, the Latin American countries are not members because of concerns about sovereignty. There's a limit on the kind of investment disputes the Center can deal with, and it does not now have any mediation or arbitration function. But I don't think it's unreasonable to begin to think now about introducing mediation and arbitration, at least mediation for investment disputes on an international level. This could only help—at least, it seems to me, it couldn't hurt—and it would be worth a great deal, not only to the home countries, but in the longer run to the host countries as well, in reducing the risks of investment.

But in general there is a problem from an international point of view of protecting expectations of people engaged in commerce, and I referred to this briefly the other day when I talked about how the non-zero-sum game in which the bargainers are engaged can end up with lawsuits from both sides too. This is a very well-known phenomenon in any dealing between people who have a great deal of power to determine what they're going to do in that relationship. For example, if we look at the arms race between the United States and the Soviet Union, they have this kind of dilemma.

There's a little paradigm in game theory that makes a good illustration. I think it's worth spending 30 seconds on. It's called the prisoner's dilemma. Imagine the police have arrested two bank robbers, and one guard was killed in this robbery, so there's a murder charge as well as a bank robbery charge that can be brought against them. The district attorney takes each prisoner, puts each in a separate cell, and says, "Notice there's a telephone in your cell. It's connected directly with my office. I'm going back to my office. The first one to pick up the telephone and give me evidence against both of you will get off with a light sentence. The one who has not picked up the telephone will be sent to the electric chair. Now it's up to each to decide whether to call first or to wait until it's too late." So he goes back to his office and waits. Now the prisoners' dilemma is that if they think they can trust each other, each in a separate cell and no means of communicating with the other—if they think they can trust each other, the benefit for both is maximized by both keeping silent. But if they don't trust each other, the benefit for each of them is maximized by turning in the other. If you add up the gains and losses for the two of them, turning in the other guy is bad for the pair together—for one thing it spoils the partnership thereafter.

This kind of dilemma, this same structure, exists in an enormous number of bargaining situations, certainly between the multinational corporation and the host country. It exists also between management and labor. Notice, however, that when management and labor are threatening each other in the short run, they ordinarily threaten each other in a limited way. For example, in a strike there's going to be limited harm done to both sides, perhaps one day's loss of work and pay per day. Over the longer run that can be much more serious, of course, because the company can go out of business and all those jobs can be lost. It can escalate to the point where both sides lose everything. We need to do something from an international point of view to deal with this situation, where the multinational corporation has all its bargaining power before it goes into a country, when it comes in and makes the presentation with all the slides to the poor little local official. At that point it can demand a lot. When it has made its investment, it's a prisoner and can be taken advantage of by the host country, and frequently is.

Ultimately we ought to be thinking about some international system of guarantee, some kinds of regulations on the timing and extent to which contracts can be renegotiated. Under what conditions is it appropriate to renegotiate? Instead of having mandatory fade-outs as we have in the Andean pact, there might be some more reasonable way of preserving for both host country and multinational corporation the advantages of continuing the flow of technology and management, and so forth. You want to keep the possibility there. One thing you don't want to do is make a contract that purports to establish for all time the bargaining relationship that existed at entry, such as 70 percent ownership for all time.

One final point I'd like to make is this. When we speak of international regulations, we must recognize that there are many biases involved, and not simply those of the corporations and of labor and of host country. There is also the ideology of Americans who are discussing this particular issue, and here again I don't want to be in the position of appearing to say that all these considerations are ideological. I want to say that among other things we ought to keep in mind that to some degree these ideas are ideological and to some degree we ought to be suspicious of them. Certainly there is some middle ground between absolute cultural relativism on the one hand, where we feel we have no right whatsoever to value our own traditions above others, and absolute cultural imperialism or arrogance on the other, where we are convinced that everything we do at home or think we should be doing at home is the right thing to do everywhere else. Some things are probably the right things to do elsewhere, even if they're not done in most places—for example, increase safety standards. We need to sort these issues out. It may be contrary to local norms to increase safety standards, but I don't think we need to feel that our values are merely relative.

One of the problems is that many Americans, especially certain kinds of well-educated, upper-middle-class, or upper-class Americans, love to feel that they are international citizens. They are cosmopolitan, they are citizens of the world, and above all nonnational. I'm not objecting to that except to some degree. The problem is that what this ideology thinks of as cosmopolitan and international very often is a disguised form not only of American interest but a disguised form of the interests of a certain class of Americans. It's very easy for people to confuse the interests of the kinds of Americans who are managers and shareholders with the interests of all Americans, and very easy to think that as long as the multinational corporations are returning a positive balance-of-payments flow, that's the main thing, and that the loss of employment is a very secondary situation. And as Liz Jager points out very forcefully, that loss of employment is likely to extend eventually to managerial and technical jobs, and when it does, it will be perceived very differently by these same people.

We have an ideological assumption that the way people can solve problems is by federating—after all, the 13 colonies got together—and one of the main forces in U.S. history has been the need for immigrant groups to assimilate and to take on the values of the dominant group in the culture. It is hard for Americans to think that this is a peculiarly American idea, but it is. People in other countries don't value assimilation the way we do; they don't value cosmopolitanism the way we do; they are nationalists in a way that we are not. (By "we" I mean upper middle-class, well-educated Americans.) They even hate each other in a way that no American would consider respectable. Upper-middle-class, well-educated Americans don't hate anybody. It's just not the right thing to do. They want to be friends with everybody and have no idea that they are exporting U.S. values. Of course you have to export values, and whenever a multinational corporation enters a country, makes an investment—and it doesn't matter actually whether it's a multinational or a domestic company—it's in the business of inculcating cultural traits that may be quite different from those that existed beforehand, and are likely to be very different in the case of a lesser developed country. Any industrial enterprise is concerned with diligence, punctuality, patience, thrift, foresight, the fundamental values of industrialization, no matter where they are, and it's intrinsic to economic enterprise to be interested in these values. And there is inevitable cultural change as a result of any investment, whether domestically or multinationally funded or managed.

So the idea that we should simply conform with local cultures is an impossibility. But the extent to which this disruption occurs ought at least to be selectively moderated. Some of the disruption may be very valuable from the point of view of the host country, because if the host country really wants to increase standards of living, this may be what it needs.

And then I think we should be aware about possible ideological biases when we consider international arrangements. Americans ought to ask themselves very carefully when they favor international arrangements to what extent they may be indulging in a kind of economic nationalism themselves in which they have confused American cultural preferences with those of the world. This is a question not only for academics and theologians and other well-intentioned persons who frequently propose international relations—it's also very much a question for the management of a multinational corporation. Very often these managers are very eager to be cosmopolitans, thinking of themselves as citizens of the world, and want to introduce what they think of as cosmopolitan standards of behavior throughout the world. What they fail to recognize is that the particular form of cosmopolitanism they are promulgating is a kind of Americanism. It doesn't follow from that that it's wrong, but it's good to be aware of the fact that it is an American set of values that's being promulgated.

I'll conclude with a famous anecdote on this point. Eisenhower had been Commander of Supreme Allied Headquarters in Europe in the immediate postwar period for some years, and then he came back to be president of Columbia University. Someone asked him what his greatest achievement at the Allied headquarters had been, and he said, "Well, for one thing I put everybody on a first-name basis." Now, I think that's a wonderful example of unconscious Americanism, because if you know Europeans, it's no favor to them to put them on a first-name basis. It is very disagreeable to Europeans to be on a first-name basis. But this was enforced. The point is, this was supposed to be a NATO headquarters. What he did was rub everyone's nose in the fact that it was an American headquarters and that you played by American rules and had the American customs there. I'm sure there were people on a first-name basis within headquarters who, when they walked out the door, called each other "Herr Doktor."

Alphonse De Rosso: I have a couple of questions for Tony Wiener. He mentioned in passing that perhaps some system should be developed to monitor disruption created by an MNC activity. I'd like him to elaborate a little bit on that. It's a rather intriguing idea, and I don't know quite where it will lead us. The other point I question somewhat is that we Americans should be conscious of the fact that our pushing for international approaches to resolution of problems perhaps reflects a class bias. This may have been the case 20, 25 years ago, but it seems to me that the rest of the world is catching up with us, and there are many countries that are pushing for that same kind of approach.

<u>Mr. Wiener</u>: Let me give you an example of the kind of thing I meant by
monitoring disruptions. When I say monitor I don't mean that you're
responsible for every consequence of your activities, but you are for
some, particularly those you are able to do something about. For example, suppose you build a plant that creates 1,000 jobs, and as a result 2,000 families come in from the countryside, from the village to
the town where your plant is located. This is not uncommon, particularly in Latin America. This in itself is a certain amount of disruption,
and many other kinds of disruption may now occur. You may find the
local intellectual writing an editorial in the newspaper saying you have
detribalized these people and disrupted their traditional way of life.
My own judgment would be that you can't help that. That's what the
plant is for, to disrupt the traditional way of life, to get these people
to become industrial workers. However, if you have created problems
for the town as a result of your economic activity having to do with
sewage systems and the sustenance of people, and so forth, maybe you
have some obligation to make some contribution to that. At any rate,
you ought to know what the range of social impact is. I didn't mean to
express as much disagreement with Chuck Powers as it might have
sounded. I think it is extremely valuable to explicate these considerations at the point where they are changing, because getting clarity
about such social factors and impacts is one of the things that facilitate the change. The point I was trying to make is that they don't become effective until they're incorporated into your own concept of business style and proper practice. They're never going to become
effective as abstract considerations on a checklist.

On the other point, on the upper-middle-class bias, let me give
you an example of how that might work. Let's suppose it turns out on
the basis of somebody's studies that you could make a good case that
the multinational corporation is operating in the world interest in increasing gross world product, but at the expense of the United States.
Now there are a lot of people in America who would have a great deal
of difficulty understanding the point. They can't understand that there's
a difference between world interest and U.S. interest. It really doesn't
occur to them very often that there is. They think of federation, internationalism, cosmopolitanism, assimilation of everyone to one thing
as necessarily both an American and a world interest.

A good example of this was our policy toward Europe of fostering
European community: It was always assumed, erroneously as it turned
out, that European community would lead to Atlantic community, and
then people came along and carried the fallacy a step further by as-
serting that European community would foster world community. Obviously the more community you have the more community you have,
so if you have community in one place you must have it elsewhere—
a non sequitur. I'm saying we ought to be very suspicious of this tend-

ency and look much more carefully at the world, because there is a real possibility that when we promote international arrangements we may be alone in our wish to make concessions to the international community. To put it very bluntly, if we don't know the difference between world and U.S. interests, we can be taken for a ride by everybody else in the game, particularly the Germans, Japanese, Russians, and others who are in direct competition.

CHAPTER

11

TWO PERSPECTIVES FROM THE CHURCHES

Howard Schomer: I have three points to make. I have been troubled throughout this meeting with the tacit identification of host country with the current government regime in that host country. Of course the de facto government, however unpopular and unrepresentative, exercises the sovereignty of that country at the moment and can in theory and in fact rebuke and throw out any foreign person or corporation. But if we are intellectually trying to understand what is really going on in the real world, and not only in the formal or the power relationship world, what about the views of the masses of the people in the villages and the urban slums in much of the developing world? Who in the long run will prove to be showing us, for example, the real will of the Brazilian people: the current military junta helped into power by the U.S. military or the Archbishop of Recife, Archbishop Helder P. Camara, and multitudes of other clergy and lay people who live in the villages and who are close to the pulse of life among their fellow citizens? I have to say in parentheses that I think our deliberations here have suffered greatly from the absence of radical Latin American voices representing not the establishments but the nonliberated peoples. They should be involved in the discussion of these very issues.

Should we blindly believe that the well-guarded enclave of the elite in various developing countries in which the political military rulers and the economic ruling class, both domestic and foreign, live in a comfortable symbiotic relationship, actually is to give guidance as to what our U.S. position should be with respect to those countries in the long run? I think we ought to be more aware of the fact that dealing with the de facto governments may not be prudent, as indeed it may not be just, if you're taking a longer look down the road.

Point two. I'm relating it directly to something Tony Wiener said. I appreciate so much of what he said, but I think it is difficult to argue, as he did, that unconscious upper-middle-class American "cosmopolitan" value imperialism is involved in any effort to echo the aspirations and repeat the demands of the vioceless masses suffering under elitist and repressive regimes. As a church shareholder I can say that in our resolutions in the annual shareholder meetings we have proposed nothing that was fabricated in Ivy League seminars or institute think-tanks. We have our people living among the unrepresented masses of Southern Africans and Latin Americans, and everything we have ever proposed has been simply an echo of a policy we didn't know was the right one to push until we were told so by authenticated popular leaders.

My last point. It is obvious, of course, that multinational corporations have not been called by providence to serve as vehicles of liberation for repressed masses of people. They are by definition not revolutionary forces. Is it not equally obvious that neither have they been chartered in the United States to reinforce the power of elite regimes, unrepresentative, in any part of the world? They have been given neither a revolutionary nor a counterrevolutionary mandate. They certainly have no authorization to use the millions of dollars of U.S. investments placed at their disposal through bonds and stocks either to make a revolution or to sustain the status quo in all of its unjust and unrepresentative character. What I've been trying to argue, in two-minute interventions on three occasions, is that the middle road, that tightrope they'd better learn to walk, is defined by internationally formulated concepts of human equality, of workers' rights, of international and interregional economic justice, some of them actually conventions that have been adopted and ratified by the countries in question. They must walk this tightrope, or they cannot be good corporate citizens of mankind. If they do not so walk, they are not likely to prove in the long run good corporate citizens of any given country.

Thomas E. Quigley: Howard Schomer has helped me by saying some of the things I wanted to say. I come not as an economist. I have not had the kind of backgrounds that most of you have, being essentially a church bureaucrat with a concern for ethics. I've been listening to all the economic discussions with great interest, and so I'm probably less innocent today than I was when I first came. While listening to these, I was also listening constantly for what ethical presuppositions might underlie some of the statements that have been made. I'd like simply to list a couple of these I have heard and conclude where I think we need to go further if this kind of a discussion can continue being fruitful. This will also pick up partly on what Chuck Powers has been suggesting.

It seems to me that the discussion has focused on two major issues: one is the international code of conduct, whether there is a possibility for such, whether there should be one, what it would consist of, and so on. The other question is perhaps symbolized best by the word "disclosure," but it really has to do with the entire question of information-gathering, dissemination, about the nature of the multinational corporation vis-a-vis every other relationship it has. It seems to me that although the ethical questions in each of these have generally been submerged, they're there and have been constant. There is an underlying ethical question in each place. And let me just cite these few lines.

Terry Hanold said, for example, that the multinational corporation is a tool of doubtful accomplishment for changing attitudes and for bettering social conditions. It may indeed be a tool of doubtful accomplishment, but it is nevertheless willy-nilly a tool. The multinational corporation is an actor, and the question must always be asked, as Howard has been asking consistently, if you're acting, how are you acting, on what side? And you can't evade the question by saying that there are different sides or conflictual attitudes on every single issue.

The question of the good citizen has been raised repeatedly. It seems to me that when you speak of good citizenship you need to ask further which people in the host country you will look to for setting the standards.

And then a further point on citizenship. The multinational corporation attempts to exercise good citizenship vis-a-vis the home country, and the question again is, to which part of the U.S. consciousness, to which U.S. consensus, do you appeal for the definition of good citizenship?

Mike Kennedy said that in the State Department there was a growing consensus on what the rationale for a program like AID was; that the United States cannot dissociate itself, cannot afford to dissociate itself, from the aspirations of the Third World. You're constantly being brought back to questions of what do the people perceive their situation to be and how do you relate to those perceptions. And that has to be ethical. Some persons here have suggested that questions of ethics are not relevant, that all our issues must be understood in terms of a shifting balance of power. Power is the name of the game, and you simply have to find where the power lies and how you're going to work with and around that. But any balance of power rests on an aggregate of human attitudes that are ethical at base. You cannot understand any balance of power without understanding popular aspirations of people that inform and limit any force that is operative within a society.

All that, it seems to me, is a necessary preliminary to the most fundamental issue having to do with the ethical attitudes of MNCs or the U.S. State Department or any other power actor. This is the question of disruption of a culture or the opposite, which may be integration or affecting positively a people in terms of their own will for development. It seems to me that we need to make a distinction among different kinds of multinational actors. An oil company or a copper company or even a pharmaceutical or chemical company can be dissociated very sharply from other kinds of influences that more directly affect the culture, the life and mores, the customs and aspirations of people. There's no disagreement in Venezuela that the oil has to be gotten out and processed. Then you can talk about justice in terms of fair and just distribution, or whatever else. But there is a very serious question as to whether McCann-Erickson or ABC should be so immediately engaged in Latin America. Business activities that directly affect communications also have an immediate influence on key cultural questions: whether the society is going to become a consumer society much like ours or whether it is going to be able to retain certain differences from that; whether the information-systems approach to certain kinds of life processes in the country are really desirable ones. These questions are raised consistently in Latin America by all kinds of people, as they try to come to grips with the question of modernization versus humanization, the question of domestication versus liberation, and so on. Such questions may seem muddy at first, but when you probe beneath them it is clear that the people are concerned about a kind of cultural disruption that goes far beyond economic issues alone. It is not just a matter of the temporary economic disruption of 2,000 families looking for 1,000 jobs; it has to do with much more fundamental issues about the direction and shape of a people and culture.

SUMMARY AND ANALYSIS

Jon P. Gunnemann

As might be expected at a conference with so many divergent points of view represented, the disagreements on the diverse issues considered outnumbered the agreements. We were not only unable to agree upon an international code of conduct for multinational corporations (an outcome of the conference hoped for by some), we could not even agree that such a code was needed. But disagreements frequently illuminate issues more than do agreements, and the conference has indeed shed light on a great number of points. I want in this summary to concentrate on the nature and sources of our disagreements; nevertheless we did seem to share some assumptions about MNCs, and we found some areas of agreement as the conference drew to a close.

The summary, then, is organized as follows:

1. a list and brief description of the common starting assumptions;
2. a list and brief description of the major disagreements;
3. an analysis of the structure of the disagreements;
4. a more theoretical interpretation of why we disagreed;
5. a concluding projection about where groups such as this might be able to reach further agreement, and why.

COMMON ASSUMPTIONS ABOUT THE MNC

We all seem to have come to the consultation sharing the following assumptions (proceeding from the most to the least obvious):

1. The MNC is a relatively new phenomenon, a new economic structure about which we do not have adequate conceptions.

2. The MNC is not something we want to eradicate. In spite of the problems posed by the MNC in both home and host countries, and in international monetary matters, no one suggested that we ought to solve the problems by trying to abolish the MNC. On the contrary, champions and critics alike have underscored the "tremendously important social function" of the MNC as a conduit for technology and information flow and as a means for capital investment in developing areas. In sum, the MNC was seen as an instrument of development.

3. The considerable conflict that now exists between MNCs and national governments is generated, in part, by corporate definitions of the essential conditions for efficient operation on the one hand and some nation-states' understanding of the conditions essential for their own development. This is not a new situation; historically there have been frequent conflicts between foreign economic interests and nation-states.

4. Present regulatory and monitoring devices for MNCs, to the extent that they exist at all, are woefully inadequate.

5. Malevolence is not intrinsic to MNCs; but as in all human institutions there is at least self-interest at work. (This is not to exclude the possibility that self-interest can sometimes breed malevolently motivated practices.)

6. The diversities among MNCs, as well as the diversities to be found among nation-states (even in the Americas), make a single international code for MNCs difficult to devise, let alone to enforce.

MAJOR DISAGREEMENTS

Any list of major disagreements invites controversy as to what is major and what is minor. The list I offer here is presented in the order the issues came up during discussion (analysis of these issues will be left for the next section). They are given here in hardened form, that is, as most sharply stated during the sessions rather than as they became refined in the course of debate. When names in parentheses are cited on a particular side of a disagreement, it is for the purpose of locating the debate rather than to ascribe the hardened position to the persons involved—I hope no serious injustice is done here.

1. In the opening presentation (by Mr. Wionczek), as well as in later statements (especially those by Mr. Muller and Mr. Schomer), the MNCs were charged with creating havoc in host nations by their practices. Specifically, transfer pricing, the introduction of new technologies, ownership controls, and consumer orientation were said to be at the root of sovereignty problems, of unemployment, of balance-of-payment difficulties, of inequitable income distribution, or of cultural disruption.

160

On the other hand, others (such as Mr. Gerstacker and Mr. Hanold) contended that the MNC is vital to the harmonious economic development of nations.

2. It was argued that the self-interest and sovereignty of nation-states could be protected only by tough bargaining and renegotiation of agreements as the balance of power shifts over time (stated most emphatically by Mr. Wionczek, Mr. Reuther, and Mr. Moran).

In contrast, some (such as Mr. Gerstacker) stressed the point that constant renegotiation of terms is an inefficient way to carry on business. Approaching the issue quite differently, others (such as Mr. Wiener) noted that in a negotiating game, where each party tries to gain the highest advantage for itself, both sides and the world may lose.

3. It was suggested that MNCs would serve host countries well by engaging in the practice of phased withdrawal, not intending to maintain ownership (Mr. Ruttenberg and Mr. Schomer, with support from Mr. Escobar).

But this suggestion was disputed (by Mr. Hanold and others) with the argument that in a complex economic world phased withdrawal could mean disaster. Modern economic structures depend upon a constant flow of information and technology so that independence could be a competitive liability. Interdependence, not withdrawal—phased or otherwise—was held to be the key (Messrs. Hanold, Bennett, and Marshall).

4. Some claimed that the most important issues for discussion concerned the relations between MNCs and their host countries (Messrs. Wionczek, Alcala Sucre, Schomer). Others said that the most important issues concerned the relations between MNCs and their home countries (Mrs. Jager, Mr. Reuther).

Another participant (Mr. Muller) suggested that one of the most important areas of MNC impact is the international monetary structure.

5. The MNC was held up as the most efficient conduit for the flow of technology and vital information to the less developed nations (Messrs. Bennett, Alcala Sucre, Hanold, Gerstacker).

But the MNC was also accused of preventing genuine transfer of technology and of overpricing technology (Messrs. Wionczek, Muller).

6. The view was put forth that MNCs must take into account the macroeconomic effects of their activities (Mr. Muller). In contrast, the view was put forth that microeconomic units cannot do this for competitive or competence reasons or that they should not do it since it is the proper role of government to gauge and regulate macroeconomic matters (Messrs. De Rosso, Hanold).

7. Sovereignty is dead as a dodo (Mr. Hanold). Sovereignty is all we've got (numerous voices).

8. A plea was heard from several participants (Messrs. Joseph, Schomer, Reuther) for the development of transnational standards for the MNC. But other participants (Messrs. Marshall, Gage, Hanold, De Rosso) held that MNCs must act contextually—that is, they must conform to the customs and laws of the countries in which they operate. To do otherwise might be counted as "arrogance"—a word whose definition and implications proved elusive throughout the conference.

9. The hope was expressed that MNCs could fulfill their responsibilities by being good citizens (Messrs. Hanold, De Rosso). But this hope was blunted by the challenge that nothing an MNC did would give it citizenship status. There would always be a conflict between the interests of the MNC and the interests of the host country, and at best an MNC should be regarded as a resident alien (Mrs. Jager).

10. Some contended that an MNC could and should be politically neutral. But others argued that an MNC would almost inevitably be an interest group (Messrs. Barnds, Muller, Powers). It was pointed out that neutrality would at least appear to be impossible in cases where an MNC operated in two countries that were in conflict with each other (Mr. Escobar).

11. Some viewed the MNC as limited in its power at all points—that it lives and moves within a complex system of constraints. In contrast, others viewed the host country as always being at a disadvantage in face of the power of the MNC. Mr. Wiener reminded us that power relations and bargaining positions change through time.

12. Several participants proposed that host nations establish standards and constraints in advance; then the MNC should decide whether it can work within this framework economically and with a good conscience. But this view was charged with containing a misleading chronology by overlooking the dynamics of power and interests not only in deciding to enter a country but also after presence is established.

13. Finally, some participants presented a model of the MNC managers working within a network of legal, economic, and political constraints out of which policy emerged. In contrast some (Messrs. Powers, Joseph, Muller) suggested that when all the constraints had been accounted for, there was still room (discretionary space) for decisions of responsibility.

It is likely that I have overlooked disagreements of some magnitude and that characterizations have not always been accurate. But by giving them in their "pristine" form, I hope to have provoked some dialectic thought. At the very least the list provides background for the interpretative analysis that follows.

THE STRUCTURE OF OUR DISAGREEMENTS

Many of the disagreements, expressed above in polar form, are rooted not no much in strict contraditions as they are in the fact that we frequently spoke and responded to each other on different levels at different times. Mr. Wiener undoubtedly spoke for more than a few of us when he suggested that, like the judge, we not only found both sides of an argument persuasive, we also were convinced of the truth of the "naive" observation that both sides could not be right. What frequently happens is that two apparently contradictory propositions turn out to be more or less true depending upon the perspective or level from which the problem is viewed.

It seems to me that most of our discussion tended to fall into four different levels of understanding the MNC—or, to put the point in another way, when we discussed the impact of MNCs, we saw four different levels of impact, which in turn reflected differing views (either explicit or implicit) of what the MNC is. This in turn influenced the way in which the critical problem areas were defined, as well as the appropriate solutions to these problems. The four levels I have isolated from our discussions are (1) total cultural impact; (2) macroeconomic impact; (3) political-legal impact; and (4) the impact of ostensible, day-to-day conduct. (It should be stressed that while these levels are expressed in terms of the impact of the MNC on host and home countries, the reverse impact of nation-states on the MNC can also be understood in terms of these levels.) These levels can be expressed schematically as follows:

Kind of Impact	Perceived Nature of Problems and Problem Areas	Perceived Solutions
1. Cultural impact		
2. Macroeconomic impact		
3. Political-legal impact		
4. Impact of ostensible conduct		

Now before proceeding to explain each of these levels (and filling in the blank spaces) I want to note that not only did most of us tend to focus on one (or two) levels rather than the others, we also tended to view the other levels in terms of the level we chose to focus on. That is to say, persons tend to make one level the hub around which the others revolve or the key by which the others are understood. It is this, I suggest, that accounts for many of the differences listed in the previous section. In what follows, each level is analyzed to show who tended to look at the corporation from that perspective; what the problems of and those created by the MNC were when viewed from that perspective; and what the perceived solutions (if any) were.

1. Total cultural impact: This is the "upper-level" approach to the impact of the MNC (one might call it the "cosmic" approach), and it is not surprising that it was articulated most often (but not always) by the philosophers, metaphysicians, and theologians present. In a sense it lurked behind the other levels of discussion during the first sessions without being clearly expressed. Thus when we first considered the question "Should MNCs conduct themselves in host nations according to home standards or local standards?" we were touching on the problem of the MNC as the nexus of interaction between two cultures.

What is at stake here is the problem of cultural imperialism, and many persons (particularly those associated with the management of MNCs), eschewing the cultural imperialism that accompanied 19th-century economic imperialism, pleaded that MNCs avoid cultural arrogance by respecting and observing as much as possible the local standards of any host nation. But others of us were uneasy with this plea, arguing that, willy-nilly, an MNC was going to have dramatic impact on a host culture simply by virtue of its presence. We contended that MNCs change consumer orientations,* uproot traditional forms of family and village life by contributing to urbanization, introduce new forms of discipline and work with concomitant values, and may contribute to the widening gap between the rich and the poor. All of this would take place independently of conscious decisions about conduct or of business policy since the changes here described are an inherent characteristic of industrialization and modernization.

Now no one suggested that MNCs should solve this problem by staying out. But there were pleas for increased sensitivity to the kinds of cultural disjunctions that can and do occur, together with attempts at working, perhaps with local governments and groups, to alleviate any suffering and injustice that might occur as a consequence of the disjunctions. And here a point was contributed by Mr. Wiener in the

---

*Incidentally, we never addressed the issue of advertising in less developed nations. For some observers—for example, those who have highlighted the American company that cultivated a taste for Barbie Dolls in one of the most impoverished areas of Brazil—this is a crucial issue.

final session: The desire to respect local customs entirely (essentially the acceptance of 20th-century views of ethical relativism) may itself be a curious form of cultural imperialism or at least of cultural parochialism. For the radical acceptance of cultural relativity, together with a cultivated tolerance for a pluralism of values, is itself dependent upon a world view peculiar to only one class of people: the cosmopolitan class of persons who, educated chiefly by Western institutions, tend to manage international corporations in the home countries and tend to welcome MNCs in the host countries. Other classes of persons may not share this cosmopolitan tolerance and may indeed expect something quite different from those in positions of power and privilege.

Thus those who talked about the MNCs from this level tended to argue for something between cultural relativism and cultural imperialism (difficult as that point may be to define) and for increased sensitivity to the consequences, foreseen or unforeseen, of massive economic presence.

2. Macroeconomic impact: There was a sizable group among us that insisted that we address ourselves to the question of the impact of the MNC, a microeconomic institution, on the total economic structures of home nations, host nations, and international monetary processes—that is, on macroeconomic systems. The frequenters of this level of analysis tended to be the professional economists, the spokesmen for labor unions, and those who were involved in research on the internal dynamics of development in Latin American countries. This group deplored the propensity to separate micro- from macroeconomic analysis and argued that the MNC, as a relatively new kind of microstructure, was creating a new set of problems for macroeconomic analysis.

With respect to host countries, these participants tended to focus on the following contentions: that transfer pricing (a procedure that is possible only for large and complex corporations) could have the effect of creating artificially (that is, nonmarket) high prices for technology and imported goods and services—and that could create balance-of-payment problems for the host country; and that various methods of tax reporting without international controls contribute further to the previous problem. They also claimed that techniques of capitalization and recapitalization had the effect of removing capital from the host country or of engendering profit for home countries from host country savings; that MNC techniques of production are less labor-absorbing than indigenous industry, thus creating both unemployment and a larger gap between the rich and the poor; and finally, that from the standpoint of macroanalysis the MNC controls the flow of technology and thus prevents full transfer of technology to the host country.

With respect to home countries, the participants concentrating on this level of analysis argued that U.S. MNCs were creating a shortage of labor here with their expansion abroad; the export of technology would inevitably mean a loss to consumers at home; MNCs, by becoming economically independent (at least to some extent) of home countries, were in effect escaping the regulatory constraints of the U.S. political system and thus operating, consciously or unconsciously, as political entities.

Finally, with respect to international monetary issues, these conferees suggested that new methods of international capitalization and transactions were changing the structure of inflation problems in the world—that inflation now had to be understood not as a structural problem in one macrosystem but as the consequence in part of international transactions.

Now in all these arenas—host, home, and international structures— those who approached the MNC on this level tended to see the solutions to the problems in the development of new regulatory and monitoring devices and in the development of more sophisticated tools of economic and social analysis. Hence these participants stressed the need for one or more of the following remedies: (a) we need new regulations on disclosure so that governments have sufficient data to determine policy that affects inflation, balance of payments, and similar matters; (b) we need legislation that permits adaptation to shifting balances of power as the economic realities shift; (c) we need the development of tools of analysis that help us to foresee the impact of microactors on macroactors both economically and socially.

Now I think two more things need to be said in order to appreciate fully what was being said on this level of approach to the MNC. First, those who took this line of thinking insisted that we must deal with averages when speaking of the impact of microactors on macroactors. That is to say, no matter what the policy or nature of a given MNC, a macroactor or national economic system has to worry chiefly about the total effect of MNCs as a group. The effect of MNCs is experienced by host, home, and international structures as a group or average effect, not as a series of isolated relationships or skirmishes.

Secondly, those who emphasized this level of approach did not deny the reality of the problems on the other levels. Rather, they said that we could not talk about the total cultural impact without understanding the macroeconomic system—that cultural values and cultural changes and questions of social justice were abstract without reference to concrete economic relationships. Political-legal problems are very real, but the exercise of power by host nations is not so much rooted in our modern concepts of nationalism as it is in the fight for survival by macroactors whose structures are threatened by microactors. And while profound humanitarian concern expressed in the day-to-day conduct of an MNC may be a good thing, it does not touch the area of greatest impact on a host or home country. In short, this level of approach suggested that pursuit of the other levels would always flounder on the shoals of inadequate perception of economic realities.

One final point. Although those who stood on this level tended to worry about the impact of MNCs on macroactors, the plea for developing new tools of analysis and control was also made for the sake of the MNCs. That is, the claim was made that MNCs could not be content with microeconomic analysis if they hoped to survive in changing macrostructures.

3. Political-legal impact: Another group, including especially the representatives of corporations, law, and the U.S. Government, had a fundamentally juridical view of the MNC. That is to say, they saw the MNC formally as a creation of political and legal orders and therefore understood the corporation chiefly in terms of the original corporate charters and the legal contracts into which it entered. Those operating on this level of analysis recognize informal relationships and constraints embodied in various constituencies such as consumers, the general public, and the labor unions, but these informal constraints are still viewed from a political-legal model—that is, they are viewed as constituencies.

From the standpoint of this level of approach the chief problems of the MNCs in relation to host, home, and international communities lie in the making, clarification, and enforcing of contractual agreements, and in balancing the claims being made by the various constituencies, both formal (such as shareholders) and informal. The difficulties, when seen from this perspective, lie in the experience that such a balancing of claims is not simple, since the constituencies often assert self-interest without recognizing the kinds of interdependency that exist in practice and that are essential for modern economic life. Thus international corporations find that they are engaged in a continual tug-of-war with a rope that has more than two ends, as host and home governments attempt to bring corporate practice into line with foreign policy, as governments change their character and their demands, as constituencies refuse to act in the light of interests other than their own.

From the point of view of this level, in order to solve the most pressing problems raised by MNCs, legislation is needed to protect contracts and investments and to regularize procedures for negotiation and renegotiation. Further, reform should be pursued within the framework of existing constitutions and laws, for without these the search for world order and efforts to achieve justice proceed without a context and are subject to whim or unrestrained power.

What were the voices speaking from this level saying about the other levels of approach? Most, it seems, were making one or both of the following arguments: (a) the rumblings of nationalism in host countries may reflect attempts to deal with averages of impact on macroactors, but the fact remains that political groups do not behave purely according to economic interests. The realities are that MNCs constantly find themselves limited by the vagaries of foreign policy and the personal moods of a vast array of political actors who may have very little insight into economic structures—and this is true at home as well as abroad. (b) The attempt to deal with MNCs on the basis of averages overlooks their diversity and can create situations where good (or helpful) MNCs are punished or impaired for the sake of an average—thus also hurting the long-range interests of the host country.

A very important point was hidden below the surface of these arguments: It may be that microactors have dramatic macroimpact and that they also have powerful cultural effects. But to ask an MNC to take into account macroimpact or cultural impact is to ask it to move beyond legal constraints and essentially to assume more power for itself—literally, to meddle in political affairs.

This last point is most interesting in contrast to the second level of analysis. Those on the second level say, "You are having a meddling effect anyway, so let's address the issue and deal with it intelligently." The third level says, "This invites more trouble because it opens the door for MNCs to become even more powerful or to take direct political action. The indirect effect of MNCs must be dealt with by political and legal action in spite of the inefficiency of governments." Whatever failings political bodies and legal structures may have, they are the only guarantee against unchecked power by other groups.

4. Ostensible conduct of MNCs: Still another level of approach to the MNC looks at the day-to-day conduct of the corporation once it is involved in a host country (or in relation to the home country). From this point of view there are critical issues in the way companies handle employees and minority groups, the kinds of determinations they make about wages and safety conditions, the extent to which they pollute or ravish the countryside, and so on. Although some of these issues overlap with concerns expressed on the other levels, they are distinguished from the other concerns by virtue of the fact that they are the kinds of activities and problems that are traditionally associated with the moral conduct of individuals—basically they have to do with how the corporation behaves as "legal person" (the concern for the "good citizen").

It seems noteworthy to me that corporate responsibility has frequently been thought of in these terms alone, and some presentations made seemed to imply that corporate responsibility has to do with what the corporation does in its spare time or in its strictly extra-business capacities. * It is perhaps because of this that when MNCs

---

*Here a distinction made by John G. Simon, Charles W. Powers, and Jon P. Gunnemann in The Ethical Investor: Universities and Cor-

were accused of upsetting macroactors, some persons thought they were being accused of bad morality on this level (and there is, as I said, some overlap). Others seemed to suggest that all the issues on this level are merely functions of problems on other levels.

But a complete understanding of the voices on this level requires us to be open to the suggestion that questions of human rights cannot always be resolved in terms of macroeconomic analysis; nor is the cause of human rights exhausted by economic considerations. (Pollution can be understood as the externalization of the cost of production, but can discrimination against blacks be understood as an externalized cost?) Furthermore, there is no guarantee that the fulfillment of the technical legal requirements of good citizenship, the keeping of contracts, and so on, will resolve the problems of human rights, since there is no guarantee that an existing legal and political system cares about those rights.

So the voices from this perspective asked for attempts to formulate and adhere to transnational standards of human rights. Inevitably such attempts drive us back to the other levels, but they also force us to see human issues in a perspective that transcends either political or economic situations.

Which of these levels is to be preferred? It will not be a surprise if I say that all four levels should be held together and in tension. In fact, the conference did begin to move in this direction. But before trying to show how, I want to reflect briefly on the philosophical basis of the different levels.

THE PHILOSOPHICAL SOURCES
OF OUR DIFFERENT PERSPECTIVES

One reason we look at the MNC from different perspectives is simply that we have different experiential perspectives—or, to put it another way, different kinds of problems cross our desks. For the MNC manager the most pressing problems probably are political—or

---

porate Responsibility (New Haven, Conn.: Yale University Press, 1972) is instructive. It is the distinction between the negative injunction not to cause social injury and the less universally required duty to seek to reach out and help others. Confusion between these two types of activity has been a major contributing factor to making the debate about corporate responsibility so obscure and poorly focused.

at least they are experienced as political problems in the sense that the manager has to deal with regulatory agencies, the state departments of various countries, politicians in power and out of power: This is the form the problems take, and the manager knows that if he does not deal with these political constraints other than in an expected or acceptable political manner, he is likely to get into deeper trouble. Host country leaders see unbalanced budgets, increasing unemployment, and demonstrations for food. Labor union leaders see fewer jobs, increased consumer costs, and less contact with the managers who make the decisions. Many church leaders are faced with starvation, illiteracy, and discrimination in their parishes or see their religiously based mandate as focusing on those issues. One of the functions of a conference such as this is to permit each of us to see what problems cross the desk (or floor) of the other guy.

But people also have different <u>moral</u> experiences, that is, different experiences of the manner in which moral questions get raised. Perhaps required reading for this conference should have been Reinhold Niebuhr's <u>Moral Man and Immoral Society</u>, [1] which, though written in the early 1930s, still illuminates critical social issues. One of the distinctions made by Niebuhr is between individual morality and group morality, and it runs something like this:

There are persons, particularly members of the middle class, who are taught a high moral code of respect for the individual, of integrity and honesty, of trust and the importance of promise-keeping. Not only are they taught this, but their experience demonstrates that this morality works—that is, it permits humane relationships and a high degree of freedom without injury to others. Thus they engage in moral persuasion, personal covenants and contracts and would prefer suffering economic loss to compromising their standards. They are deeply suspicious of mass movements and decisions that are made on the basis of coercion and pressure.

There are other persons, particularly members of the working classes (but including many more) who find that moral issues arise not so much in interpersonal contacts but in relationships between groups. By experience they have learned that justice is not a function of their individual situation but rather of the situation of the group to which they belong. To the extent that they have access to the good or humane life it is the consequence of a <u>concerted</u> effort to fight for higher wages, better retirement plans, shorter hours, and so on. To put it another way, <u>they feel moral issues in terms of averages</u>. What counts is not the keeping of promises but the average quantifications of their situation in relation to the averages of other groups. They are deeply suspicious of those who advocate high individual morality, not because such advocacy is insincere (though it may be), but because it does not improve their averages or the averages for those about whom they are concerned.

According to Niebuhr, each of these moral experiences has both strengths and weaknesses. The former makes possible deep and constructive human relationships but, in trying to apply individual morality to the relationships of groups and classes, overlooks the extent to which justice is a function of economic power. The latter view understands power relations very clearly and knows that power can be met only with power in the pursuit of justice, but it tends to forget that human dignity is not simply a function of economic situation. I think we all tend to work out of one of these camps more than the other, and it accounts in part for our different perspectives.

But there is a third reason for our differences. What we call modern capitalism was born in the 17th century in a philosophical tradition in England called "philosophic radicalism" (is it not wondrous that the first capitalists were called "radicals"?). The philosophic radicals, including Jeremy Bentham, Adam Smith, James Mill, and David Ricardo arrived at certain theses about individual and concerted human action, which they then applied to economic issues and political and legal reform.[2] We all share to some extent the major assumptions of their work, and it may be helpful here to delineate just two of these. The first (and most famous) assumption or thesis is that in the economic realm individual pursuits of self-interest will blend with each other to form a natural identity of interests. The market system will assure that no one individual's interest will violate others. But the second assumption is that in the political realm there is no natural harmony of interests. At most we can hope for the artificial identification of interests through the creation of political institutions and laws that force the individual to consider and pursue the common good.

Now if we accept these premises, we will always tend to view the political realm as the arena of the less beautiful human passions and as the source of most human conflict. And we will expect of political institutions, as inefficient as they may be, at least the attempt to free economic institutions so that the needs of mankind can be satisfied. In this view the problems that beset MNCs and the economic structures they live in are not rooted in economic issues as much as they are in political wilfulness and ineptitude.

But not everyone here seems willing to accept these premises unquestioningly. They are sufficiently influenced by some version of neo-Marxism (I trust I can use this term without raising hackles or causing fear) to question particularly the first assumption of the philosophic radicals and to suggest that we have no guarantee that there is a natural identity of interests in the economic realm. The source of many of our ills may lie in economic structures themselves, and

171

therefore stabilizing political conditions and securing contractual arrangements will not be sufficient. (Note, incidentally, that one would become a full Marxist in the usual sense of the term only if one also denied the second assumption of the philosophic radicals—that is, if one denied that there were sources of human conflict independent of the economic realm. No one at the conference appeared to take that position.)

So we have different problem experiences, different moral experiences, and perhaps different philosophical perspectives. Yet in spite of these differences we did seem to move toward the awareness that all four levels of approach to the MNC had to be held together. First we tried to be conscious of the different perceptions of the MNC that were at work in our utterances; then we tried to look at the MNC as a system of relationships and, within that system, to find where there would be the freedom and power to act for beneficial change. But when we tried to look at the system as a whole, we discovered that we still used different maps as our guides. As Mr. Wionczek suggested, the MNC is engaged in an nth dimensional war—the total system of relationships and the total process of action are far too complex for the analysis and remedies for the problems they uncovered to emerge from a four-day discussion.

PROGNOSIS AND FURTHER AGREEMENT

Apart from the positive tendency just mentioned, there was movement toward consensus on some of the following:

1. Unbridled bargaining, where each party seeks to gain the highest advantage for itself, does not work to the benefit of any party in the long run. This was clearly stated by a corporate manager, by a representative of Latin American countries, and by a game-theorist.

2. Given the pluralism of problems and relations, as well as the diversity of MNCs, continued bargaining and renegotiation are inevitable as the balance of power continually shifts.

3. Therefore an informal system of countervailing power will develop much as such a system developed in response to corporate growth in this country. And Mr. Escobar reported that countervailing powers are already discernible.

4. There is and will be increasing pressure for the development of more formal international regulatory devices for MNCs. The source of this pressure comes chiefly from macroactors—as host countries and groups within them reanalyze the impact of MNCs on their interests and as those responsible for international monetary problems try

to come to grips with a changing financial structure. But the MNCs themselves are looking in this direction and were encouraged to do so for their own self-interest.

5. If such mechanisms do emerge, there was growing consensus that they will focus on three levels of international control:

(a) Regulations governing <u>conduct</u> and the keeping of contracts and agreements.

(b) Regulations on <u>information</u> (disclosure, tax-reporting).

(c) Institutions or centers to formalize conflict and bargaining.

The pattern that emerges from all these developments—some already in process, some projected—is one in which the multinational corporation will find itself under increasing pressures and restrictions. As the less developed countries in Latin America and elsewhere become more sophisticated in their economic analysis, in the development of regulatory devices, and in the training of civil servants to utilize those devices, the balance of power will shift in their direction and a good number of MNCs may find their situations too restrictive. If LDCs combine their knowledge and join together for bargaining leverage (as the oil countries have done), multinationals may soon find that they are the first to get on the bandwagon for international controls as a way of protecting their own interests.

This analysis and projection may be carried a step further: A large number of participants in the consultation, representing many different points of view, expressed the concern that the governments of the less developed nations are passing those of the more developed nations (usually home countries of the MNCs) in understanding and controlling the activities of the large multinationals. If this is indeed the case—and I believe the evidence for it is strong (see, for example, Ronald Muller's paper in Chapter 7)—then very soon the multinational corporation is going to be the chief instrument by which less developed nations "squeeze" the advanced nations economically. At this writing, that squeeze has already begun in dramatic form by the oil-producing countries. While extraction industries are almost surely the most susceptible to such a squeeze (indeed, foreign-owned extraction companies may soon be a thing of the past), there is no reason to assume that similar pressure, perhaps more subtle in form, cannot be exerted on other forms of multinationals as well. [3] This is certainly the case once a company has become "captive"—that is, when it has made a capital investment in a country but has not realized a return sufficient to cover that investment.

We are faced then with a remarkable irony: Whereas many people in the debates presented above and in other places have worried about the extent to which multinational corporations represent a threat to the "Third World," there is good reason to believe that many of the less developed nations will take care of themselves, at least as economic national units. One might argue therefore that the ethical concern for justice, human rights, and other values expressed by many in relation to MNC activity is unfounded—such concern applies to a transitory period in the life of less developed nations. Such a view, however, totally misses the complexity of the problem of human justice and the human good in relation to economic structures. The fact that certain national units can hold their own in relation to the huge MNCs in no way guarantees that there will be concomitant economic justice and concern for human rights. On the contrary, many human problems will be exacerbated, others simply shifted from one place to another. Consider the following areas of concern.

As the oil crisis demonstrated, powerful national units can tighten belts and hold their own, but within those national units certain groups of people may suffer disproportionately. In this country inflation does not affect all groups with equal force, a point always appreciated by labor unions but now seen by others. The outlook for those large numbers of Americans who stand outside the large institutional structures of our society (and the labor unions constitute one of those institutional structures), for the "other America," is drastically dismal.

So also there are entire nations that are dependent in secondary and tertiary fashion upon oil in order to feed their population. That people in India should starve to death because U.S.-produced fertilizer has been priced out of reach now becomes a problem not just for the United States, or for U.S.-based companies but for the Arab countries as well. The remarkable interdependence of the world economy does not dispense with issues of economic and social justice but makes the issues more complex.

Moreover, there are many countries and populations that lie outside the kind of power struggle and "squeeze" here depicted. Many of these, such as countries in sub-Saharan Africa, have neither the natural resources nor the political, social, and economic infrastructure to attract multinationals, to attract capital investments at all. They have always fallen outside the development process promised by the champions of multinational enterprises, and there is every indication that their plight will worsen in the squeeze process. In other words, the distinction between the "haves" and the "have-nots" will soon apply to groupings within what has in the recent past been considered a homogeneous world of "have-nots."

Finally, national governments can achieve considerable power in relation to MNCs without distributing their gains equitably to their populations. It is a reasonable hypothesis, however, that governments that are most sophisticated in the analysis of their internal economic difficulties, and committed to economic development for the benefit of all, will also be the most sophisticated in dealing with and regulating foreign-owned companies. Multinationals may find that, at least for a short time span, the easiest countries to deal with are those in which the ruling classes are least interested in the welfare of the general populations. I leave it for the reader to decide whether the complex U.S. involvement in Chile reflects this dilemma.

In short, the shifting balances of power in relation to the multinational corporation and among nation-states will make questions of economic and social justice more complex; the questions will not disappear. If the problems that persist, and the new ones that arise, are not to be treated merely with finger-in-the-dike emergency relief programs, if multinationals are to make a positive contribution to human development, if multinationals are not to align increasingly with regressive governments, if multinational corporations survive at all— all these questions are likely to depend for their answer on the capacity of the MNCs to entertain new kinds of economic and social questions. Plant location may be more important than ever before. Attempts to fit production requirements to local labor and social requirements may be critical for long-term tenure. The ability of a corporation to anticipate and articulate in advance the kinds of economic and social problems a host nation will face may be decisive in that country's determination of the helpfulness or unhelpfulness of a foreign presence. This may engage multinational corporations in kinds of analysis to which they are not accustomed. But if they do not do this on their own, they will be forced into it by ever tighter regulations and controls—or they will be forced out.

NOTES

1. New York: Scribner's, 1932.
2. See Elie Halevy, The Growth of Philosophic Radicalism (Boston: Beacon, 1934). Some of the terminology I use here comes from Halevy.
3. A full analysis of the susceptibility of multinational corporations to the pressures of national governments and private competition would require a breakdown of types of multinationals according to structure, financing, product (or sector of economy), market, and so on. Increasingly, such distinctions are being made. For example, Jack N. Behrman in many of his writings has distinguished among the colonial form of investment (which establishes a subsidiary in a foreign country for the purpose of exploiting the resources there for the home country), the "international holding company" (which has a subsidiary for the purpose of serving the host market), and the genuine multinational enterprise (which integrates financing, market,

product, and so on across national lines). The first two are most sus-
ceptible to host country pressures. See "Social Investment Issues
Raised by Foreign Operations of Multinational Enterprises," People/
Profits: The Ethics of Investments, ed. by Charles W. Powers (New
York: Council on Religion and International Affairs, 1972).

THE IMPACT OF MULTINATIONAL OIL COMPANIES
ON VENEZUELA: THE OIL COMPANIES IN GENERAL
AND GULF OIL CORPORATION IN PARTICULAR
Luis Alcala Sucre

In recent years the multinational companies have become a favorite subject of numerous distinguished authors, and many and varied are the opinions that the latter have formed and expressed regarding the influence that those companies exert on the economic and even the political life of the less developed nations where they operate.

Venezuela, notwithstanding the significant progress it has made in the last four decades, is still far from being a fully developed country, and it has felt and is still feeling the impact of the multinational enterprises. The purpose of this Appendix is to discuss this impact, and this will be done by focusing on the international oil companies, because for years oil has been this country's lifeline, and there is no doubt that this situation will not change significantly in the foreseeable future. Furthermore, in order to exemplify what the oil companies have done or failed to do particular attention will be given to the activities of the Mene Grande Oil Company (a Gulf Oil Corporation subsidiary commonly known by the abbreviated name Meneg), especially in Eastern Venezuela, where this company is the principal producer. Throughout the Appendix, Gulf's Venezuelan subsidiary will be referred to as Meneg, even though prior to 1937 it was known as Venezuela Gulf Oil Company.

It should also be pointed out that in 1937 International Petroleum Company bought 50 percent interest in Meneg and later sold half of its purchase to Shell. Meneg, however, is the operator and is fully responsible for the actions of the company. The same holds true for the so-called Vengref refinery at Puerto La Cruz, which is owned two-thirds by Gulf and one-third by Texaco and is operated by Meneg. Therefore, when the term "Meneg-operated" is used in the paper in connection with statistics, it covers Gulf's as well as the partners' share of the particular item.

Finally, it should be understood that unless otherwise noted specifically, the opinions expressed in this Appendix are strictly the writer's own.

VENEZUELAN POLITICAL BACKGROUND
AND DEMOGRAPHICS

It is believed that for a better understanding of what will be covered in the following sections of this Appendix, a brief summary of the political history and demographics of the country should prove helpful.

Political Background

To trace the political history of Venezuela from the year 1830, when General Jose Antonio Paez became the country's first president, would lengthen this presentation unduly without serving a truly useful purpose, so we will begin with the era of General Juan Vicente Gomez, because it was during his regime that the international oil companies arrived.

General Cipriano Castro, president and dictator since 1899, made the mistake of taking a long European trip, and General Gomez took advantage of this to engineer a bloodless and successful coup in November 1908. He promulgated the first Law of Hydrocarbons on June 19, 1920, and the second approximately one year later.

General Gomez died on December 17, 1935, and General Eleazar Lopez Contreras assumed control of the country. He was elected president by the National Congress on April 25 of the following year and governed until April 28, 1941, when the National Congress elected General Isaias Medina Angarita to succeed him. It was during the latter's tenure of office that, on March 13, 1943, the Congress passed a new Law of Hydrocarbons, the implications of which will be mentioned in another section of this Appendix.

General Medina Angarita did not serve out his term of office. A group of army colonels led a coup that deposed him on October 18, 1945. However, contrary to the tradition of military control of the government, they did not keep the power but formed a "revolutionary junta" and installed Romulo Betancourt, a civilian, as its president. At the time, he was the head of Accion Democratica, a left-of-center political party he had founded several years earlier. One of this junta's first steps that affected the oil companies was taken on December 31, 1945 and consisted of the levying of an extraordinary tax of (U.S.) $22.3 million on their profits.

Betancourt went on to organize a genuinely free election in 1948, in which his party's candidate was Mr. Romulo Gallegos, a world-renowned novelist, who won the presidency by a substantial majority.

Gallegos, however, held office less than a year, for the same group of colonels who in 1945 had made Betancourt chief of state staged another coup on November 24 and placed the government under the control of a three-man military junta headed by Lt. Col. Carlos Delgado Chalbaud. Betancourt was exiled, and his Accion Democratica was outlawed.

Lt. Col. Delgado Chalbaud was assassinated on November 13, 1950, and a civilian, Dr. German Suarez Flamerich, became president of the junta. But the power behind the throne was Col. Marcos Perez Jimenez who came out in the open as a dictator on December 2, 1952. In 1956 and 1957 his defacto regime granted extensive oil concessions, which gave new life to the petroleum industry.

A popular uprising, with military support, deposed Perez Jimenez on January 23, 1958, and a provisional government junta, headed first by Rear Admiral Wolfgang Larrazabal and then by Dr. Edgar Sanabria, was established. It called for elections, and on December 7 of that year Mr. Romulo Betancourt won them handily. However, even before he took the oath of office on February 13, 1958, the first hard "democratic" blow was struck at the oil companies when, on December 19, 1958, Acting President Sanabria, no doubt with President-elect Betancourt's knowledge and blessing, issued a decree by which the income tax underwent a drastic upward revision.

Mr. Betancourt was succeeded by Dr. Raul Leoni, another leader of the Accion Democratica, who was elected president on December 1, 1963, and was sworn in on March 11 of the following year. As a whole, his regime was fair to the private oil industry in that it recognized the international competitive aspects of the business and refrained from swamping it with a flood of oppressive and discouraging legislation.

Elections were held again in 1969, and on December 1 of that year Dr. Rafael Caldera, the leader of the Social Christian Party, COPEI, defeated several candidates and became president-elect. Nine days later he announced the adoption of a nationalistic oil policy, which, as we shall see later, has characterized his regime.

Venezuelan Demographics

Venezuela is 352,051 square miles in area. Politically, it is divided into one "federal district," two "federal territories," and 20 states. Table A.1 lists Venezuela's population for selected years.

Table A.1 has been included to give an idea of the rapid growth of Venezuela's population, especially since 1950. The increase has multiplied the social needs of the country, and ever larger budgets

TABLE A.1

Venezuela's Population

Census Year	Population
1971	10,721,522
1961	7,523,999
1950	5,034,838
1941	3,850,771
1936	3,364,347

Source: Annual Report of the Ministry of Development for the Year 1972.

TABLE A.2

Population by Age Group

Age Group	Number	Percent of Total
19 and under	6,072,948	56.64
20-34	2,230,574	20.82
35-49	1,377,128	12.84
50-64	725,259	6.76
Over 64	315,613	2.94
Total	10,721,522	100.00

Source: Annual Report of the Ministry of Development for 1972.

based principally on fiscal income from hydrocarbons are required
to satisfy them. This fiscal income comes primarily from payments
made by the oil companies, and as a result they are continually ex-
posed to pyramiding demands for the lion's share of their profits.

Of at least equal significance is the division of the population by
age groups. Table A.2 shows the distribution of the total determined
by the 1971 census.

Evidently, Venezuela's is predominantly a young population. This
fact increases the demands for educational facilities on one hand and
jobs on the other. Any political party that has been victorious at the
polls and aspires to reelection must meet these demands, and it does
so by undertaking ambitious school construction programs, which is
commendable, and more often than not by implementing extensive and
expensive bureaucratic plans to create employment opportunities,
which is not so commendable. The millions required for this must
come from the nation's coffers, and in the case of Venezuela the
inflow into those coffers stems mainly from the taxes and other economic burdens that are placed on the private oil companies.

THE BIRTH AND GROWTH OF THE OIL INDUSTRY
IN VENEZUELA: ITS DIRECT IMPACT ON THE
ECONOMY OF THE NATION

History of the Industry

Oil and asphalt seeps were observed in Venezuela long before
the arrival of the international oil companies. As a matter of fact,
historians assert that upon landing in Venezuela toward the end of
the 15th century Columbus used the asphalt to caulk his ships. They
also report that the Venezuelan Indians attributed medicinal properties
to the oil and smeared it on their heads and bodies. However, oil
was ignored as a commercial product until 1878, when Don Antonio
Pulido and five associates founded the Compania Petrolia del Tachira
in what is today the State of Tachira, and obtained a 250-acre concession in the Rubio District of that state.

One of Pulido's associates traveled all the way to the Pennsylvania oilfields to learn how to drill a well and brought back a drilling
rig. It was hauled piece by piece on mule back to the concession, but
the rig was damaged on the first attempt to use it and was discarded.
The partners turned to picks and shovels and dug pits where the oil
would gather and from which it was pumped with an old-style hand
pump. Eventually the company built a primitive still with a daily

capacity of 15 barrels per day, and the kerosene obtained was sold in the neighboring communities.

Petrolia del Tachira lasted until August 8, 1934, when the concession rights lapsed. At the end it was not much more than when it started, but there are Venezuelans who remember it with pride and, being unfamiliar with the intricacies of the modern oil business, say, "We were the first to produce our oil; we should be producing it now."

Venezuela's first oil well was drilled by the Bermudez Oil Company, a subsidiary of General Asphalt, in the State of Sucre. On August 15, 1913, at a depth of 615 feet the bit struck oil. The initial rejoicing disappeared soon, because the oil was so thick and heavy that it could hardly be pumped. Other wells were drilled on the concession, but they yielded the same kind of undesirable crude.

The Caribbean Petroleum Company, a subsidiary of Shell, had better luck. On July 31, 1914, the company completed the first truly commercial oil well in Venezuela. The well came in at Mene Grande, a community in the State of Zulia. This well's initial production was 250 barrels per day, but, more significantly, it discovered the oil-rich Lake Maracaibo Basin. The company quickly drilled other producing wells and laid a pipeline to the lakeside town of San Lorenzo, where it also built a refinery and a terminal. It was from there, in September 1917, that the first export of Venezuelan oil was made.

But the well that really started the Venezuelan oil boom was Shell's Barroso no. 2. This well was drilled on the outskirts of the village of La Rosa, about three-quarters of a mile from the lake shore, and on December 14, 1922, it came in so strongly and unexpectedly that control was lost. The "blowout" lasted nine days, during which the well spewed an estimated 850,000 barrels of oil.

The news of the discovery was soon flashed around the world. The New York Times, in describing the gusher, called it "the most productive in the world." The rush to acquire concessions was on, but the newcomers found themselves facing a discouraging fact: Shell had title to every square inch of land in the District of Bolivar, and that is where the oil was. The only unleased land in the Maracaibo Basin was the floor of the lake itself. Even a portion of that was under lease, but not by anyone who intended to drill it. It had been taken by companies and individuals who dealt in the buying and selling of leases. They had taken the acreage in order to acquire concessions considered to be more valuable. Like most everyone else they felt that drilling in Lake Maracaibo would be a foolish if not impossible task.

Gulf did not share that view and on March 23, 1923, formed the Venezuela Gulf Oil Company, later to be known as the Mene Grande Oil Company (Meneg). It acquired its first concessions in the so-called kilometer Strip, a zone that encircled the lake and extended from the shore one kilometer out into the water.

TABLE A.3

Venezuelan Oil Production
(thousands of barrels)

| Period | Meneg Operated | | | Total Venez. All Companies | Percent of Total Ven. Operated by Meneg |
	West. Ven.	East. Ven.	Total		
1917-69	997,407	2,949,294	3,946,701	24,948,617	15.8
1970	59,737	122,289	182,026	1,353,420	13.4
1971	60,438	115,285	175,723	1,295,406	13.6
1972	56,336	112,429	168,765	1,178,487	14.3
Totals	1,173,918	3,299,297	4,473,215	28,775,930	15.5

Sources: Annual Report of the Ministry of Mines and Hydrocarbons for the Year 1972 and Meneg's Production Department Files.

TABLE A.4

Venezuelan Oil Production by Region
(thousands of barrels)

| Region | 1971 | | | | 1972 | | | |
	Meneg Oper.	Others	Total	Meneg Percent of Tot.	Meneg Oper.	Others	Total	Meneg Percent of Tot.
W.V.	60,438	990,952	1,051,390	5.7	56,336	893,433	949,769	5.9
E.V.	115,285	108,130	223,415	51.6	112,429	97,574	210,003	53.5
C.V.	—	20,601	20,601	—	—	18,715	18,715	—
Totals	175,723	1,119,683	1,295,406	13.6	168,765	1,009,722	1,178,487	14.3

Sources: Annual Report of the Ministry of Mines and Hydrocarbons for the Year 1972 and Meneg's Production Department Files.

On August 31, 1924 Gulf completed its first commercial well, and the ensuing intensive drilling program produced one success after another. An oceangoing terminal was built at Las Piedras on Paraguana Peninsula in the State of Falcon, and the first export of crude was made from there on March 21, 1925.

Meneg, because its attractive acreage in Western Venezuela was, and is, small compared to that held by Shell and the Creole Petroleum Corporation (a subsidiary of today's Exxon), the two giants in that area, never attained the importance of those two companies, at least not from the standpoint of production. In Eastern Venezuela, however, the story is different. There, on June 16, 1937, the company discovered the fabulous Central Oficina field in the State of Anzoategui and soon thereafter became the most important oil company operating in that region. These and other facts are brought out in Tables A.3 and A.4.

In addition to quantifying the fact that as regards production Meneg is comparatively small in Western Venezuela but is large in the Eastern part of the country, both preceding tables show indirectly that the 1970-71 and 1971-72 interannual declines in Meneg's production were less than those corresponding to the industry as a whole. It is important to call attention to this, because the declines in the industry's production were severely criticized by politicians of most parties and in not a few instances were interpreted maliciously.

Impact on the Economy

Before the start of the commercial production of oil, and even during the first eight years of the latter, Venezuela was primarily an agricultural country. Its main exports were coffee and cocoa, and it was not until 1925 that, based on value, oil became the number-one export product. As the years passed, the role played by hydrocarbons gained importance, as evidenced by Tables A.5 and A.6.

The preceding figures have not been converted to U.S. dollars because to do so would be misleading, since the rate of exchange of the petroleum dollar, that is, the rate at which the oil companies must buy bolivars from the Central Bank of Venezuela, has fluctuated through the years. For example, in 1960 it was B 3.09/$1, for 1970 and 1971 it was B 4.40/$1, and in 1972 it became B 4.30/$1. Actually the principal significance of the table is that it shows how the fiscal income from hydrocarbons has grown not only in absolute terms but also as a percentage of the total.

The contribution of oil and gas to the gross national product has also been substantial, as indicated in Table A.7.

TABLE A.5

Composition of Value of Exports
(in percentages)

	1968	1969	1970	1971
Hydrocarbons	92.8	91.3	90.2	92.2
Iron ore	4.1	5.2	5.5	4.5
Coffee	0.3	0.5	0.5	0.4
Cocoa	0.3	0.3	0.3	0.2
Fish	0.2	0.2	0.4	0.4
Iron products	0.7	0.7	0.6	0.3
Aluminum	0.1	0.2	0.3	0.2
Others	1.5	1.6	2.2	1.8
Totals	100.0	100.0	100.0	100.0

Source: Annual Report of the Central Bank of Venezuela for the Year 1971 (the Report for 1972 has not been issued as yet).

TABLE A.6

Ordinary Fiscal Income

Year	Total Income (millions of bolivars)	Income from Hydrocarbons (millions of bolivars)	Percent Corresponding to Hydrocarbons
1920	82	1	1.2
1930	244	47	19.3
1940	330	98	29.7
1950	1,917	901	47.0
1960	4,968	3,248	65.4
1970	9,498	5,774	60.8
1971	11,637	7,760	65.3
1972	12,192	7,967	67.1

Source: Annual Report of the Ministry of Finance for the Year 1972.

TABLE A. 7

Gross National Product

Year	Total GNP (millions of bolivars)	Percent Corresponding to Hydrocarbons
1968	42,119	17.2
1969	43,665	16.3
1970	46,744	14.6
1971	52,350	16.1

Source: Annual Report of the Central Bank of Venezuela for the Year 1971.

Still another parameter by which the importance of hydrocarbons to the Venezuelan economy can be measured is the inflow of foreign exchange, summarized in Table A. 8.

The contribution of the oil industry in general and of Meneg in particular to the economic and social welfare of the nation will be discussed in the next section.

TABLE A. 8

Inflow of Foreign Exchange
(millions of dollars)

	1970	1971
From all sources	2,640	3,421
From hydrocarbons	1,686	2,165
Percent from hydrocarbons	63.9	60.4

Source: Annual Report of the Central Bank of Venezuela for the Year 1971.

CONTRIBUTIONS OF THE OIL INDUSTRY IN GENERAL AND OF MENEG IN PARTICULAR TO THE ECONOMIC AND SOCIAL WELFARE OF THE COMMUNITY

This section will be divided into six parts, entitled and defined as follows:

1. Direct economic contributions to the government: These are the payments made to the government for concession rights, as well as the disbursements covering royalty, taxes (income, surface, and so on) and other miscellaneous items such as customs duties.

2. Indirect contributions to the government: These include technical assistance and training of government personnel.

3. Direct economic contributions to the employees: These cover all cash payments, including wages and salaries, share in the profits, housing allowance, vacation bonus, overtime and night work bonuses, and other miscellaneous payments of lower relative importance. Also in this category, but shown separately, are the capital and operating expenditures in facilities such as schools, housing, and hospitals for company personnel.

4. Indirect contributions to the employees: These comprise training, counseling, and all other assistance not in the form of cash payments made directly to the working force.

5. Direct economic contributions to the rest of the community: These are the cash contributions made to nonprofit organizations (educational, cultural, religious) that serve the community. Likewise included, but again shown separately, are the capital and operating expenditures in facilities such as roads and bridges, churches, and recreational areas.

6. Indirect contributions to the rest of the community: These include all noncash contributions, such as assistance in organizing firefighting units, donations of land and equipment, city planning advice, preference for local goods.

Direct Economic Contributions to the Government

Table A. 9 shows Meneg's payments for its concession rights.

After 1950 the only years of concession acquirements were 1956 and 1957, when, under the Perez Jimenez regime, 13 companies (including Meneg, which obtained 226,000 acres), received 2,029,000 acres of new leases, mainly in the Lake Maracaibo area.

TABLE A.9

Cost of Concessions
(millions of dollars)

Period	Western Ven.	Eastern Ven.	Total
1923–50	6.3	15.5	21.8
1956–57	137.6	—	137.6
Totals	143.9	15.5	159.4

Source: Meneg files.

TABLE A.10

Other Direct Economic Contribution to Government
(millions of dollars)

Year	Total All Companies	Meneg Oper.	Meneg Percent of All
1966	1,099.1	135.9	12.4
1967	1,240.9	141.3	11.4
1968	1,252.9	155.2	12.4
1969	1,255.9	147.2	11.7
1970	1,409.1	141.8	10.1
1971	1.715.0	212.9	12.4
1972	1,961.2	226.7	11.6

Sources: Annual Report of the Ministry of Mines and Hydro-carbons for the Year 1972; and Meneg files.

Table A. 10, covering the period 1966-72, pertains to the direct economic contributions to the government other than payments for leases.

A tabulation of the years prior to 1966 would be superfluous, but to complete the Meneg picture it is in order to mention that its direct contributions to the government from the beginning of its operations in 1923 through 1972 totaled $3.3282 billion.

The seven years listed are sufficient to illustrate a trend: The government's "take" rose in 1967 as a consequence of an increase in the income tax and of the five-year tax reference value agreement between the National Executive and the companies, and then it leveled off until 1970, when a sharp interannual climb started as a result of higher income tax obligations and substantial rises in the tax reference values. Additional comments on these developments will be made in another section of this paper.

Indirect Contributions to the Government

Referring now only to Meneg, the company has offered and given specialized training to personnel of the Ministry of Mines and Hydrocarbons. For example, a reservoir engineering course prepared by Meneg's Production Department in Eastern Venezuela was made available not only to company personnel but also to Ministry engineers.

Also, in its various facilities the company has provided summer vacation work and training opportunities for university students sponsored by the Ministry of Mines and Hydrocarbons.

Direct Economic Contributions to the Employees

The numerical fluctuations in the oil industry's and Meneg's personnel and those in the remuneration paid by Meneg are reflected in Table A. 11 year by year for the period 1966-72.

Table A. 11 refers only to personnel on the companies' payrolls. Reliable statistics pertaining to the personnel of contractors who work exclusively or predominantly for the oil industry were not available. As regards the steady decrease in the number of workers, it can be attributed to a combination of causes, the principal ones being curtailment of some operations and consolidation of others.

It should also be noted that the decision not to compare the remuneration paid by Meneg with the industry average was prompted by the

TABLE A.11

Oil Industry and Meneg Personnel: Meneg Yearly Remuneration

| | Number of Employees | | | Meneg Oper. Remuneration | |
| | All Cos. | Meneg Oper. | Meneg Percent of All | Total (millions of dollars) | Per Capita (dollars) |
Year					
1966	29,448	3,619	12.3	24.9	6,880
1967	27,022	3,200	11.8	23.1	7,220
1968	25,419	3,106	12.2	22.7	7,310
1969	24,521	2,969	12.1	26.8	9,030
1970	23,993	2,876	12.0	25.5	8,850
1971	23,714	2,782	11.7	25.8	9,280
1972	22,584	2,726	12.1	26.8	9,830

Sources: Annual Report of the Ministry of Mines and Hydrocarbons for the Year 1972 and Meneg files.

existence of several distorting variables such as, for example, the fact that some companies pay somewhat higher base salaries but charge realistic rentals for housing in their camps, whereas others (Meneg among them) subsidize the house rent. However, the take-home pay of Meneg workers is well in line with that received by the personnel of the rest of the industry and certainly exceeds by far the national average for all industries.

Finally it is important to point out that a new three-year collective contract was subscribed to by the oil industry and the Federation of Petroleum Workers on July 20, 1973 and that, in addition to expanding several fringe benefits, this contract will increase the take-home pay of the oil industry personnel by approximately 15 percent.

In Table A.12 capital outlay and expenses for maintaining facilities for personnel are shown with a breakdown for Western and Eastern Venezuela.

Approximately 80 percent of the capital expenditures were incurred during the first thirty years of Meneg's life (1923-52). This is understandable, because it was during that period that most construction of housing, schools, hospitals, clubs, commissaries, and so on, took place in Western Venezuela (mainly in Maracaibo, Cabimas, Lagunillas, and Las Piedras) and in Eastern Venezuela (mainly in San Tome, Oficina, and Puerto La Cruz).

Indirect Contributions to Meneg Personnel

Early in its life Meneg launched a scholarship program for its eligible workers and members of their families (as well as for a number of carefully selected outsiders, many of whom joined the

TABLE A.12

Capital and Operating Expenditures in Facilities
for Meneg Personnel, 1923-72
(millions of dollars)

	Capital	Operating
Western Ven.	359.3	14.1
Eastern Ven.	890.4	53.5
Totals	1,249.7	67.5

Source: Meneg files

191

TABLE A. 13

Meneg Investment in Training and Education, 1923-72
(millions of dollars)

	West. Ven.*	East. Ven.	Total
Scholarships	1.9	0.4	2.3
Other	4.7	4.3	9.0
Totals	6.6	4.7	11.3

* Includes Caracas.
Source: Meneg files.

company following graduation), which produced quite a number of
engineers, geologists, accountants, nurses, technicians, teachers,
and so on. Side by side, it initiated a program of training and education for company personnel, their relatives and some outsiders, in
various educational centers located in the United States and abroad.
The investment in the latter program is listed as "other" in Table A.13.

Not included in Table A.13, because from the existing records they
would be difficult to quantify in terms of money outlays, are the many
and varied intracompany educational programs sponsored by the company—to name but a few: on- and off-the-job training in various trades
such as welding and instrument repair, basic mud engineering, and
language instruction (English for the Venezuelans and Spanish for the
Americans). One very important and tangible result of this program,
coupled with intensive recruiting of Venezuelan graduates of both
local and foreign colleges and universities, is that Meneg has approached its goal of "Venezuelanization" of its personnel. Table A.14
shows the progress in this direction.

But Meneg's Venezuelanization program has gone beyond impressive increases in the ratio of nationals to expatriates. The multinational companies are often accused—and the oil industry in Venezuela
is no exception—of withholding the positions of responsibility from the
citizens of the countries where they operate. In Meneg, the Western
Venezuela District is managed by a Venezuelan, and 80 percent of the
departments in the East and West are headed by Venezuelans.

Meneg was also the first foreign oil company to have a Venezuelan
as its president. And Gulf's promotion of nationals has even extended
abroad. Thus the present head of the Western District at one time
managed one of Gulf's U.S. Districts, and the corporation's operations
in Ecuador are directed by a Venezuelan.

Meneg Personnel, by Nationality

Year	(a) Venezuelans	(b) Foreigners	Total	Ratio (a) to (b)
1950	6,027	856	6,883	88/12
1960	4,960	538	5,498	90/10
1970	2,729	147	2,876	95/5
1972	2,607	119	2,726	96/4

Source: Meneg files.

In the area of housing Meneg has also made substantial contributions to the workers. This reference is not to the houses that the company has built in its areas of operation and for the use of which it charges its workers a token rental (as low as $5 per month) but to those it donated to its personnel in Puerto La Cruz, where the refinery and export terminal are located. Originally the two camps established there were well separated from the town, but as the town grew and spread, they came within the city limits. It was therefore decided to integrate them into the community, and of the total 447 houses, 437 were deeded to the workers occupying them. The donation of the rest of the houses and of the other facilities in the camps will be referred to in other sections of this paper.

Direct Economic Contributions to the Rest of the Community

Meneg's contributions are quantified in Tables A.15 and A.16

TABLE A.15

Cash Contributions to Nonprofit Organizations, 1923-72
(millions of dollars)

Area	Contribution
Western Venezuela	3.0
Eastern Venezuela	5.9
Total	8.9

Source: Meneg files.

TABLE A.16

Capital and Operating Expenditures in Facilities
Benefiting Community, 1923-72
(millions of dollars)

	Capital	Operating
Western Ven.	1.6	7.3
Eastern Ven.	7.5	11.1
Totals	9.1	18.4

Source: Meneg files.

As will be described in the next subsection, these direct contributions and expenditures, coupled with the indirect ones, fostered
the development of the urban and rural areas in Western and Eastern
Venezuela, especially in the latter.

Indirect Contributions to the Rest of the Community

It has been stated already that in Western Venezuela Meneg plays
a secondary role behind Creole and Shell. Nevertheless, it has done
its share and is well regarded in this part of the country, where, in
addition to its contributions to the construction and maintenance of
facilities benefiting the community, it has made the following three
important donations:

1. In 1960, when the dredging of the Lake Maracaibo bar had
made it unnecessary and impractical to tranship the crude to oceangoing tankers at Las Piedras in the State of Falcon, the company
deeded its approximately 285-acre terminal site to the autonomous
institute Banco Obrero for the construction of low-cost housing.
2. In 1966 Meneg donated its Cabimas Terminal loading dock,
and all installations thereon, to the Municipality of the District of
Bolivar, State of Zulia. This dock was to be reconditioned for use
by a Lake Maracaibo fishing fleet.
3. In 1969 Meneg ceded the housing and other installations in its
Taparito Camp, State of Zulia, to a nonprofit educational organization
called Fe y Alegria. The land on which the camp was built, owned by
Shell, was donated by that company to the same organization.

No comments will be made on other contributions in the West, because all in all they were similar, although on a smaller scale and less directly connected with Meneg in the public's eye, to those made in Eastern Venezuela, which will be described forthwith.

In the mid-1920s, when Meneg started geophysical work in the State of Anzoategui, the village of El Tigre consisted of nothing more than a telegraph relay station and a handful of huts. The company was obliged to install some provisional facilities for its technicians, and the village started to grow in disorderly fashion as family after family arrived in search of employment. The growth was accelerated by the discovery of the gigantic Central Oficina field, and today the population of El Tigre is estimated to stand at between 50,000 and 60,000.

Later, when the company became fully convinced of the attractiveness of the region's oil future, it looked for a site to establish permanent headquarters for its operations, and selected San Tome, a location approximately 10 miles from El Tigre, which by now was called "city" and not "town" by its proud inhabitants. However, eventually some of these plus a number of newcomers decided that it would be better to be closer to the company's center of operations, and they founded the town of Tigrito, approximately halfway between El Tigre and San Tome, which today has an estimated population of about 25,000.

But what really gave impetus to the development of Eastern Venezuela was the construction, by Meneg, of the black-top highway between Oficina (near El Tigre), where the company had installed a large tank farm, to Puerto La Cruz, which became the site of the company's export terminal and where its refinery went on stream in 1950. Started in March 1938 and completed near the end of the following year, this highway, 100 miles long including the San Tome-Oficina extension, literally transformed the roadway communities, the principal ones of these being, in addition to El Tigre and Tigrito, Cantaura, Anaco, San Mateo, and Naricual.

Through three decades of town building and expansion Meneg has repeatedly cooperated in many essential ways. Streets and roads, plazas, water systems, and diverse other public works in the highway communities and others nearby have been designed and built by the company.

Of them all perhaps the development of Puerto La Cruz is the most dramatic. In 1937 this community had a mere 3,000 inhabitants; today there are over 100,000, and the city has surpassed the state capital, Barcelona, whose inhabitants numbered 75,000 according to the 1971 census. From a fisherman's village Puerto La Cruz has grown to be Venezuela's most important eastern port.

Two very important fields in which Meneg has done much to assist the communities where it operates are medical care and education. In those communities, which owe much of their growth and progress to the petroleum industry, medical facilities were nonexistent or utterly inadequate prior to the arrival of the oil companies. Meneg for one built and operated several hospitals and clinics, the significance of which is best described in the words of Dr. T. Briceno Maaz, the Eastern District's medical director from 1942 to 1965, who said:

In the early days especially, Mene Grande hospitals rendered a real social service by giving good medical attention not only to employees and their families but to outsiders as well. The hospitals have been educational, with emphasis on sanitary education, not just for workers, but for the surrounding communities also.

The 52-bed hospital in Puerto La Cruz was turned over to the Social Security Institute in 1965, but the company continues to operate the 110-bed unit in San Tome, as well as several clinics in its smaller camps.

As regards education, the company owns and runs six grammar schools in Eastern Venezuela. Of the total 1,478 students enrolled during the 1972-73 school year, 195, or 13.3 percent, were outsiders, that is, not relatives of company workers. Two other schools, both in Puerto La Cruz, were donated to the Ministry of Education in 1969, when Meneg's camps became an integral part of the community.

Meneg also contributed to education in rural areas by donating, through the El Tigre Rotary Club, 15 prefabricated houses to serve as elementary schools.

Other forms of assistance rendered by Meneg, such as the donation of material for the construction of public buildings and the paving of streets and the construction of sewage disposal systems, will not be detailed. However, before concluding this section of the paper, it is deemed to be desirable to refer to a pair of specific projects from which the community has derived ample benefits.

The first is the fire-prevention and fire-fighting program conducted by the company. The prevention part of it consisted of a "table-top" demonstration, using specially made equipment to illustrate the more common causes of fires, especially in the homes, and to explain how they could be prevented. This demonstration was given at hundreds of schools and clubs throughout the country.

The fire-fighting portion was geared more to the training, by the head of Meneg's own fire control units, of inexperienced members of the municipal fire departments in El Tigre, Puerto La Cruz, and

Barcelona. Equipment, including fire engines, was also donated to these departments.

The second project was not even remotely related to oil. Throughout the 1940s there were repeated governmental efforts to diversify national industry and strengthen agriculture for the purpose of reducing the nation's dependence on imported goods. As early as 1940, in the interest of this effort, Meneg invested several thousand dollars to set up seven agricultural projects—farms, chicken farms, and cattle ranches—all in the State of Anzoategui. An agronomist spent a year on the scene, but the original experiments failed, mainly due to the characteristics of the soil and the lack of controlled irrigation. Several years later, however, it was determined that the area was ideal for the growing of peanuts, and many acres are now covered with peanuts. The crops are good, and a plant for the extraction of peanut oil is in full operation.

Meneg has surface rights over much of the land planted with peanuts, but under the terms of the Law of Agrarian Reform it cannot keep the growers out and much less evict them (nor would it want to do so) so long as they do not interfere with the company's operations. This has happened on occasion, but the company has learned to live with the relatively minor problems and has proved its willingness to cooperate with this agricultural effort, which is a step forward toward the diversification of the economy of Anzcategui.

The merits of the contributions that have been outlined are generally recognized, but the type of cooperation thus far described, no matter how liberal, is not by itself sufficient to create a truly favorable image for an industry or an enterprise, particularly a multinational company. More important are the relations that a company establishes and maintains with various sectors of the community. What Meneg has done in this regard and what it has gained therefrom will be discussed in the next section of this Appendix.

MENEG'S RELATIONS WITH THE COMMUNITY:
WHAT THE COMPANY HAS GAINED FROM THEM

For purposes of this discussion, the community will be divided into the following seven sectors: the government; the political parties; the employees; the labor unions; the competitors; the general public (sectors of the community other than the five above and the press); and the press.

The Government

Meneg has always been on cordial and mutually respectful terms with all branches of the government. In the days of absolute dictatorships the important thing was to maintain good or at least neutral relations with the man in power and his relatively few really trusted friends. It was also rather easy for the oil companies to conduct their business, because on one hand the government officials, being unsophisticated and totally unfamiliar with the petroleum business, were willing to agree to almost any company proposal and on the other the iron-fisted regimes such as that of Gomez did not tolerate strikes or disruptive movements of any kind.

The then prevailing situation can be illustrated with the words of President Gomez who, according to chroniclers of his period, said more or less the following in connection with the preparation of the first Law of Hydrocarbons promulgated in 1920: "Let the companies write it; they have the experts and we know nothing about petroleum." Meneg was not in Venezuela at that time and did not participate in the drafting of this law.

As time passed the government became more and more aware of the need to keep an eye on the development of the resource, which was rapidly becoming its main source of income, and in June 1930 it created the Technical Office of Hydrocarbons and attached it to the Ministry of Development. Over 20 years later, in December 1950, the military junta then in power decreed the creation of the Ministry of Mines and Hydrocarbons. This ministry is not the only government entity with which the oil companies have to discuss important aspects of the conduct of their business; others include the ministries of Finance, Labor, Development, and Communications. In the states where they operate, the companies also have to deal with the governors' offices, the branches of the various ministries, and the municipal councils.

Meneg's conduct vis-a-vis the Ministry of Mines and Hydrocarbons is typical of that which it observes in its contacts with all government branches. The enforced policy is that the company's representatives must make it a point to

1. Maintain a sound business and social relationship with the officials of the various government agencies;

2. Never bypass a lower-echelon official to whom one or another problem should be taken first in an effort to get quickly to the man at the final decision-making level;

3. Refrain from taking advantage of the lack of experience and/or specialized knowledge of the man across the table, to the extent of

trying to "snow" him with weighty and complex technical or economic arguments that are not wholly based on truth;

4. Admit that an argument advanced by the other side is valid when it is so;

5. Never threaten and never overreact to threats; and

6. Avoid making dire predictions of what the consequences of this or that governmental step will be, especially when it is not certain or even likely that such consequences will materialize. Companies that have made such predictions have ceased to enjoy much credibility.

The above is not a complete list of do's and don'ts, but it does illustrate the basic principles on which Meneg's relations with the government rest. Sometimes their observance does not suffice to resolve differences of opinion, and when this happens and Meneg feels that its rights are being violated, it takes its case to the highest court in the land. For example, in 1963 the Ministry of Mines and Hydrocarbons issued two resolutions fining Meneg for having dismantled two gathering stations without having requested "proper authorization" from the ministry to do so. The fines themselves did not amount to much, but the wording of the resolutions was precedent setting, and its acceptance by the company would have opened the way to serious interference with its operations. Meneg tried to get the ministry to revoke the fines or at least to change the text of the resolutions, but the discussions, cordial as they were, bore no fruit, and so the company took the matter to the Supreme Court, which on the following year ruled completely in its favor.

Meneg, along with other companies, has also gone before the Supreme Court to challenge the constitutionality of several laws, regulations, and ordinances adopted during President Caldera's "democratic nationalism" regime, among them the Reversion Law, the Regulation on Conservation of Hydrocarbon Resources, and the Commercial and Industrial Patent Ordinance of the State of Anzoategui's District of Sotillo. Although some of these suits were filed almost three years ago, the Court's decisions are still pending.

The aforementioned actions have not soured the government against Meneg, and neither have they adversely affected the company's relations with the officials. But has Meneg gained anything from those relations? One answer to this question might be another query: What would the company have lost had it not maintained them? Actually there is a better reply. The gains have been tangible, though not measurable in dollars and cents. For instance, the company's requests for discussion of problems of mutual interest are usually honored promptly, and more often than not the results of those discussions are compromises that both sides can live with. This of course is not saying that one or another government agency bends the law to the breaking point in order to favor the company. Meneg neither expects nor wants this. What it does strive for, often successfully, is the best possible treatment under legislation that places implementation flexibility in the hands of the enforcing agency.

The Political Parties

Venezuelans are a bit like the man who was lost in the desert, went without food and drink for several days, eventually found his way back to the town, staggered into a restaurant, ordered everything on the menu, gorged himself, and got indigestion. During the many decades of dictatorship Venezuelans lived in a political desert, without the food and drink that is the right of expression and freedom of association, and when it became available with the arrival of democracy, they decided to make up for lost time and consume it to excess. There are those who argue that the point of indigestion has not been reached as yet, but the fact is that political parties are a dime a dozen and that an almost incredible 14 of them nominated candidates to compete in the December 1973 presidential elections.

Regardless of the boasts and claims of the aspirants, the race will probably be decided between the nominees of the two traditionally strongest parties: Accion Democratica and COPEI. This notwithstanding, Meneg is not courting the two giants, openly or disguisedly, and this not because of fear that there may be a David among the other 12 but because by adhering to a strict hands-off policy and not giving rise to suspicion that it favors some candidacies and dislikes others, it has avoided accusations of interference in the internal affairs of the nation.

This does not mean that Meneg refuses to have anything to do with political parties during an election year or at any other time. If any one of them, large or small and whatever its ideology may be, expresses a desire to meet with representatives of the company to exchange views on, say, the international oil situation, the meeting is not shirked. It is held, and it is kept objective and apolitical. The result of this policy is that the party in power at any particular time may not be a bosom pal of the company, but neither is it an enemy.

The hands-off policy applies only to Meneg as a company and not to its employees, over whose political preferences it has no control. Their views are their own, and nothing is done to try to influence them, but campaigning on company premises is not allowed.

The Employees

Meneg's direct and indirect contributions to its employees were described above. As shown, they are considerable, but the company realizes that it cannot buy the loyalty of its personnel by offering good wages and attractive fringe benefits. More is needed and more is given: respect for the dignity of the worker as a human being and treatment of him as a person and not as a part of a machine.

The company's program is to maintain, through its supervisors, two-way communication with its workers. Plans and policy changes that may affect them are to be made known and explained to them, and their suggestions, grievances, and problems, including those of a personal nature, are to be heard and handled fairly. The goal is to make the worker feel that he is part of the company, that the rules of discipline he must observe have been made not solely to benefit his employer but also for his own good and that of the community, and that his well-being and the progress of the company are interdependent.

The task is a big one. At one time it was made more difficult by the fact that most supervisors were foreigners who spoke little or no Spanish, not a few of whom acted according to the self-created belief that the Venezuelans were members of an inferior race. Now the language barrier has disappeared because the few remaining foreign supervisors are completely bilingual or at least have learned sufficient Spanish to communicate with their subordinates on subjects other than those directly related to the job and have also learned to appreciate the skill and personality of the nationals.

The plan has not always worked smoothly and is not working perfectly now. Occasionally a supervisor—and he may well be a Venezuelan—adopts an arrogant and intolerant attitude, or a subordinate refuses to react to fair treatment and makes up his mind that the company is abusing him, and friction occurs. But these situations are not common. Continuous efforts are made to prevent them, and corrective measures are applied as quickly as possible when they do arise.

An indication of the success of Meneg's personnel policy is the length of service of its employees. Table A.17 shows that nearly 70 percent of the workers had 15 or more years of service with the company as of December 31, 1972.

The Labor Unions

The Syndicate of Oil Workers and Employees of Cabimas was the first petroleum workers' union to be organized in Venezuela. It

Length of Service of Meneg Personnel as of December 31, 1972

Years of Service	Number of Workers	Percent of Total
Less than 5	318	11.7
5 to less than 10	209	7.7
10 to less than 15	355	13.0
15 to less than 20	617	22.6
20 to less than 25	531	19.5
25 and over	696	25.5
Totals	2,726	100.0

Source: Meneg files.

came into being late in February 1936, less than three months after the death of General Gomez, and before the end of its first year of existence it instigated a general strike. President Lopez Contreras put an end to the strike by a decree that granted the workers a wage increase of 20 cents a day.

A second strike was averted in November 1944 when President Isaias Medina decreed a 40-cent-a-day across-the-board salary increase but rejected the demands for social benefits. The following year the companies and the unions did get together in the office of the Labor Inspector in Maracaibo, and a few months later in the Ministry of Labor in Caracas, and signed agreements whereby certain social benefits were granted to the workers. In those days the negotiations between the companies and the unions were one-sided, because in practice the latter did not have the right to call strikes and, further-more, the government, for political reasons, did not want them to gain strength.

The situation changed in 1946 when, some five months after Romulo Betancourt became president of the revolutionary junta, the Federation of Petroleum Workers (Fedepetrol) was established in Caracas. Collective contracts were signed with the federation in June 1946 and again in February 1948.

Following the overthrow of President Gallegos in November 1948, and during the ensuing decade of dictatorship, the unions were stifled and ceased to exist as effective representatives of the workers. But after Perez Jimenez was deposed in 1958 they resurged with a ven-geance, and with the tacit support of sympathetic governments inter-ested in gaining popularity they confronted the companies with long lists of demands, some not unreasonable and others completely absurd.

Five collective contracts, at approximately three-year intervals, have been negotiated since the days of Perez Jimenez. The industry's negotiating team is made up of representatives of Creole, Shell, and Meneg, and those of the latter have participated very actively. Their effectiveness has been enhanced by the good relations with the labor leaders through the years.

The cordial Meneg-union relations have not been cultivated with liberal donations by the company, although from time to time Meneg has contributed to worthy union projects such as the establishment of vacation colonies for workers. It has also helped the syndicates by giving them places for their field offices and for their general assemblies. For instance, when the Puerto La Cruz camps were integrated into the community, several houses and two club houses were ceded to them. These cordial relations are the result of the company's policy to abstain from trying to weaken the unions by discouraging its workers from joining them (65 percent of Meneg's workers are unionized; the average for the industry is about 1 percent less) and to keep the door open for frank discussions of any problems the syndicate leaders may wish to present.

In the area of management-union relations perhaps the best compliment that a company can receive is that voiced by a high official of Fedepetrol, who not long ago told the writer: "We respect Meneg; it is tough but it is also fair." Toughness and fairness have paid off. In the last seven years Meneg has experienced only three strikes, the longest of which lasted two days and the shortest, three hours. The The total time lost amounted to 2,300 man-days. Two of the strikes, involving a loss of 550 man-days, were not directed against Meneg but were called to show solidarity with the striking workers of other oil companies.

The Competitors

Many of the problems stemming from governmental and labor actions as well as from other sources are common to the entire oil industry, and therefore it is natural and logical for the companies to exchange views on these problems and to seek solutions that would be acceptable to all. Needless to say, this is done judiciously, and extreme care is taken to avoid any intercompany collaboration that may be interpreted, even stretching the imagination, as a violation of U.S. antitrust legislation.

Meneg participates in the discussions, and there are times when its points of view prevail and times when they do not. Usually, however, there is a quid pro quo, perhaps not immediately but in the future, for any concession that the company may make to satisfy others. But Meneg does not hesitate to fight a battle that may not be to the liking of one or more of its competitors, when the issue is one of discrimination against it. An example of this is the Law to Encourage Desulphurization.

In 1967 the Venezuelan Congress was considering a bill to encourage desulphurization of heavy crudes, and one of its provisions was that "The National Executive is authorized to enter into special tax reference price agreements covering the Venezuelan heavy fuel and heavy crudes exported for processing in the traditional refineries in the Caribbean area." In the Exposition of Motives the "traditional" refineries were defined as those operating in Aruba (Creole), Curacao (Shell), and Trinidad (Texaco). Thus the owners of those refineries would be able to use them for "processing" (which means refining and not strictly desulphurization) Venezuelan heavy crude at special (that is, lower) tax reference values.

Meneg felt that the bill was discriminatory because it excluded refineries such as Gulf's very traditional one in Puerto Rico, which for many years had processed nothing but Venezuelan oil. Therefore, the company's representatives argued before the ministers of Mines and Hydrocarbons and of Finance, and eventually before a congressional committee, that the bill was unfair and should be generalized as a first choice, or killed as a less desirable alternative, so that a qualified company would not be placed in a potentially disadvantageous competitive position vis-a-vis others.

Meneg's efforts were unsuccessful in that the bill was passed and became law in November 1967, with only one change: "processing" was qualified by the addition of the words "and desulphurizing." The companies favored by the law were somewhat upset by Meneg's actions, but they recognized the validity of its arguments and could not help but respect its defense of its legitimate interests. That in itself was a plus for Meneg, but the industry as a whole gained because Meneg's conduct helped to dispel the common, erroneous, and unhealthy Venezuelan belief that the oil companies are members of one and the same big and powerful family and that there is no competition between them.

The General Public

The term "general public" covers all sectors of the community, other than the five already discussed, and the press, to which the final subsection will be devoted.

Meneg's contributions to the "rest of the community" have been outlined above. They have helped the company's image, but by no means have they been the sole foundation of the good relations with the community. Meneg has established these relations by avoiding isolation and emphasizing association.

The company's employees, nationals and foreigners alike, participate actively in numerous community activities. Some are members of clubs such as the Rotary and the Lions, others belong to cultural and athletic associations, and still others take part in the work chambers of commerce and industry. And Meneg employees become involved in the fund-raising drives of many organizations that serve the community: the Red Cross, the Fight Against Cancer Society, the Antituberculosis Institute, the Blood Bank, the YMCA, and so forth.

In short, Meneg has been able to win friends. The company celebrated its 50th anniversary this year, and several of the congratulatory messages it received reflected appreciation for the role that it has played in the community. The words with which the El Tigre Rotary Club concluded an editorial published in its news bulletin are indicative:

> Today, when the 50th anniversary of the beginning of this company's operations in the country is being commemorated, we, the rotarians of El Tigre, leaders and representatives of this community, cannot fail to make public our sincere and warm expression of appreciation for the work carried out by Mene Grande.

The Press

Discussing the relations with the press last does not signify that they are considered to be less important than those with the other sectors. On the contrary, a good press will give fair and objective coverage to a company's positive attitude and actions, whereas a bad one will either ignore or report them in a less than favorable light.

Meneg does not believe in flooding the newspaper and other communications media with releases on minor company activities and accomplishments. Nor does it believe in holding press conferences when there is nothing truly significant to announce. It speaks only when what there is to say is worthwhile and should be of interest to the public. The press knows this and in general prints Meneg's releases fully and accurately. Any errors that may creep in are accidental.

When the news media take the initiative, that is, when they are after views and opinions on one subject or another and ask questions, Meneg does not resort to evasive tactics. It replies factually, and on those occasions when the company feels that a question is improper for this or that reason and should not be answered, it explains why it feels obliged to withhold comments.

After reading the preceding, one would think that since Meneg, and more than likely most if not all the other foreign oil companies as well, are respectful and respected members of the community, there is nothing to worry about. Unfortunately there is much reason for concern. The future of the private oil industry in Venezuela is most uncertain and not very bright. The big questions are, Will the industry, and Meneg as part of it, be able to survive until 1984, when most of the concessions expire? What, if any, will be the role of Meneg and of other foreign oil companies after 1984? An attempt to answer these questions will be made in the final section of this appendix.

THE FUTURE OF THE FOREIGN OIL COMPANIES OPERATING IN VENEZUELA

The Future until 1984

As may be gleaned from Table A.18, a total of 3,893,296 of the 5,455,551 acres (71.4 percent) of concessions held by the industry as of December 31, 1972, will lapse by 1984, in accordance with the terms of the concession agreements. Meneg will be affected even more seriously, for it will lose 1,231,801 acres, or 84 percent of the 1,466,558 acres it now holds.

Approximately 68.2 percent of Venezuela's present total production and 70.5 percent of Meneg's come from the leases that will revert by 1984, so the companies have an obvious reason for wishing to retain their acreage at least until then. Will they be able to do so, or will they be nationalized before the legal expiration date? Let us take a look at the following principal accusations that are made against the multinational companies and that singly or combined are alleged to constitute justification for expropriation and see to what extent, if any, they could in fairness be aimed at the international oil companies operating in Venezuela:

1. The companies are exploiting the nation.
2. The companies are wasting the hydrocarbon resources of the nation.

TABLE A.18

Expiration of Concessions in Force as of December 31, 1972

Year of Expiration	Meneg (acres)	Rest of Industry (acres)	Total (acres)
1975	—	1,235	1,235
1977	—	4,166	4,166
1983	—	435,491	435,491
1984	1,231,801	2,220,603	3,452,404
1985	21,711	566,856	588,567
1986	5,068	34,291	39,359
1988	31,367	424,498	455,865
1989	55,622	57,426	113,048
1990	—	7,852	7,852
1991	—	5,336	5,336
1996	120,989	114,993	235,982
1997	—	116,246	116,246
Totals	1,466,558	3,988,993	5,455,551

Source: Annual Report of the Ministry of Mines and Hydrocarbons for the Year 1972.

3. The companies obtain an excessive return on their invested capital.

4. The companies meddle in the internal affairs of the nation.

5. The companies finance at least part of their activities with borrowed local capital, thereby curtailing the availability of money for use by national enterprises and causing increases in interest rates.

6. The companies keep their national employees in subordinate positions, so as to prevent the development of local managerial talent to the extent that the operations may eventually be run by nationals.

7. The companies play one country against the other by increasing or decreasing production as they see fit.

Exploitation of the Nation

In her book The Growth of Firms, Middle East Oil and Other Essays, Dr. Edith Penrose, a well-known economist and professor at the School of Oriental and African Studies, University of London, states:

Even if we conclude that "exploitation" cannot easily be given a clear objective meaning, however, we cannot ignore the fact that the sense of being exploited is one of the powerful reasons for much hostility towards foreign investment. It might, of course, be said that if all gain goes to the foreign firm, the country obtaining nothing is being exploited, but this is not what is meant by those who complain of exploitation. The notion is rather that the foreign company is obtaining a disproportionate gain—a gain greater than it ought in some sense to get when it is compared with the gain accruing to the receiving country. In other words, it is a feeling of "unfair" treatment. . . .

In this respect, the introduction by the international oil companies in the Middle East of fifty-fifty—the equal sharing between governments and companies of profits attributed to crude oil production—was a stroke of genius, for equality of sharing has a distinct ring of fairness about it.

Dr. Penrose does not say that what she calls a "stroke of genius" actually originated in Venezuela. Reference to it is made in the 1943 Law of Hydrocarbons, which increased the participation of the nation in the profits of the oil industry by raising such taxes as those on exploration, surface, consumption, transportation, and exploitation and at the same time allowed for the conversion of the old concessions to new concessions, giving the latter a life of 40 years from the date of the conversion.

In the Exposition of Motives of the aforementioned law, it is stated that "according to numerous and careful calculations made, the 16-2/3 percent tax on exploitation, together with the other taxes, is equivalent in our country to 50 percent of the benefits of the extractive petroleum industry." The intent of this was to consecrate the principle of "50-50," which was later fully cemented by the November 1948 Income Tax Law. This law established the so-called additional tax which was a 50 percent tax applicable to any amount by which a company's after-normal-tax profits exceeded the sum of the normal taxes payable in accordance with the pertinent legislation.

Over the 10-year period 1948-57 most members of the industry, including Meneg, had to pay additional tax in order to attain the 50-50 goal. Thereafter the sum of normal taxes has exceeded the industry's net profits. The year-by-year distribution of the income from oil for the 10-year period 1963-72, on a per barrel basis, is the subject of Table A.19.

Meneg did better than the industry average, the 1972 ratio of government take to its income being in the order of 81/19.

Distribution of Income per Barrel of Oil Produced

Year	Income (dollars)		Ratio of Govt.- to-Industry Income
	Government	Industry	
1963	0.88	0.45	66/ 34
1964	0.90	0.45	67/ 33
1965	0.89	0.47	65/ 35
1966	0.88	0.46	66/ 34
1967	0.94	0.44	68/ 32
1968	0.94	0.45	68/ 32
1969	0.94	0.39	71/ 29
1970	1.03	0.29	78/ 22
1971	1.30	0.39	77/ 33
1972	1.62	0.21	89/ 11

Source: Annual Report of the Ministry of Mines and Hydro-carbons for the Year 1972.

At any rate, if, as Dr. Penrose declares, equality of sharing has a distinct ring of fairness about it, then the distribution tabulated above should, from the government's point of view, have a peal of ultrafairness.

Waste of the Hydrocarbon Resources of the Nation

The industry produces crude oil in accordance with sound technical principles and has seldom been accused of abusing the oil reservoirs, but the amount of gas flared has been criticized frequently, particularly by laymen who cannot or will not realize that the cost of gathering widely scattered associated gas would be prohibitive for the nation as well as for the companies. Admittedly, in the early days appreciable volumes of gas were wasted unnecessarily, but this situation ceased to exist years ago, and in 1972 stood as shown in Table A.20.

Overall, Meneg has done better than the private industry as a whole, and the latter has by far surpassed the National Oil Company (CVP), which in 1972 produced 17,572.7 million cubic feet of gas and flared 16,202.5 million cubic feet, or 92.2 percent.

The industry and Meneg have made substantial investments in gas injection plants that contribute much to gas conservation and, additionally, are effective reservoir pressure maintenance vehicles. Data pertaining to these plants appear in Table A.21.

TABLE A.20

Gas Produced and Flared by Industry and by Meneg, 1972

(millions of cubic feet)

	All Companies			Meneg. Oper.		
	Produced	Flared	Percent Flared	Produced	Flared	Percent Flared
Western Ven.	913,387.2	386,314.3	42.3	44,999.0	37,511.6	83.4
Eastern Ven.	710,905.1	126,049.8	17.7	339,536.1	46,795.9	13.8
Central Ven.	565.0	448.5	79.4	—	—	—
Totals	1,624,857.3	512,812.6	31.6	384,535.1	84,307.5	21.8

Source: Annual Report of the Ministry of Mines and Hydrocarbons for the year 1972.

210

TABLE A. 21

Gas Injection Plants in Operation as of December 31, 1972

	All Companies	Meneg Oper.	Meneg Percent of All
Number of plants	54	23	42.6
Installed horsepower	691,135	111,960	16.2
Orig. cost (millions of dollars)	302.4	41.0	13.3

Source: Annual Report of the Ministry of Mines and Hydrocarbons Year 1972.

TABLE A. 22

Net Fixed Assets and Percentage of Return
(millions of dollars)

Year	Average Net Fixed Assets	Percent Return
1964	1,802.2	31.0
1965	1,742.0	34.4
1966	1,658.6	34.3
1967	1,547.7	36.9
1968	1,525.9	39.5
1969	1,615.2	31.9
1970	1,684.3	23.5
1971	1,692.5	30.2
1972	1,691.1	14.5

Source: Annual Report of the Ministry of Mines and Hydrocarbons for the Year 1972.

In addition, 118,390 horsepower (26.6 percent Meneg operated) have been installed, at an original cost of $105.4 million (12.7 percent Meneg operated), to compress gas for delivery to, and usage at, various facilities.

A valuable recognition of Meneg's conservation efforts is contained in the following telegram which Dr. Baltazar Gimon Ron, Technical Inspector of Hydrocarbons for the State of Anzoategui, sent on the occasion of this year's commemoration of Meneg's 50th anniversary:

> In the name of this Technical Inspectorate of Hydrocarbons and in my own, I am pleased to congratulate the Mene Grande Oil Co. for having completed 50 years of activities in Venezuela, where it has contributed efficiently to the development of the petroleum industry and has collaborated amply in the application of measures of conservation established by the Ministry of Mines and Hydrocarbons.

Clearly, then, a charge that the private oil companies are wasting the hydrocarbon resources of the nation could not be substantiated.

Excessive Return on Invested Capital

Table A.22 shows the return on the oil industry's net fixed assets year by year for the period 1964-72.

Meneg's 1972 percentage of return was above the industry's average for that year but below it for 1971.

It should be stressed that the Venezuelan Government does not recognize as deductible such expenditures as those incurred in foreign marketing of the Venezuelan crude and products, research projects conducted abroad for the benefit of the local companies, and so on, nor does it permit revaluation of the assets in the light of inflation or use of a replacement value factor. All the more reason, therefore, why the returns listed in Table A.22, based on the net book value of the assets, do not deserve being called "excessive." Furthermore, even the most bitter critics of the companies' profits aver that a 15 percent return would be in order, and so the 1972 results should please them no end.

Meddling in the Internal Affairs of the Nation

Among those who accuse the private oil companies operating in Venezuela of meddling in the internal affairs of the nation there are many whose only argument is the following: "They did it in other countries; they must be doing it here." The case of the International Petroleum Company (IPC) in Peru is one of their favorite springboards. Perhaps they have read the book The Multinational Corporation as a Force in Latin American Politics: A Case Study of the International Petroleum Company in Peru by Dr. Alberto J. Pinelo, Assistant Professor of Political Science at Northern Kentucky State College, who, in his conclusions, says the following about the anti-IPC argument:

> It had logical validity. Asked why he disliked IPC, an unidentified Peruvian general with the present government responded: "They bribed ministers, corrupted governments, and promoted revolutions." Evidence pointed to the truth of this charge, at least during the period covered in the available Department of State diplomatic correspondence between the U.S. Government and the American Embassy in Lima up to 1939. As Richard Goodwin stated, however, "it takes two to make a bribe, and you cannot corrupt the incorruptible." Nevertheless, the generals who carried out the coup and subsequent seizure of La Brea y Parinas in 1968 were aware of IPC's historic role in Peruvian politics—as the rescuer of doomed incompetent Cabinet officials, as the underwriter of any government which promised no interference with the company, and as the promoter of international intrigues designed to bend the will of Peru's public officials.

The correctness or lack of it of Dr. Pinelo's conclusion is beside the point. What is relevant is the fact that notwithstanding the unsupported oral and sometimes printed allegations made by a number of Venezuelans whose feelings border on xenophobia, a similar conclusion could not be rightly drawn from the behavior of the foreign oil companies in Venezuela. Meneg has never contributed directly or indirectly to a political campaign, although on occasion it has been asked to do so, nor has it ever interfered in the internal affairs of the nation in any other form. Actually, Meneg itself has never been accused by name, as at least one other company has been, but it is tacitly included when the charge is fired at the foreign oil companies in general.

But what really counts is not what an industry or a company does but what the influential nationals and the general public believe it does. In this regard, it is fortunate that for the most part the Venezuelan wielders of the interference argument are not in the influential category.

Borrowing of Local Capital

A June 1969 decree issued by the Ministry of Finance stipulates that if a foreign company borrows local capital, it must repay the loan in full before it can export even a penny of its profits. This effectively closed the door to such borrowing, but even before 1969, the oil companies, rightly or wrongly, never availed themselves of the local money market. What is more, through the years they have added to that market by investing in national financing enterprises and purchasing government bonds of various types. Meneg itself has made such investments and purchases in an amount totaling slightly over $10 million.

Placing Managerial Positions beyond the Reach of National Employees

The progress of Meneg's Venezuelanization program has been described above. The other oil companies have also encouraged the advancement of their nationals. Some examples are as follows: Creole Petroleum Corporation's executive vice president plus three of its directors are Venezuelans, and so are two vice presidents of Mobil Oil Company of Venezuela, the second vice president and four directors of Shell Oil Company of Venezuela, and the general manager of Venezuelan Sun Oil Company.

Obviously, then, argument that the oil companies in Venezuela relegate their national employees to positions of secondary importance does not hold water.

The Companies Play One Country Against Another

The international oil companies established in Venezuela also have sources of supply in other parts of the world. The production in the various countries fluctuates in accordance with the international market situation at a given time. In Venezuela the output in 1971 was 4.3 percent lower than in 1970, and in 1972 it was 9 percent below that corresponding to 1971. At the same time several other oil exporting nations registered production increases. The drops in the Venezuelan production were due largely to the curtailed international demand for high-sulphur heavy residual fuel, which is the principal yield of the large volumes of Venezuelan crudes that are high in sulphur, vanadium, and nickel content.

At this point it is timely to interject that late in 1970 President Caldera's regime of "democratic nationalism" became a carnival of laws and decrees, during which the various political parties, including the one in power, competed for the anti-private-oil-industry-legislation championship. The following is a list of the most onerous legislative measures, in chronological order:

1. Partial modification of the Income Tax Law: On December 17, 1970, the Income Tax Law promulgated on December 16, 1966, was amended to empower the National Executive to establish unilaterally the export values of hydrocarbons for periods of up to three years each. These values are those the companies must report as realization values for income tax purposes, unless they should have sold at prices above the government-established export values—a most unlikely occurrence—in which event the actual realization values would be reported.

The amended law also taxed the annual profits of the oil companies at a rate of 60 percent.

2. The Reversion Law: In accordance with the terms of the concession agreements and of the Law of Hydrocarbons all the permanent works and installations on the concessions will become the property of the nation at expiration time. However, the new brand of politicians concluded that this was not enough, and because of their fears—totally unjustified on the basis of experience—that the companies would strip the concessions of most assets prior to their expiration, Congress passed a bill covering those assets subject to reversion. On July 30, 1971, this bill, with the signature of Dr. Caldera, became the Reversion Law.

The worst feature of this legislation is that it goes much beyond the scope of the subject that gave it its name. Some of its most objectionable provisions are as follows:

a. It extends the principle of reversion to all assets, including those not on the concessions themselves.

b. It limits the right to contract by stipulating that a concessionaire may utilize third-party assets on the concessions only in special cases and subject to the National Executive's prior authorization, which may be granted only if the value of such assets does not exceed 10 percent of that of the net fixed assets of the concessionaire. It also makes the latter responsible for the maintenance of the third-party assets used by him.

c. It calls for the establishment of a Guarantee Fund to be composed of 10 percent of the cost accepted by the Income Tax administration for purposes of depreciation of the assets subject to reversion.

d. It obliges the concessionaires to explore their acreage in accordance with such programs as the Ministry of Mines and Hydrocarbons may dictate, or to return said acreage if they fail to do so.

e. It gives the National Executive the right to demand the return of concession areas the exploitation of which may have become uneconomical, even temporarily, for the concessionaire.

f. It empowers the Ministry of Mines and Hydrocarbons to impose fines of from $12,000 to $240,000 for each infraction.

3. The Gas Nationalization Law: The administration, not to be outdone by the opposition that had sponsored the Reversion Law, came

up with a Gas Nationalization Bill, which President Caldera announced to the nation with great fanfare and which his minister of Mines and Hydrocarbons subsequently presented to Congress, where it underwent several drastic changes that made it even more onerous.

As amended, the bill became law on August 26, 1971. Its most significant stipulations are as follows:

a. That the concessionaires of hydrocarbons shall be obligated to turn over to the state, at the time, in the measure, and under the conditions determined by the National Executive, the gas produced in their operations.

b. That the National Executive shall establish the measure and the conditions under which the hydrocarbons concessionaires may use in their operations the gas that is produced in association with oil.

c. That if the state should decide to assume the operations of gathering, compression, and treatment in plants now owned and run by the concessionaires, it shall pay to the latter a compensation equivalent to the unamortized portion of the book value of the installations and equipment that it may require for those operations, or to their actual value if this should be less than the former.

d. That any infraction of the law shall be punished with a fine of from $6,000 to $120,000.

The fact that the beginning and continuation of the decline in Venezuela's oil production coincided with the aforementioned avalanche of legislation prompted several congressmen to accuse the companies of adopting reprisal measures. Some of them went so far as to call for nationalization if the companies should "persist in maintaining a rebellious attitude against the sovereign acts of Congress."

The companies went out of their way to explain the existing international market situation and to deny any relation between the congressional actions and the production cutbacks. Their explanations and denials were supported by the president and the minister of Mines and Hydrocarbons, and this proved enough to quiet the critics. There was actually a distinct calm after the storm.

If, then, none of the seven principal charges that are frequently preferred against the multinational enterprises can, as reasoned herein, be justly aimed at the oil companies operating in Venezuela, is it certain or probable that some or all of the latter will be nationalized by 1984?

Not a few Venezuelans and foreigners, including some connected with the oil companies, feel that complete nationalization is just around the corner. They base their judgment largely on the pronouncements of several political parties that have committed themselves unqualifiedly to nationalization if they should ever come into power, on a recent statement by the minister of Mines and Hydrocarbons to the effect that Venezuela is already able to handle all aspects of the exploitation and marketing of its national resources, on declarations by the two presidential candidates with the best chance of winning the 1973 elections (one of them said, "My pulse would not shake if I should feel that signing a nationalization decree would be in the nation's best interests"; the other stated, "Reversion before 1983-1984 is one of the alternatives that merits consideration"), and on conclusions such as those reached by the Congress of Economists held in Caracas in July 1973, which recommended that the oil industry be nationalized "progressively."

The writer desagrees with those who believe that total nationalization is imminent. The reasons for this difference of opinion will be given together with the definitions he considers are applicable to the various forms of possible nationalization.

1. Total uncompensated expropriation: This form of nationalization, of which the expropriation of the International Petroleum Company in Peru is an example, involves the confiscation of a company's total assets without the payment of any compensation whatsoever. Expropriation followed by the payment of inadequate compensation may also be included in this category. Even the most rabid critics of the foreign oil companies operating in Venezuela do not advocate such nationalization.

2. Total compensated expropriation: An example of this form is the nationalization of Bolivian Gulf Oil Company in 1969. The Bolivian Government and the company reached agreement on the amount of compensation and the method of payment, and the agreement has been respected.

As regards Venezuela, the nation's Constitution stipulates that nationalization, accompanied by adequate compensation, may be resorted to if it should be deemed to be in the public interest. The foreign companies operating in the country have always been aware of this provision and therefore should not be overly shocked if and when it should be applied. They would, however, have the right to insist on prompt and adequate compensation, but it is possible and even probable that their views and those of the government as to what constitutes promptness and adequacy would differ substantially.

Be that as it may, the writer's opinion is that in Venezuela the question is moot. It is true that, as has been mentioned, some political personalities have voiced a certain degree of inclination toward nationalization, but in many instances this is nothing more than election-year talk and the speakers mean little or nothing of what they say. Furthermore, there are also those—among them the presidential candidates of the Movement toward Development, the National Democratic Front, and the National Opinion parties—who have pronounced themselves against "premature reversion," that is, against nationalization before 1983-84, and those who, like the present minister of Finance, are more cautious in their comments about expropriation. During a press conference on August 3, 1973, he answered a question about nationalization prior to 1983 in the following terms: "This cannot be a capricious decision, and it would have to depend on the conditions within which the petroleum activities might be able to be conducted at a given moment."

Also worth quoting are the following paragraphs from the August 6, 1973, essay in the widely read column "Petroleum Thermometer," which appears daily in the Caracas newspaper El Universal.

> The statements made by the Minister of Mines and Hydrocarbons, Dr. Hugo Perez La Salvia, to the effect that nationalization could take place before the reversion dates, that is, before 1983, create uneasiness, surprise, and even perplexity.
>
> Uneasiness because anything that sounds like nationalization alarms certain sectors which are larger than they may seem and which encompass not only those who own big or small companies, but also the employees and the laborers who are aware of how the nationalization of the tin, the copper, etc., became starting points for the collapse of the economic bases of certain countries.
>
> Furthermore, nationalization must make one think, with concern, that the large international companies which explore, produce, transport, and market the crude oil so efficiently, might be replaced by a Venezuelan Petroleum Corporation which, notwithstanding all its virtues, has neither the personnel nor the experience nor the capital to engage in such an extremely complex and exacting business. And all the more so when we all know that in order to do what it does, which isn't much, the Venezuelan Petroleum Corporation employs several foreign firms which have their own well-qualified and well-paid personnel.
>
> In addition, one must view with grave concern the possibility that the flourishing oil industry, which keeps us at our present level (in these times of lean cows in almost all of Latin America and in many other parts of the world), may become an Autonomous Institute of the State comparable, say, to the Venezuelan Petrochemical Institute or to another of the sixty which produce incalculable deficits.

The opinion that total nationalization is not impending does not, however, rest on the relative weights of pro- and antiexpropriation arguments such as those mentioned above. It is based on economic realities. Thus if in 1972 the government obtained, without investing a penny or running any risks whatsoever, $1.62 from every barrel of oil produced, while the companies averaged a net income of only $0.21 per barrel (see Table A.19), it would not make sense to expropriate and pay adequate compensation running into hundreds of millions of dollars for assets that, at reversion time some 10 years hence, the nation would get at no cost to it.

3. Partial uncompensated expropriation: This form differs from total uncompensated expropriation only in that some but not all phases of a company's operations and the corresponding assets would be nationalized. It has no sincere supporters in Venezuela.

4. Partial compensated expropriation: This form of nationalization has already been applied through the gas Nationalization Law and even more recently, on June 21, 1973, through the Law Reserving to the Nation the Internal Market for Refined Products. The latter provides that all the service stations now in the hands of the private oil companies must be ceded to the State Oil Company by no later than December 31, 1976. Some have already been transferred, and reasonable compensation has been paid.

Meneg, with only 60 stations, or 3.3 percent of the total 1,822 in the country, is not seriously affected by the aforementioned provision, but Creole and Shell, who between them control 1,150 retail outlets, or 63.1 percent of the total, are indeed hurt. What may affect Meneg as well as the other private oil companies that conduct refining activities in the country is the stipulation that they will have to supply products to the monopolist, the Venezuelan Petroleum Corporation, in quantities and at prices established unilaterally by the National Executive.

In conclusion, and for the reasons cited, the writer does not believe that total nationalization, compensated or uncompensated, will occur prior to the expiration of the majority of the concessions in 1983-84. The same opinion applies to further partial nationalization, again compensated or uncompensated, because there do not appear to be other phases of the operations of real immediate political or economic interest to the government.

On the other hand, the industry may be subjected to additional financial burdens in the form of higher taxes, increased export values, and so on, and harassed further through such legislation as (1) the recently promulgated Law of Protection and Development of the National Merchant Marine, Article 9 of which reads: "The National Executive shall reserve for national ships the transportation of a percentage of not less than 10 percent of the crude oil and refined products exported and imported, and shall gradually increase said percentage to 50 percent; and (2) the Bill on Contamination Derived from Activities Related to Hydrocarbons, now before Congress, which consists of 33 Articles, many of which are objectionable to varying degrees.

In other words, the goose that lays the golden eggs has been hurt; its neck has been squeezed and may be squeezed ever harder in the future, but not to the point of strangulation.

The Future after 1984

The first question that may be raised is, Why look beyond 1984? Will there be enough hydrocarbons left in Venezuela to make trying to continue operating in the country worthwhile? The answers to these questions may be found in Table A. 23.

Evidently the reserves dwindled somewhat in the 10 years since 1963. However, the fact that the proven reserves stood at 17,014.5 million barrels as of December 31, 1963, that since that time 12,680.6 million barrels have been produced, and that 13,875.7 million barrels of reserves still remained as of December 31, 1972, clearly indicates that new reserves were discovered during the 10-year period in question, although not in sufficient volumes to offset completely the depletion resulting from production.

During the next 10 years the rate of new discoveries in areas now under concession is almost certain to be lower than it was during

TABLE A. 23

Proven Crude Oil Reserves
(millions of barrels)

Year	Remaining Reserves as of 31 Dec.	Production-to-Reserves Ratio (percent)	Reserves-to-Production Ratio (years)
1963	17,014.5	7.0	14.4
1964	17,196.9	7.2	13.9
1965	17,247.2	7.4	13.6
1966	16,869.8	7.3	13.7
1967	15,957.7	8.1	12.3
1968	15,668.4	8.4	11.9
1969	14,713.5	8.8	11.3
1970	14,039.0	9.6	10.4
1971	13,762.5	9.4	10.6
1972	13,875.7	8.5	10.8

Source: Annual Report of the Ministry of Mines and Hydrocarbons for the Year 1972.

Proven Natural Gas Reserves
(millions of cubic feet)

Year	Remaining Reserves as of 31 Dec.	Production-to-Reserves Ratio (percent)	Reserves-to-Production Ratio (years)
1963	30,330,690	2.5	40.5
1964	30,740,886	2.6	38.9
1965	30,015,336	2.7	36.8
1966	29,173,051	2.8	36.2
1967	27,826,964	3.3	30.4
1968	26,749,444	3.4	29.8
1969	32,866,830	2.8	35.7
1970	32,750,661	3.1	32.8
1971	38,428,014	2.5	40.9
1972	41,128,311	2.2	46.1

Source: Annual Report of the Ministry of Mines and Hydrocarbons for the Year 1972.

the last decade, but it is equally almost certain that by 1983-84 there will be enough recoverable oil in the ground to warrant the continuation of operations on the "old" concessions as well as on the "new" ones, which do not lapse until 1996. In addition, of course, there is the Orinoco Heavy Oil Belt, not now leased to any company, which, in a very preliminary and not too reliable manner, has been estimated to contain in situ reserves in the order of 700 billion barrels, of which 10 percent, or 70 billion barrels, is estimated to be recoverable.

The natural gas reserve situation is even more promising (see Table A. 24).

Despite the production of 8,722,135 million cubic feet of gas during the 1963-72 decade, the proven reserves were 305,795 million cubic feet higher at the end of that 10-year period than at the beginning of it.

It is true that by virtue of the Gas Nationalization Law and so long as the law is not ruled to be unconstitutional, the gas belongs to the nation. Nonetheless, there is always the possibility that the government will find it desirable and perhaps even necessary to resort to joint ventures for the exploitation and utilization of gas. Actually there are many prominent Venezuelans who favor such joint ventures, not only for the production and utilization of gas but for that of oil as well. Some are in favor of Venezuelan-Government/Venezuelan-private-capital associations, while others prefer the tripartite form—that is, Venezuelan-Government/Venezuelan-private-capital/foreign-private-capital. However, all of them are against a state monopoly. One reason for this opposition was expressed by a highly respected Venezuelan, former Minister of Development Dr. Manuel R. Egana, who at a forum on the subject of Nationalization of Oil in Venezuela, held in Caracas in May 1971, declared:

> Why do I prefer the mixed enterprise rather than the direct management by the State? The reason is very simple: I am horrified by the bureaucratic monster, and I believe that the oil industry, producer of 3,500,000 barrels per day at present, with 23,000 workers, would become an industry manned by 100,000 voters within 5 years, and by one million within 10. With the mixed enterprise there would be some control, although I wouldn't say an absolute control.

The writer may be accused of being overly optimistic, but he believes that after 1984 at least some of the foreign oil companies will continue to operate in Venezuela, not merely as purchasers and marketers of government-produced oil and gas, but as partners of the nation in joint ventures encompassing the various phases of the oil business. Such ventures may extend not only to all present concessions, including those that lapse as late as 1996, but also to new acreage not now leased, as, for example, the Orinoco Heavy Oil Belt.

The companies that can hope to retain a firm foothold in the country will be only those that learn how to roll with the punches, how to adapt themselves to inevitably changing situations, and how to impress on all sectors of the Venezuelan community that while they are in business to make a reasonable profit for their stockholders, they will try to reach this goal without disregarding the best interests of the nation. Meneg expects to be one of those companies.

BIBLIOGRAPHY

Central Bank of Venezuela. Annual Report, 1972.

Mene Grande Oil Company files.

Edith Penrose. The Growth of Firms, Middle East Oil and Other Essays. New York: Frank Cass.

Adalberto J. Pinelo. The Multinational Corporation as a Force in
    Latin American Politics: A Case Study of the International Petro-
    leum Company in Peru. New York: Praeger Publishers.

Anibal R. Martinez. Cronolgia del Petroleo. Caracas: Ediciones
    Libreria Historia.

Fernando Mendoza G. Ensayos de Economia Petrolera. Caracas:
    Cromotip.

Venezuela. Ministries of Mines and Hydrocarbons; Development;
    and Finance. Annual Reports, 1972.

IBM IN LATIN AMERICA
Robert A. Bennett

The purpose of this Appendix is to describe briefly IBM's operations in Latin America. It will be a factual description of how IBM conducts its business, the policies and principles under which it operates, and the unique characteristics of the Latin American environment that affect these operations.

The objective of the CRIA Corporate Consultation Program is to gain a broader understanding of corporate social responsibility, particularly as it pertains to the growing influence of multinational corporations in the developing world. With this objective in mind, I will attempt in this paper to highlight those aspects of IBM's activities in Latin America that intersect the issues of social responsibility.

It is difficult to evaluate which of the many aspects of IBM's business, or in fact of any other multinational enterprise, most clearly intersect the issues of social responsibility to be discussed. Milton Friedman would argue that a sound profit plan and success in achieving it are the major elements of corporate responsibility. He and others who subscribe to this school of thought believe that social activities should be undertaken by corporations only when such activities are necessary to the corporations' well-being. Others would argue that the large successful multinational company must have a conscience and voluntarily go far beyond profit objectives or legal requirements to pursue a truly altruistic course in addressing social responsibility. In any case, whichever position is argued, it appears that social awareness in directing the day-to-day activities of multinational companies, as well as specific socially oriented programs, is prerequisite to successful operation. As a basis for discussion I will describe both IBM's approach to achieving its business objectives in Latin America, as well as its social programs.

GENERAL DESCRIPTION OF LATIN AMERICAN OPERATIONS

The IBM Corporation is in the business of developing, manufacturing, marketing, and servicing computing equipment and office products such as typewriters, dictating machines, and copying machines. Its business is conducted in the United States and in 126 other countries throughout the world. Twenty-six of these countries make up the Latin American operations, which represent about 6 percent of the business volumes outside of the United States. Each of the 26 country operations has its own personality and unique environment, and they are constantly changing. For example, eight years ago IBM Brazil was a relatively small company representing 20 percent of Latin American business and had no growth. Import restrictions prohibited the importation of all equipment but a few spare parts. The 50-man sales force had nothing to sell. Today IBM Brazil is the fastest-growing IBM subsidiary in the world and generates 50 percent of the company's business volumes in Latin America.

Very often the point is made that "there is no such thing as Latin America." Until now, IBM's experience would support that view. A trip through four or five of the countries is always a reminder of how different they are in spite of many things in common. Nevertheless, in recent years a change has begun to take place, and a growing regional and subregional nationalism is evident, which already is having significant influence on the companies doing business in the region.

Over 8,000 people are employed in IBM's Latin American companies, virtually all of whom are indigenous to the area. Foreign assignees from outside of Latin America are brought in occasionally in technical/advisory roles, but there are no North Americans in top executive or second-level executive positions in any of the Latin American countries. There is a Latin American Area Headquarters with 28 professional employees, only seven of whom are North Americans, including the area general manager. The assistant general manager is an Argentine.

IBM conducts its marketing operations in the 26 countries from 81 branch offices. Data processing (computer) products are manufactured in Argentina and Brazil, and typewriters are manufactured in Mexico, Colombia, and Brazil. Regional Education Centers are located in Brazil and Mexico. In addition, there are 11 local education centers in various countries in the region. The products marketed in Latin America are the same as those marketed throughout the world and are of the latest, most modern technology. The products manufactured in the Latin American plants are also of the latest technology, and much of the production is exported throughout the world. Country companies are wholly owned subsidiaries or branches of the IBM World Trade Corporation, which is a subsidiary of the IBM Corporation.

BASIC PRINCIPLES

IBM is a growth-oriented commercial enterprise. Thomas J. Watson, Sr. founded the company on three equally important business principles: adequate return for the stockholder, respect for the employee, and service to the customer. More recently, Thomas J. Watson, Jr., as chairman of the board, added social responsibility as the fourth basic principle of corporate philosophy. This set of beliefs is as valid in IBM Argentina and IBM Honduras as in IBM U.S. or IBM France.

Activities in the area of social responsibility are gaining in importance, and the company is currently involved in a wide spectrum of projects throughout the world in fields such as education, science, medicine/health, the environment, and community affairs. The principal criteria in selecting and funding projects in the social responsibility area are basically threefold: (1) the project should be of vital interest to the particular country in which it will be implemented (or of worldwide interest, as, for example, work being done in cancer research, in biomedical image processing for assisting physicians in diagnosing illness, or in air pollution); (2) the company should have something unique to contribute in terms of scientific/technical expertise; and (3) the project should not have direct business connotation.

The following outline of IBM's business in Latin America will also attempt to highlight how operations there follow the basic principles of the company.

IBM's ENTRY INTO LATIN AMERICA

IBM's first entry into Latin America was in 1917, when a dealership was established in Brazil to market the early punched card (Hollerith) machines. The success of that venture prompted Mr. Watson, Sr. to visit the area during the 1920s and early 1930s and establish subsidiaries in most of the countries in the region. For example, Dutch Guiana became the 78th country outside of the United States in which IBM operated in 1931, and IBM Brazil began manufacturing electric accounting machine parts in the same year. The growth of these companies was quite slow, but before World War II Latin American operations represented a significantly larger portion of the company's business outside of the United States than it does today. By the beginning of the war IBM had established technical schools for its employees as well as customer education programs in several countries.

A significant point in this history is that IBM started operations in Latin America early in its corporate development. Between 1917 and 1941 it established subsidiaries or branches in over 20 Latin American countries. This fact, combined with the high-technology product and business practices that established it as a good corporate citizen, has allowed IBM to maintain almost normal operations in spite of recent legislation directed toward controlling foreign companies and foreign investment in many countries in the region. New companies attempting to enter the Latin American market very often encounter limitations and restrictions. The "rules of the game" are frequently different for new companies than for established companies.

GOVERNMENT RELATIONS

Government relations have naturally developed as a most important aspect of IBM's activities in Latin America, perhaps more so than in other parts of the world. Latin American governments frequently control basic industries such as electric power, petroleum, steel, transportation, communication, and so on. Therefore, over 50 percent of IBM's business in the region is in the government sector.

Governments have changed frequently, and often there is a new economic "game plan" that may affect the operations of local and foreign business. Foreign exchange regulations, price control and wage policies, import duty rates and licensing arrangements, royalty and technical assistance policies, tax rates, export reimbursement incentives, local content requirements for manufacturing licenses—all may be subject to change in a very short time frame. Indeed, the basic philosophy of government toward foreign companies and foreign investment has been subject to change in many Latin American countries.

In response to this uncertainty, IBM attempts to keep government officials continually updated on its operations and acquainted with its policies. Over time, it has been the company's experience that fair, reasonable rules of the game may be established when a government completely understands its activities. This story is communicated to government officials formally by the country general manager through the vehicle of a "white paper," which describes how the business works and explains how IBM believes its approach makes a contribution to the country.

HOW THE BUSINESS WORKS

Except for the four Latin American companies that have a manufacturing function, the subsidiaries and branches perform mainly a marketing and service function. Products in the computer line are provided by one or more of the 17 countries that have manufacturing facilities, including those in Latin America. These countries of course also market the full line of products. Products are purchased from the manufacturing countries at an intercompany billing price (transfer price), which is equal to the production cost plus a markup approximately equal to the company's pretax profit margins worldwide. The purchasing country pays the manufacturing country in U.S. dollars. The product is then sold outright or rented by the purchasing company to customers at a standard worldwide base price billed in local currency. Sometimes there is a small price uplift to cover extraordinary costs of doing business in that country, such as the import duties on spare parts. This system provides for reasonable profit both for the manufacturing company and the marketing company. Thus, both companies grow in their own countries, hire and train more people, pay more taxes, and, in the case of manufacturing companies, increase exports.

The parent company enters into royalty agreements with the subsidiaries, under which the subsidiaries remit a portion of total revenue as a payment for the research and development done by the parent company. There is no charge for research and development in the intercompany billing price from the manufacturing companies. All of the latest products and technical support are available to the Latin American market.

Subsidiaries and branches reinvest the majority of their profits in the local business but are expected to remit a part of their profits to the parent company for distribution to stockholders. These remittances are in dollars. Many Latin American countries do not have free exchange, and there are frequently problems of converting local currency to dollars for the purposes of royalty and dividend remittances.

THE SERVICE ASPECT OF THE BUSINESS

IBM's business is primarily a service business. Customers receive support from field systems engineers, who provide assistance in systems design, installation, applications, and programming support. The equipment and the programs are maintained by the field customer engineers. Customers are also offered a wide variety of educational programs in two regional education centers located in Brazil and Mexico, or in any of the 11 local education centers in various countries in the region.

All told, customers received 92,000 man-days of education in Latin America in 1972. In addition, the company's Latin American employees received 82,000 man-days of education in the Latin American Centers or in the United States or in other parts of the world. That's a total of 174,000 man-days or 870,000 man-hours of instruction, in 1972. This training was made up of education in various aspects of computer technology and programing systems and applications and 4,000 man-days of management development.

Education is an extremely important aspect of the company's operations. In addition to professional instructors, the company uses young employees with high management potential. An assignment in an education center is very often one of the prerequisites for advancement. Thus the quality of education is maintained, and future managers develop an understanding of the importance of education through personal experience in teaching.

MANUFACTURING IN LATIN AMERICA

Particularly in the case of the typewriter business, manufacturing within LAFTA (Latin American Free Trade Association) is essential to maintain a competitive price in the region. Import duties on typewriters from outside of LAFTA are very high.

IBM has manufacturing plants in four Latin American countries. Mexico supplies the Latin American needs for typebar typewriters, with the exception of Colombia, which manufactures for its own requirements. Brazil manufactures the single-element-type typewriter for Latin America and in July 1973 shipped its first System 370/145 computer, the latest medium-scale computer in the IBM product line. Brazil has the mission to supply the 370/145 to Latin America and Japan. The acceptance by Japan of the Brazilian 370/145 is a result of expanding trade relations between Japan and Brazil. This added trading partner for the Brazilian 370/145 will greatly assist in reducing the cost of that machine to the rest of the Latin American countries. The sorter and the printer for the System/3, the latest small-scale computer in the IBM line, are manufactured in Argentina for Latin America and for half of the world.

IBM's policy is to manufacture the requirements of its foreign subsidiaries outside of the United States. No plant manufactures the entire product line, nor in fact an entire computing system. In order to take advantage of economies of scale, plants are assigned one or more specific "boxes" to be produced for export. Thus one plant, as in the case of the Brazilian plant, will produce the main frame of a computer, whereas the computer tapes, printers, disc units, terminals, and other peripheral equipment that make up the total system may be produced in one or several other plants throughout the world. Not only does this approach result in reduced production costs, but also, and very importantly, it generates exports from the manufacturing countries. For example, IBM has been the major exporter of nontraditional goods from Argentina ($14 million are expected to be exported in 1973) and Brazil ($20 million in 1973) for several years, and thus it has contributed significantly to the balance of trade of both countries. In addition every manufacturing plant relies on local subcontractors for parts that initially must be imported from other IBM plants. These subcontractors are progressively brought up to the high quality standards embodied in the company's technology. Thus an IBM manufacturing plant not only contributes to the balance of trade of a country like Brazil, Argentina, or Mexico but also stimulates the development of local manufacturing enterprises that must satisfy high standards of quality.

PERSONNEL POLICIES AND PRACTICES

IBM's personnel policies in Latin America are consistent with those in the United States and throughout the rest of the world. Because of the very advanced and sophisticated nature of the technology many Latin American employees are university graduates with a wide variety of professional backgrounds. Through the technical training provided, these people become experts in the latest aspects of computer technology. Many of them are members of local university faculties (on their own time or on company time) teaching subjects or conducting seminars related to their particular expertise (systems analysis and design, mathematical techniques, model building, programing languages, and so on). The company encourages this type of activity because it makes available to a much wider audience advanced technical knowledge that would otherwise be limited to those directly involved with it. It is considered an important part of the company's technological contribution in Latin America.

The companies' compensation programs are based on a "pay for performance" concept and a merit increase system. This means that an employee is paid on the basis of performance in a particular job and the length of time in that job. Positions are defined by levels that are consistent throughout IBM's worldwide organization. Pay for those levels, however, varies from country to country depending on the local pay scale. Salary surveys for all levels are conducted annually, and IBM's pay scales are compared to those of other "leading companies" in the area. The company attempts to maintain a pay position that is equal to, or slightly better than, the other companies. It is interesting to note, for example, that, due to boom conditions in Brazil in recent years and the resulting competition for qualified people, some of IBM's pay scales there are higher than for similar positions in the U.S. IBM company.

Benefit programs are also compared to those of other leading companies, and an attempt is made to stay competitive in the area of benefits. In addition, benefits are tailored to the local situation. Because Latin American society in general is very family oriented, the company's social and recreational programs are slanted toward this orientation. Company facilities are made available for recreational purposes for the families, and, in Argentina, for example, the company provides a summer camp program for the children of employees.

The IBM company has always tried to be sensitive to the need for good downward communications. All of the vehicles for this purpose, such as Think magazine and various company publications for managers, are translated into the Spanish language and distributed throughout Latin America.

As a general principle, the company has found that it is equally important to pay close attention to grievance channels and other methods of upward employee communication. Employees everywhere, including Latin America, have strong opinions and attitudes concerning their jobs, their working conditions, their company, their management, and the slow, steady growth of frustration and resentment that can result in operational difficulties. Several ways of systematizing this upward communication are working in Latin America. I will describe them all, generally going into some detail on one program, that of employee opinion and attitude surveys, giving some data that might prove interesting.

First, communication is promoted at the man/management level through the appraisal and counseling program. Any employee may take any problem to his manager at any time, but at least once a year both of them must formally sit down to discuss performance, objectives for the coming year, and employee problems. The results of this formal interview are recorded and reviewed by high-level management, and a performance rating is assigned to the employee. In this way every employee knows where he stands with respect to the company and his manager and has an opportunity to express his opinion on this. Employees can disagree with their performance rating and receive a hearing at higher management levels.

In cases in which the employee prefers a confidential communications channel to submit complaints, questions, or comments on any company-related subject the "Speak-Up!" program may be used. There are forms for this purpose at each IBM location, which are filled in with the employee's complaint and submitted to a speak-up coordinator. Signed forms receive a response directly to the employee's home. Responses to unsigned submissions may be posted on the bulletin board or published in local company newspapers. Even in the case of signed speak-up submissions, the employee remains anonymous, since the coordinator removes the identification before assigning the submission to a manager for response.

A third upward grievance channel has a very long history in IBM and is based on the principle that every person has a right to appeal the actions of those who are immediately over him in authority. Should any employee have a problem he believes the company can help solve, he first discusses it with his immediate manager or the location personnel manager. If the matter is not resolved, or if the matter is of such a nature that he prefers not to discuss it with local management, he has the right to go to his local general manager, regional manager, president, or general manager, and, in fact, as far up the management line, including to the chairman of the board, as he feels is necessary to receive a satisfactory answer.

Finally, in this line of upward communication and grievance channels there is an extensive employee opinion- and attitude-survey program in Latin America, which interests me very much and which I would like to describe in some detail. Here about once every two to three years, employees have the opportunity to express themselves on a wide range of topics relative to their business life—their jobs, their management, their work-load and work procedures, their pay, their advancement, working conditions, and so on. This process employs a questionnaire of about 180 questions in length, which covers just about every topic that could be of interest to employees and which is open-ended in the sense that employees may add comments and points they feel are not covered in the survey. The employees who answer the questionnaire remain anonymous. The survey data are combined and analyzed into groups sufficiently large so as to protect employee anonymity, yet sufficiently small so as to enable specific action to be planned to improve problem areas. The important thing about this program is that the data are communicated to employees and discussed with them. For example, in Venezuela in 1972 a total company opinion survey was held. After the data were analyzed, some 80 meetings were held between managers and employee groups to discuss and elaborate on the data. Booklets were prepared containing total opinion survey results and distributed to employees. Employees had the feeling of participation and in fact were actually brought into the data analysis and action planning process.

There are some real advantages to this program, some of them extremely important for Latin America: (1) In general, the relationship between subordinates and managers in Latin America is not as easy and open as it is in the United States. For example, first names are not frequently used, and although an employee may have strong opinions, he may find it uncomfortable to communicate them to his immediate manager. The opinion survey data provide a structure for this type of discussion. By that I mean the data are presented at meetings during which employees are supposed to respond and comment. This is particularly valuable in Latin America. A great deal of meaningful communication would probably never take place without this opinion survey data feedback structure. (2) The opinion survey data enable the company to assess the "fit" of its policies to different cultures and countries. It serves as an early warning system to country management and can help pinpoint where policies are not working properly. (3) Since the survey program is worldwide, there is an opportunity to compare the various operating units around the world. Surveys done in different years enable evaluation of trends.

I'd like to give you an idea of some of the data gathered through opinion and attitude surveys that personally interest me. One area of interest is management style, and the question is what management style is most preferred by employees. Paragraphs describing four different kinds of managers were constructed. They were the authoritarian, the informative manager, the consultative manager, and the participative manager. We asked which type of manager they would prefer to work under. The results are as follows, and I give them here for Latin America, with Europe as a comparative.

	Percentage Response	
	Latin America	Europe
Authoritarian	6	2
Informative	23	19
Consultative	38	49
Participative	33	30

We can see a moderate but clear tendency for Latin American non-managers to prefer authoritarian and informative managers over the consultative and participative variety to a greater extent than their European counterparts. (These results are statistically significant.)

As a companion question we ask which of the four types of managers most closely corresponds to the respondent's manager, and we get the following results:

	Latin America	Europe
Authoritarian	20	17
Informative	28	30
Consultative	28	28
Participative	12	10
None of the above	12	15

The picture that employees have of their managers in Latin America and Europe is strikingly similar. In both cases employees apparently perceive more authoritarian and informative management than they would like. This is a clear message on which the company is working in its management development programs.

Some other questions were asked that point up interesting cultural differences, and here I will include the Far East by way of contrast. For example, the survey asks the extent of agreement with the following statement: "A Corporation should have a major responsibility for the health and welfare of its employees and their immediate families." The results are as follows:

	Percent Agree and Strongly Agree		
	LA	Europe	Far East
Corporate responsibility to employee and family	81	78	93

Again the picture between Latin America and Europe is fairly similar, but the Far East, in which Japan is heavily weighted, shows much stronger agreement with this statement.

Approaching the corporate responsibility point from a different angle the survey asks for the extent of agreement with the following: "A Corporation should do as much as it can to help society's problems (poverty, pollution, etc.)," with the following results:

	Percent Agree and Strongly Agree		
	LA	Europe	Far East
Corporate responsibility to society	73	72	91

We can see that the feeling in the Far East that companies have responsibilities to individual employees and their families extends also very strongly to the area of social responsibility, in some contrast to Latin American and European employees, where this feeling is not as strong.

I would like to emphasize that these are averages and that within them are some strong and very interesting differences by country. Even so, I think we can say with some confidence that IBM work populations are more alike than they are different. They are a young, highly educated, and motivated work force practically everywhere, and their beliefs (and, from another set of questions, their goals) show a great deal of commonality.

CORPORATE RESPONSIBILITY

The area of "corporate responsibility" has been addressed briefly in this Appendix. This section will give some examples of programs being supported both by the Latin American companies and other IBM companies throughout the world.

A wide range of computer applications dealing directly with social problems of national and international concern is carried out in various IBM Scientific Centers throughout the world. These centers usually consist of some 10 to 20 IBM scientists and engineers working together with local government agencies, research institutions, and universities on specific projects of mutual interest. For example, air pollution problems are being studied in IBM Scientific Centers in Italy, Japan, Mexico, and Spain. In addition, representatives of these four countries have formed a task force that works with the United States Scientific Center in Palo Alto, California, on the problem of air pollution. Water pollution is being studied in the Swedish Scientific Center. The Heidelberg Center is involved in testing the hearing capabilities of infants and test animals, as well as in cancer and liver disease research. The Tokyo Center is working to prove the feasibility of a computer system assisting physicians in diagnosing illness through the technique of biochemical image processing. The Venice Center is working with the National Research Council of Italy on a study of the unique environmental problems of that city, and the Pisa Center is studying flood control techniques for the Arno River.

Very often the results of these various studies are applicable in Latin America. In addition there is a scientific center in Mexico, and there are plans for one in Brazil. The Mexican Center, for example, is right now developing projects in the areas of air pollution, agricultural models, and the application of terminal-oriented APL (Automatic Programming Language) in education. It is anticipated that the activities of these centers will grow in size and scope, directing their attention to specific problems of the Latin American social and economic environment.

The company also sponsors and supports scientific conferences. For example, two years ago IBM worked with the National Bureau of Economic Research in New York and several leading research institutions in Latin America (Colegio de Mexico in Mexico, Getulio Vargas Foundation in Rio, and the Di Tella Institute in Buenos Aires) in developing and supporting an international symposium on the Role of the Computer in Social and Economic Research in Latin America. This conference provided a medium to discuss the "state of the art" on quantitative research and computer technologies and their application to the solution of some of the socioeconomic problems affecting the Latin American region. It was held in Cuernavaca, Mexico, in November 1971 with the participation of some 200 scientists and researchers from most of the Latin American countries, Canada, the United States, Europe, and Asia. As a follow-up to the Cuernavaca Conference IBM is now sponsoring and supporting a series of workshops being organized also by the National Bureau of Economic Research, together with leading Latin American researchers, to discuss specific work being done in universities and research institutes in Latin America and elsewhere in this relatively new area of technology as it applies to the social sciences. It is expected that these professional exchanges will make available to a regional audience new and improved analytical tools applicable to the study of socioeconomic problems susceptible of quantitative analysis and will thus accelerate the application of latest computing techniques to the solution of some of the problems facing developing countries.

Emphasis is put on education activities. Contributions and grants are made to universities; fellowships and scholarships are supported. Postdoctoral fellowships are granted whereby junior faculty members from local universities are given extended assignments with IBM research facilities in the United States and Europe. Senior IBM scientists are brought from IBM laboratories to local universities. For example, recently an expert in microelectronics from one of our laboratories in the United States spent a year at the University of Sao Paulo teaching and helping to build (with the help of Brazilian students) a laboratory microcomputer.

The company has a 100 percent tuition refund program for its employees who wish to further their education. Also highly qualified employees are granted leaves of absence with pay to pursue research and teaching activities at leading educational institutions.

IBM sponsors annual tours for Latin American university professors to visit selected U.S. and Canadian universities and IBM locations. These tours acquaint the professors with the operation and management of computer centers and expose them to latest techniques and curricula innovations of potential use in their own universities. These tours often serve as a catalyst for potential "twinning" relationships between institutions of higher learning, which very often result in joint programs, professional exchanges, and other activities of mutual interest.

Much of the company's efforts in corporate responsibility programs are left to the individual company managers, who pursue those areas they feel are most significant in their countries. In Brazil, for example, the company works with the Literacy Institute, which is attempting to solve the grave illiteracy problem in the Brazilian Northeast. In Colombia the wives of IBM employees have established a school in a section of Bogota where no public school existed. In addition to financial support they provide teaching assistance. A similar school has been founded in Ecuador. Local managers are also authorized to grant employee-initiated leaves of absence for the purpose of working full time on jobs of a social service nature. In Latin America employees in Argentina and the Bahamas have taken advantage of this program.

This is a brief overview of our business philosophy and practices throughout the world, with particular emphasis on "corporate responsibility" as it applies to the Latin American region. It should be noted that many of the policies and activities just described have been in effect for many years. The fact that "social responsibility" is the fourth basic principle of IBM's corporate philosophy has given momentum to something the company has always attempted to do but until now never completely defined. It is my hope the discussions in Aspen will help in the development of this definition.

INDEX

AID (see Agency for International Development)

Agency for International Development, 70, 114, 154

Alcala Sucre, Luis: on impositions of standards, 53; on international federation of petroleum workers, 53; on multinational oil companies in Venezuela, 177-223

Alessandri, Jorge, 11-12

Allende, Salvador, xix-xx, 10, 12, 29, 38

Anaconda Aluminum Company, 9, 22

Andean Group, 136, 147

antitrust laws, 45

Argentina: printers, 38

"arrogance": of MNCs in host countries, 41, 46, 48, 57-58

Automotive workers, world council, 51 (see also United Auto Workers; Victor G. Reuther)

Bahamas, 19

balance of payments, 45, 64, 116

balance of trade, U.S., 90

Ball, George, 88, 136

bargaining power: of LDCs, 105-06 (see also labor unions)

Barnds, William J., on power balance, 26-27 passim; on renegotiation of contracts in Latin America, 36; on safety standards, 47

Behrman, Jack, 139

Bennett, Robert A.: on IBM in Latin America, 224-37; on international regulations, 38; on phase-out by home country, 37

Blumenthal, W. Michael, 135

Bolivar, Simon, 6-7, 9

Bolivia, 9

Brazil: 7, 29, 50, 69, 74, 118; prosperity, 5; technological education system in, 15

Bretton Woods, 87, 88

bribery of foreign officials, 145

Burke-Hartke bill, 109, 110, 119

Canada: automobile workers union, 51; Wheat Board, 115

Chile, xix-xx; 29, 69 (see also Salvador Allende, Dow Chemical Company)

China, 29

collective bargaining, 30

Colombia, 111

copper, 9-10, 12

corporate responsibility (see social responsibility of corporations)

Council on Religion and International Affairs: study of corporation and transnational corporation as instruments in achieving justice, vi; as planners of conference, xxii

cross-subsidization, 92-106 passim

Cuba, 18

dependencia, 24, 32, 34; in Latin America, 20-22

De Rosso, Alphonse: on renegotiation of contracts, 26
Diebold, John, 88
Dillon, Douglas, 114
disclosure, 117, 118, 122-25,
144, 154
Dominican Republic, 18
Dow Chemical Company, 28,
30, 68; in Chile, 9-14, 21-
22, 29, 30, 33, 144
Dusseldorf conference on international organization for
investment (see foreign investment, international
regulations and standards
for MNCs)

Ecuador, 26
Eisenhower, Dwight D., 149
Escobar, Luis: on international regulatory agency for
MNCs, 134-40; on needs
for development of econo-
mies in Latin America, 35
ethical issues, xxv, 41, 47,
57-58, 63, 74, 78, 143,
153-55
ethical standards, 45, 47, 59,
64, 65
Eurodollar market, 89
European Community, 136,
139
expropriation, threat of as
bargaining lever, 78-79;
in Venezuela, 217-19

Fedepetrol, 53
Fiat, 35
Finn, James: on "good citizen"
concept applied to corporations, 49-50; on Latin
American concept of sov-
ereignty, 31
Ford Motor Company: in England, 52; in Germany, 52;
in Soviet Union, 34, 52, 72

foreign investment, 73; conference in Dusseldorf on international organization for,
134, 139; "export platform,"
function of, 96; in Latin
America, 20-21, 33
Frei, Eduardo, 10, 11

Gage, Harlow W.: on local government restrictions in host
countries, 15; on what makes
a "good citizen," 50
Galbraith, John Kenneth, xix
GATT (see General Agreement
on Trade and Tariffs)
General Agreement on Trade and
Tariffs, 87, 88, 135, 139
General Motors, 30, 38, 126-27,
142; in Latin America, 49
Germany, 27, 52, 125-26
Gerstacker, Carl A.: on dealing with governments unrepresentative of their people,
74-76; on Dow Chemical in
Chile, 4-16, 30-31; on renegotiation of contracts,
36, 38
GM (see General Motors)
"good citizen" concept, 43, 49-
50, 64, 153, 154
Group of Eminent Persons, 134,
138, 140
Gulf Oil Company, Venezuela,
177-223
Gunneman, Jon P.: summary
and analysis of points of disagreement by conference
participants, 159-75

Hanold, Terrance: on approach
to foreign investment, 65-66;
on concept of sovereignty,
31-33; on export of flour and
wheat, 114-16; on information
and technology, 34-35; on
transfer-pricing, 112-13

Hellman, Rainer, 136

IBM (see International Business Machines)
independencia, 34
India, 76
inflation: as affected by global corporations, 102-03, 116
interdependence, xx, 32, 37, 41, 46, 54-55, 77, 87-90, 106
Internal Revenue Service, 93, 122, 125
International Business Machines, 23-24, 68, 111; in Latin America, 224-37
International Center for the Settlement of Investment Dispute, 138 et seq., 146
ICSID (see International Center for the Settlement of Investment Dispute)
international regulations and standards for MNCs, 16-17, 24, 41, 46, 73-74, 122, 146, 147, 149-50 (see also International Center for the Settlement of Investment Dispute)

Jager, Elizabeth: on Burke-Hartke bill, 109-10; on different meanings of "multinational," 68-69; on export of employment out of U.S., 107, 148; on social justice, 108
Japan, 27, 68, 95-96, 125-26
Joseph, James: on General Motors in Latin America, 49; on transnational values, 51

Katzenbach, Nicholas de B., 139

Kennecott Copper Corporation, 9, 22
Kidder Peabody & Company, 36
Kennedy, Moorhead C.: on role of U.S. Government re MNCs, 70-71
Keynes, John Maynard, 93, 98, 102, 103

labor: bargaining power of in host countries, 147; international, xxiii, 98
labor unions, U.S., xxi, 47, 108; bargaining power, 98, 102; responsibility to employees, 45
labor relations: impact of MNCs on, 30
Latin America: conflict of U.S.-based MNCs with governments, 18-20; nationalism and character of Latin Americans, 6, 7 (see also individual countries)
Latin American Free Trade Association, 20

Maisonrouge, Jacques, 88, 122
Malaysia, 74-75; Chinese majority in, 74-75
Marshall, Burke: on "arrogance," 58 passim; on corporate responsibilities, 44-46; on interdependence, 37, 46; on international standards for MNCs, 43-46; on legal practices, 143; on safety standards, 46-47, 48
Marxism, 22, 30, 110
Meneg (see Gulf Oil Company, Venezuela)
Mexico, 33, 66, 72, 115
Middle East, xx
Moran, Theodore H.: on global standard of taxation, 119; on Latin American sovereignty,

33; on nationalism and dependencia, 20–25; on Overseas Private Investment
Corporation, 69–70; on renegotiation of contracts,
26–27 passim, 36–37; on
transfer-pricing, 118
Muller, Ronald E.: on development goals, 63–64; on
disclosure, 117–25 passim;
on employment in U.S.,
108–09; on global corporate
operations, 84–106; on
multinational corporate
executive, 122; on nego-
tiation of contracts and
bargaining power, 27
multinational corporations,
U.S.: number and percent-
age on global scale, 86,
100

nationalism, 32; economic,
22–23, 28, 119, 149; vs.
internationalism, 88, 93
nationalization, 23, 215–19
Neuhauser, Paul M.: on interdependence, 46; on power
relationships, 37
Nicholson, H. P.: on bal-
ance of payments, 64

oil: developments in Middle
East, xx; (see also Organi-
zation of Petroleum Ex-
porting Countries; petro-
leum workers, interna-
tional confederation of;
Suez Canal pipeline;
Venezuela)
Oil, Chemical, and Atomic
Workers International
Union, 53
OPEC (see Organization of
Petroleum Exporting
Countries)

OPIC (see Overseas Private In-
vestment Corporation)
Organization of American States,
6–7
Organization of Petroleum Export-
ing Countries, 89–90, 105
Overseas Private Investment
Corporation, 69–70

Panama, 19
Peru, 9, 18, 72
petroleum workers, international
confederation of, 51, 53
Petroquimica Chilena, 10 (see
also Petrodow)
Petrodow, 11–14 (see also Dow
Chemical Company)
pollution: control of, 50, 75;
global guidelines, 49; in Sao
Paulo, 50, 123
populism, 22
power relations, xxiv
Powers, Charles W.: on "arrogance," 48, 57–59 passim, 63;
on economic and moral issues,
42; on interdependence, 54–
55; on precision about ethical
issues, 78; on sustenance
standards, 59–60, 63, 64
PQC (see Petroquimica Chilena)
price-fixing, 19

Quigley, Thomas E.: on ethical
issues, 47–48; on international
code of conduct for MNCs,
153–55

research and development costs,
111–12
Reuther, Victor G.: on collective bargaining processes, 51–
52; on Ford Motor Company in
Soviet Union, 34; on negotiations MNCs-LDCs, 28–30; on
unemployment benefits and
social security, 126–27

Ricardo, David, 90-92, 94
Rodo, Jose Enrique: on anti-
 U.S. feeling in Latin
 America, 5
Rostow, W. W.: classifica-
 tion of economies, 66
rubber production: Brazil and
 Far East, 8
Rubin, Seymour, 134
Ruttenberg, Stanley H.: on
 legal constraints by U.S.
 Government on MNCs, 72;
 on phased withdrawal and
 renegotiation of contracts,
 33, 37; on problem of U.S.
 export trade, 106-07

safety standards, 47-49, 75-
 76, 148
Schomer, Howard: on development of international
 standards, 73-74; on foreign investment as arm to
 U.S. foreign policy, 73;
 on negotiation of contracts,
 34; on U.S. position to-
 ward repressive regimes,
 152-53
shareholders, 47; responsibility to, 44, 53, 55, 58
Smith, Adam, 90-91, 94
social responsibility of corporations, xxii, 43-44, 45-
 46, 51, 143-44, 145
social security, 60-61
Solomon, Anthony, 139
Soviet Union, 29, 34, 69, 74
 (see also Ford Motor Company)
Suez Canal pipeline, 36

tax laws, 45, 104
taxes, corporate, 92, 100-01,
 104, 139

technology: capital-intensive
 vs. labor-intensive, 62;
 control over by MNCs, 21, 24,
 86-87; international transfer
 of, 95; value of to LDCs, 8-9,
 35
Tomic, Radomiro, 11
trade unions (see labor unions)
transfer-pricing, 19, 21, 92-94,
 111-17 passim, 118, 144

UAW (see United Auto Workers)
United Auto Workers, 126-27
United Nations: on establishing
 international standard of con-
 duct for MNCs, 24, 52, 74;
 report on multinational cor-
 porations and currency crisis,
 xix; resolution by Economic
 and Social Council to Study
 Role of MNCs, 134 (see also
 Group of Eminent Persons)
U.S. Steel, 23
Universal Declaration of Human
 Rights, 73-74, 128

Veblen, Thorstein, 96
Venezuela: federation of petroleum unions, 53; flour mills,
 113-14; oil resources and
 production, 43-44, 58, 177-222

Wiener, Anthony: on expropriation, 78-79; on interdependence,
 77; on multiple interests in international bargaining, 141-49
Wionczek, Miguel S.: on Burke-
 Harke bill, 110; on controlling
 factor of technology, 31; on
 relations between MNCs and
 LDCs, 16-20; on research and
 development costs of MNCs,
 111-12; on technologies U.S.
 and European, 62

ABOUT THE EDITOR

Jon P. Gunnemann is Assistant Professor of Religious Studies at Pennsylvania State University. He earned his A.B. at Harvard University, his B.D. at United Theological Seminary, and his M.A. at Yale University. Mr. Gunnemann is currently a Ph.D. candidate at Yale.

EXPROPRIATION OF U.S. INVESTMENTS IN
CUBA, MEXICO, AND CHILE
Eric N. Baklanoff

EXPROPRIATION OF U.S. PROPERTY IN SOUTH
AMERICA: Nationalization of Oil and Copper
Companies in Peru, Bolivia, and Chile
George M. Ingram

THE MULTINATIONAL CORPORATION AND
SOCIAL POLICY: Special Reference to General
Motors in South Africa
edited by Richard A. Jackson

THE MULTINATIONAL CORPORATION AS A
FORCE IN LATIN AMERICAN POLITICS: A Case
Study of the International Petroleum Company in
Peru
Adalberto J. Pinelo

THE POLITICAL RISKS FOR MULTINATIONAL
ENTERPRISE IN DEVELOPING COUNTRIES:
With a Case Study of Peru
Dolph Warren Zink